Liberal Protestantism

Liberal Protestantism

Realities and Possibilities

EDITED BY
Robert S. Michaelsen
AND
Wade Clark Roof

The Pilgrim Press
NEW YORK

Library of Congress Cataloging-in-Publication Data
Main entry under title:

Liberal Protestantism.

Bibliography: p. 269.
    1. Liberalism (Religion)—Addresses, essays,
lectures.   2. Protestantism—Addresses, essays, lectures.
I. Michaelsen, Robert S., 1919–   II. Roof, Wade
Clark.
BR1616.L53   1986   280′.4   85-32091
ISBN 0-8298-0584-2

The Pilgrim Press, 132 West 31 Street, New York, NY 10001

Contributors

Peter L. Berger is university professor at Boston University and an adjunct scholar at the American Enterprise Institute for Public Policy Research. His eleven books include *Pyramids of Sacrifice*, *The Heretical Imperative*, and *The Sacred Canopy*. He is currently writing a book on the social and political theory of capitalism, *Capitalism and Society*.

Michael Burdick is a United Methodist minister and doctoral student in religious studies at the University of California, Santa Barbara. He recently published an article in *Christian Century* entitled "My Close Encounters with Monasticism."

Edwin S. Gaustad is professor of history and acting dean of the College of Humanities and Social Sciences at the University of California, Riverside. He has authored numerous books, including *A Religious History of America*, as well as edited several others, including *A Documentary of Religion in America*, volumes I and II.

Phillip E. Hammond is professor of religious studies and sociology and current chairman of the department of religious studies at the University of California, Santa Barbara. He is organizer and editor of *The Sacred in the Secular Age* and is the current president of the Society for the Scientific Study in Religion.

Joseph C. Hough Jr. is professor of ethics and dean of the school of theology at Claremont and professor of religion at Claremont Graduate School. His works include a recently published book, *Christian Identity and Theological Education*, written with John Cobb.

William R. Hutchison is Charles Warren professor of the history of religion in America at Harvard Divinity School. His publications include *The Modernist Impulse in American Protestantism*.

Benton Johnson is professor of sociology at the University of Oregon. His numerous articles and books on religious development in America include "Liberal Protestantism: End of the Road?"

recently published in the *Annals of the American Academy of Political and Social Science*.

Patrick J. Mahaffey is a Ph.D. candidate in religious studies at the University of California, Santa Barbara, writing a dissertation on "Religious Pluralism and the Question of Truth." A previous article on American civil religion was selected for publication in *Church Divinity 1984* through the National Student Essay Competition in Divinity.

William McKinney is director of educational programs at Hartford Seminary and his publications include *Varieties of Religious Presence*, written with Jackson Carroll and David Roozen.

Robert S. Michaelsen is professor of religious studies at the University of California, Santa Barbara. His published works include *The American Search for Soul*.

Donald E. Miller is associate professor of religion and dean of the School of Religion at the University of Southern California. His published works include *The Case for Liberal Christianity*.

D. Keith Naylor is a former university administrator and currently a doctoral candidate in the department of religious studies at the University of California, Santa Barbara.

Wade Clark Roof is professor of sociology at the University of Massachusetts. He is the coauthor, with William McKinney, of a forthcoming volume on denominational trends in religion in America to be published by Rutgers University Press.

John K. Simmons is a doctoral candidate in religious studies at the University of California, Santa Barbara, writing a dissertation on "Mormonism and Christian Science in California: Religious Development in the Pluralistic Cultural Environment." He recently published an article in *Christian Century* titled "Pilgrimage to the Wall."

Leonard Sweet is president of the United Theological Seminary in Dayton, Ohio. His most recent publications include *The Evangelical Tradition in America*, of which he was editor, and *The Minister's Life: 19th Century Evangelicalism*.

Barbara Brown Zikmund is academic dean and professor of church history at Pacific School of Religion in Berkeley, California. She recently edited the book *Hidden Histories in the United Church of Christ*.

Contents

Preface

Most of the chapters in this book were initially prepared for a symposium on the question, Does liberal Protestantism have an American future? which was held at the University of California, Santa Barbara, in the spring of 1985. The chapters by Peter Berger and William Hutchison were prepared in connection with a dialogue that immediately preceded the symposium and that was sponsored by the Robert Maynard Hutchins Center for the Study of Democratic Institutions and the department of religious studies at the University of California, Santa Barbara. (Because of circumstances beyond his control Professor Berger was unable to participate in the dialogue.)

The dialogue and the symposium developed out of a longer range project on trends in Protestantism and its relationship with American society, which has been funded by a grant from the Lilly Endowment and directed by Prof. Phillip Hammond and me. Professor Hammond and I express gratitude to the Lilly Endowment for this support and to Dr. Robert Wood Lynn, senior vice-president, religion, for his continuing interest and encouragement.

The longer range project on trends in American Protestantism has included an ongoing seminar taught by Professor Hammond and me and including among its guest participants Prof. James D. Hunter, now of the department of sociology at the University of Virginia; Prof. Armand Mauss, department of sociology at Washington State University; and Prof. Wade Clark Roof, department of sociology, University of Massachusetts. We are grateful to these scholars for their valuable contributions to the seminar and to Professor Roof for his willingness to assume an editorial role for this book. We are also grateful to the students who have participated in the seminar and, especially, to Michael Burdick, Patrick Mahaffey, Keith Naylor, and John Simmons, whose essays are included in this book. Keith Naylor and John Simmons have also served as research assistants for the project, and John Simmons assisted in the editorial process and prepared the Bibliography.

Finally, Professor Roof and I express appreciation to Cindy Nunn and Casandra Heiland for their assistance in preparing the manuscripts for publication.

Robert S. Michaelsen
Santa Barbara, California

Liberal Protestantism

Introduction

Robert S. Michaelsen
Wade Clark Roof

As Tom Lehrer used to say, "the future lies ahead." It is tempting to leave it at that. Still, with the gift of memory and retrospection comes the possibility of anticipation and prospect. Hence we ask, What are liberal Protestantism's prospects? And we are led to do so because we have some sense that the subject may have fallen on hard times.

But first what is the subject? We understand by liberal Protestantism (1) an attitude or outlook or mode of thinking, (2) a movement within Protestant Christianity, and (3) the institutions in which the outlook has been most consistently expressed and the movement most clearly embodied.

To speak of liberal Protestantism is to imply that there is also a conservative Protestantism. And to speak of Protestantism is to suggest protest—against something in the name of something. Historically, we understand this movement as having developed out of Martin Luther's protest against the Roman Catholic Church under the banner of biblical authority and Christian liberty. Although Luther, who was grasped by a profound sense of God's grace, was able to hold these thrusts together, they have, in the subsequent development of Protestantism, at times become divided. Biblical authority may become overly rigid. This is not liberal. Christian liberty may veer off into anarchy and relativism. Nor is this liberal. Liberal Protestantism comes down somewhere in between these extremes.

Understood theologically, we mean by liberal Protestantism a view that has stressed freedom, liberation from earthly authoritarianism, closed systems, in the name of the ultimate authority whose way is dynamically disclosed in and through the Bible. The vitality and dynamism that has characterized this view was clearly implied by the Leyden separatist John Robinson in his words to that migrant band later called Pilgrims: "The Lord hath more light yet to break forth out of his Holy word" (quoted in Mather, 1977:144). This view stands in contrast to the view that understands God's truth to be fully and exclusively contained in the written word of the Bible and is confident that properly instructed human beings can fully appropriate that truth.

Protestantism is, indeed, a religion of the word. Protestants have understood God's revelation not only in terms of the word made flesh, but also in terms of the word embodied in or made evident through the canonical scriptures. But as liberal Protestants such as Horace Bushnell have emphasized, words are pointers or symbols that are best understood in a poetic or figurative sense rather than in a literal sense. And as Friedrich Schleiermacher, the father of liberal Protestantism, insisted, experience precedes words and words must always be reinvigorated through experience.

The inadequacy of words to express fundamental truths is most dramatically implied in the Christian understanding that God's ultimate and most intimate expression to humankind came (and comes) in the form of a human person: the word made flesh. Liberal Protestants have understood that expression to mean, among other things, that human beings have an ultimate worth, that their lives as individuals have infinite value, and that their life together is blessed. Hence life in this world is supremely worthwhile. Hence, because God is both creator and redeemer, this world is itself enormously precious. Thus Christianity is understood to be, as the late Archbishop Temple pointed out, the most materialistic of religions. These convictions have led liberal Protestants in the past to stress the immanence of God, to be optimistic about the prospect of humankind, and to join with the power of God in improving themselves and the world.[1]

Serendipitously, Protestantism has also been experience centered. People are justified by grace through faith—in the classic understanding. All believers are understood to be priests, i.e., capable of relating directly to God on their own behalf and in behalf of others. Hence there occurs in Protestantism a dialectic between word and experience.

Defined in these terms, the phenomenon we examine is bound to be unstable or at least mobile. Again, this is a characteristic inherent in the thrust of Protestantism itself. No institutional embodiment can outlast the acids of protest, analysis, and change that this movement has brewed. Yet, paradoxically perhaps, Protestantism has been a strongly social movement—one that has not only taken shape in and through various ecclesiastical forms, but has also sought to shape society as well as be shaped by it. Puritan Protestants, so important to American beginnings, sought to build biblical commonwealths in the new world. So strong and pervasive was Protestant influence in American beginnings and subsequent development that American culture came to be dominated by it. But a fundamental split occurred within American Protestantism in the late nineteenth century between those who continued to seek to shape the society of which they were a part—to build the kingdom of God on earth, as some put it—and those who understood the Christian call to entail escape from this corrupt world into the kingdom that is not of this world.[2] The social concern that motivated the former and that provided the impetus for the Social Gospel movement became another of the distinctive marks of liberal Protestantism.

In the early years of the twentieth century, Protestantism was rent by controversy between those who accepted and embodied all or most of the views of liberal Protestantism as described here and those who, in the name of biblical literalism and other "fundamentals"—such as the view that Jesus Christ would soon return to judge this failed world—rejected them. Protestant denominations were often the primary arenas of this controversy. For the most part, the liberals "won" these denominational battles. Enough so that one can describe what came to be called "mainline" or "mainstream" denominations, such as the Congregational, the Presbyterian, the Episcopal, the Christian or

Disciples, and the northern Baptists and Methodists, as "liberal" at least in their leadership.[3] These denominations may also be described as "ecumenical." They constituted the majority of the membership of the Federal Council of Churches and its successor, the National Council of Churches. This is another mark of their liberal tendencies. It is these denominations, plus two large Lutheran bodies (The Lutheran Church in America and The American Lutheran Church), that constitute the main institutional focus of this book.

Some preference is now expressed for "oldline" as against "mainline" to describe these denominations (see Hutchison's and Sweet's essays, for example). This may imply a somewhat narrower focus. In their discussion of liberal Protestantism, William McKinney and Wade Clark Roof concentrate on the Episcopal, Congregational, and Presbyterian denominations, those truly "oldline" in the sense that they were the predominant groups of the colonial period. These authors also introduce the category "moderate Protestant" in which they include such less "oldline" groups as the Methodists, Disciples, Northern or American Baptists, and Lutherans.

"Oldline" may also suggest that what was once "main" has ceased to be so. This brings us to the immediate rationale for our basic question concerning the future of liberal Protestantism—the unmistakable evidence of internal loss in membership and support by the mainline or oldline denominations and subtler evidence of decline in their public influence since the 1960s.

Evidence that shows a noticeable internal decline in liberal Protestant denominations from the mid-sixties to the present is summarized in the McKinney and Roof essay in this book. Although varying interpretations of this evidence are offered (Hutchison's essay, for instance), no one denies the obvious— that liberal Protestant churches have clearly declined in numbers and in other ways in the period considered. What happened? Theologians, historians, and sociologists are still trying to understand the shifts—religious and cultural—in the mid-1960s. To describe what happened is fairly easy; to explain why is much more difficult.

Beginning in 1966, membership declines for many of the large ecumenical Protestant denominations became apparent. Well-established churches with long-standing records of growth and prosperity, some dating to colonial times, not only ceased growing, but also experienced major institutional downturns. To cite some prominent examples, the Episcopal Church, the United Presbyterian Church, the United Methodist Church, the Christian Church (Disciples of Christ), and the United Church of Christ all began reporting losses beginning about the mid-1960s. These churches had grown in the earlier post-World War II period, but they lost members during the late 1960s and 1970s. Especially in the 1970s, the losses were staggering, with many of these bodies declining by 10 percent or more. Lutherans joined the list of mainline bodies with net losses in this decade. By the end of the 1970s, at least ten of the largest Protestant denominations had experienced membership losses of a substantial sort.[4]

Membership decline was but one of a larger set of indicators pointing to a loss of institutional vitality. Attendance at worship services declined steadily throughout the 1960s and well into the 1970s after a period in the 1950s when religious participation had reached new heights. The declines in attendance among Protestants were greatest for those of moderate-to-liberal theological persuasion—for Methodists, Lutherans, Presbyterians, Episcopalians. Both religious giving and church school enrollments declined, and disproportionately so for the liberal churches. Like other "establishment" structures at the time, the liberal mainline churches suffered from a lack of appeal.

Dean Kelley, in his book *Why Conservative Churches Are Growing* (1972), was among the first to describe the changes that were underway. He argued that the churches that were growing were those which made strong demands on members; those that were declining did not. Growth was a correlate of religious commitment, and the plight of liberal churches was due to their diffuseness and openness and their general lack of the "traits of strictness"—absolutist belief, moral conformity, and enthusiastic spirit. Thus sectarian-minded, exclusivist churches should flourish in a secular context, Kelley postulated, while more established, ecumenical churches would fail in providing a satisfactory basis for personal meaning and commitment.

Others have argued that contextual, not institutional, factors were primarily responsible for the liberal declines. American society underwent some fundamental shifts in the 1960s—both demographically and culturally. A large baby boom cohort began to mature in the late 1960s, the largest cohort ever of youth in the nation's history. In the 1950s churches and schools expanded to accommodate these children; later, as the children grew into adolescents and young adults, the years when many persons drop out of churches, they did drop out in record numbers. Value shifts as expressed most visibly in the counter-cultural protests of the period also swept across the country. Quests for self-fulfillment and a strongly individualistic, "Me Generation" ethos led many young adults out of the churches and into new religious experiences or, as was often the case, secular indifference. A climate of freedom and expressiveness, of experimentation and self-realization prevailed that shaped new norms of churchgoing and encouraged more "privatized" religious forms; the currents of change were strong, especially for middle-class America, and, as Hoge and Roozen (1979) point out, "hit the churches from the outside."

That some major realignments of religion and culture were occurring at the time is underscored by two further considerations. One was the simple matter of timing. The drop in membership and participation occurred at about the same time for all these churches. Whatever brought about the declines lay outside any single church or tradition and cut across institutions. Widespread shifts in value commitments and life-styles hit all the churches, but the hardest hit were those most closely identified with the mainstream culture. Also, the declines were a result mainly of decreasing numbers of new members rather than of an increase in "drop-outs." Proportionately fewer persons were joining after the mid-1960s, and among those joining, fewer were becoming active participants and faithful supporters. This was especially true among the young. Fewer youth and young adults under thirty-five were recruited into membership, too few in many instances to keep the church rolls constant much less to grow.

In the meantime, liberal Protestants watched with fascination or horror as conservative growth and public influence accelerated. Sunday schools of conservative churches were packed. Youth flocked to Young Life, the Navigators, Campus Crusade, and the Inter-Varsity Fellowship. The Jesus Movement enjoyed a brief period of dramatic growth and public attention. Mainline Protestants were baffled or affronted by that movement, especially by its counterculture disdain for the mainline churches. As one Children of God hymn put it:

O Lord, have mercy on me.
I hate that damned old sound
Of the Church bells ringing
And the people coming from miles around.
　　　　　—Quoted in Marty, 1984:468

Pentecostalism experienced renewed vitality and a wider following than it had ever had. Fundamentalist preachers became increasingly visible in the media and exercised mounting influence in public life.

Given such developments it is little wonder that liberal Protestant reaction ran the gamut from shock to outrage to despair. What seemed at stake was not merely denominational survival, but the public role of liberal Protestantism. The roles of liberal and conservative seemed to be reversed. The conservatives were now vigorously and successfully asserting a public role in America while liberal Protestants were under fire or, even worse, ignored. Was anybody listening? Indeed, even the conservatives now focused their fire, not on liberal Protestantism, but on secular humanism.

Is the time ripe for a late twentieth-century Oliver Wendell Holmes to satirize the collapse of another classic vehicle? Not quite, suggest the scholars asked to respond to the question, Does liberal Protestantism have an American future? The mainline or oldline denominations may experience continuing difficulties. They definitely will have to adapt to a new status— curiously enough, a denominational status. That is, they will have to accommodate to modest size and role. No longer the custodians of the culture in quite the way they once were, they must now truly accept the fact of pluralism and face religious and secular realities unlike any before.

The question of the future of liberal Protestantism has stimulated a wide range of responses. It is addressed in this book from many vantage points—social and cultural, historical, theological, programmatic. But there are overlapping themes and shared views that surface in the essays, itself significant and indicative of a broadly based concern for the liberal churches and the challenges they now face.

The essays are organized into four sections. Part I describes the contemporary liberal Protestant scene in the United States. Each of the essays here focuses on broadly based shifts of one sort or another in modern society all affecting religion and the liberal Protestant tradition in particular. Peter L. Berger's lead essay offers a general overview of recent religious and cultural changes, with attention primarily to shifts in the class structure and the polarization within Protestantism. The present ferment in liberal Protestantism is part of a broader set of ideological and moral struggles, arising out of the realignments of religion and class in the post-World War II years. He attaches particular importance to the rise of the "new class," or sector most closely identified with the generation and distribution of knowledge in modern society, and the split in values and ideology between this group and the more traditional bourgeois class.

William McKinney and Wade Clark Roof look at the weakened demographic base for the liberal churches in this period. The constituencies of these churches are aging and have fewer children than either Catholics or conservative Protestants, and thus below-average rates of natural growth. Also, liberal Protestantism benefits less now than it once did from interdenominational religious switching and suffers severely from losses to the ranks of the disaffiliated. Another shift described by Phillip E. Hammond is what he calls a process of "extravasation," or the seeping out of the sacred from the vessel of the church. Historically, liberal Protestantism inspired great ventures in foreign missions, in higher education, and in the health and well-being of people; however, in the late twentieth century the links between these thrusts and religious motivation are no longer evident. Much of what was once defined as religious, or as religiously inspired, now passes as part of the taken-for-granted, secular humanistic culture.

In response to these sociological analyses of contemporary religious changes, historian William R. Hutchison cautions against overgeneralizations about the institutional declines of the 1960s and against nostalgia about some earlier, serener moral and religious period in the American past. He calls for a clearer understanding of liberal Protestantism's diminishing numbers and influence throughout this century and its evolving status as a minority religious subculture. This new status offers new challenges and opportunities for the rich theological tradition of liberal Protestantism. Hutchison sees as its distinctive contribution, perhaps more fully realizable now than in the past, a truly positive and forthright theology of pluralism.

The chapters in Part II are historical and seek to shed light on the present dilemmas within the tradition by looking to its past. Edwin S. Gaustad reviews in some detail a classic Protestant work first published in 1885—Josiah Strong's *Our Country*—using it as a benchmark against which to evaluate current trends and analyses. The situation is, of course, far different now than then, and Gaustad shows just how striking are the contrasts; but he also points to some parallels, most notably a sense of justice and social concern, that have characterized this tradition for at least a century. Most important, he warns against easy and uncritical interpretation of current trends, in hopes that commentators now will be less culture-bound in their views than was Strong.

Other chapters focus on selected aspects of liberal Protestantism's historic accommodation to the culture. Because it has sought to extend influence and to engage the culture creatively, it has also been vulnerable to changing contexts and shifting moods. Michael Burdick examines the decline in liberal Protestant missions abroad and seeks to explain it in terms of a new mission field. Rather than a "failure of nerve," he argues that a changing geopolitical situation since World War II and new strategies to accommodate the needs of younger, third world churches account for their diminished role. D. Keith Naylor looks at higher education and describes how campus ministry in the 1960s became increasingly marginalized, or cut off from the religious communities supporting it. Events and developments in the period since have forced ministries in higher education to establish closer ties with the churches and to celebrate more deeply their religious and spiritual roots. Patrick J. Mahaffey examines the rise of the self-fulfillment, narcissistic ethos of the 1960s and 1970s and its challenge to liberal Protestantism. His analysis points to the need for the churches to address the deeper spiritual forms of personal quest and to restore the cure of souls as a rightful concern in this tradition.

Part III is theological and theoretical; all the chapters are concerned with liberal Protestant faith or potential in the present context. Joseph C. Hough Jr. argues that the optimism about the future of human history that once characterized liberal Christian faith in America collapsed after World War II. Aside from being alienated from American democratic faith, liberal theology today confronts an even deeper problem—the possibility of the end of all history. The nuclear age forces Christians to live under conditions of uncertainty of a sort never known before and has led to theological reflection far more pessimistic about the future of the world. As a result, Hough foresees little chance of a neoliberal consensus of Christian faith emerging in America but holds out hope of a resurgent theistic perspective that will challenge the easy optimism of secular humanistic faith and the self-righteous moralism of conservative Christian faith.

John K. Simmons is more optimistic in his assessment of liberal Protestant faith. Drawing on systems theory, he is hopeful of new configurations of meaning. Given the liberal Protestant predilection for the inductive mode of theological reflection, he sees the dynamics of complementarity, communication, communion/community, and consensus as descriptive of the religious pattern of organization, and thus a move toward some new adaptation within the culture. Even though liberal

Protestantism may not regain its dominant position in society, he sees it as a creative minority in an emerging, more pluralistic context. For Barbara Brown Zikmund, pluralism is a more troubling reality within the liberal churches. Growing social and religious diversity undermines traditions and erodes religious and cultural unities. Yet, as she argues, diversity and pluralism may force liberal Protestantism to discover religious meaning in the world of religious language and metaphor. She advances a cultural-linguistic model of theology in a postliberal age: religious meaning as grounded in the language and communal life of a people, and not in some universally common experience diversely articulated by different religions. The future of liberal Protestantism, as she sees it, lies not in its ability to translate the faith into new categories as old-style liberal theology attempted to do, but in effectively teaching the language and practices of faith and by celebrating the capacity of human beings to live in diverse, yet meaningful, communities of faith.

The essays in Part IV emphasize programmatic themes and new institutional directions that may revitalize the tradition. Donald E. Miller identifies various target audiences for liberal Protestant recruitment: disillusioned evangelicals and Catholics, young upwardly mobile professionals, political liberals, those seeking counseling within a transcendent context, and those who find today's utilitarian individualistic culture empty and lonely. The liberal church can provide, he believes, religious community for those with a postmodern mentality and serve as a prophetic witness to traditional liberal values such as pluralism, tolerance, and freedom of expression and choice. Benton Johnson charts a recovery course for winning "lost sheep," that is, the young of the predominantly white middle-class constituencies who make up these churches. He calls for programs consistent with the broad cultural traditions and resources of liberal Protestantism and that address the concerns, worries, and aspirations common to young middle-class whites. It is within this sector that popular therapies designed to enhance people's ability to take control of their lives flourish. Liberal churches must, as he sees it, come to terms with these

(13)

quests for personal growth and power and do so in a manner that provides moral guidance and mobilizes personal energies for public causes.

Somewhat more generally, Leonard Sweet asks, Can a mainstream change its course? and proposes a fourfold agenda for the revamping of oldline American Protestantism: (1) a reconstructed theology, (2) a revitalized ecclesiology, (3) a rehabilitated patriotism, and (4) a reconstituted supernaturalism. He sees signs of renewal along these lines but leaves the question unanswered; if the course changes, it will come, as he notes, not without the "pain" of reconstruction, revitalization, rehabilitation, and reexamination. The future is open, very much dependent on the choices made by those within the churches and the particular chord struck by liberal faith in its contemporary, and emerging, context.

What about the future? Perhaps the most positive affirmation is that of William Hutchison, that the liberal spirit is not dead, but alive and well. Liberal Protestantism's greatest strength may be its capacity to question the way things are. "Our hearts are restless until they find rest in Thee" wrote Augustine. That kind of restlessness is characteristic of liberal Protestantism at its best. Because it is satisfied with nothing less than God and God's ways it encourages and welcomes change in lesser ways. Hence in these past two decades of rapid change in this country, liberal Protestantism has not been quiescent or played a passive role on the sidelines. Liberal Protestants have continued to espouse the cause of justice, a concern as old as the Hebrew prophets and as new as the issue of apartheid in South Africa. It may be true, as Peter Berger suggests, that they have sometimes become nothing more than chaplains to one side in a class war. Identifying injustice is difficult enough; knowing what is most effective in countering it is even more problematic. It may also be true that the liberal Protestant witness has really not been particularly effective in addressing some of the major issues of the time, such as the status of ethnic minorities in American society. Nonetheless, as Barbara Brown Zikmund points out, the most evident areas of growth in liberal Protestant churches today are among ethnic minorities. Furthermore, possibly the most significant social advance made within liberal Protestant churches in recent decades has been the increased leadership role of women.

The future of liberal Protestantism cannot be assured merely on the basis of response to social issues, however. Liberal Protestantism may be something of a barometer. It registers approaching storms early. But the figurative role of barometer is insufficient. Something of the gyroscope is also required. Several of the following essays reach for this more positive and directed role. Peter Berger preaches *metanoia*, repentance and reform, turning from secular idols to the God of Abraham, Isaac, and Jacob. Similarly, in somewhat less specific language, Leonard Sweet writes of the need for a renewed transcendence and a revitalized worship. Barbara Brown Zikmund calls for a new or rediscovered language of faith that springs from Christian community. Joseph Hough proclaims the need for a recovered ultimate optimism about the human prospect. Benton Johnson and Patrick Mahaffey see the need for a renewed attention to the cure of souls. William Hutchison and John Simmons challenge liberal Protestants to embrace and celebrate pluralism. All these point to long-standing liberal values and affirmations. It remains to be seen if they can be proclaimed anew with sufficient vitality and force to assure the future of the heritage.

PART

I

THE
CONTEMPORARY
SETTING

1

American Religion: Conservative Upsurge, Liberal Prospects

Peter L. Berger

Intellectuals, when addressing any topic of public import, have the tendency to fall into a peculiar rhetorical style that might be called the crisis-sermon. It consists of first giving an exceedingly gloomy picture of the situation at hand—in other words, proclaiming the existence of a grave crisis—and then suggesting, just before the end, that the advertised calamities might yet be averted if only people repented and accepted the speaker's point of view. Intellectuals do this, of course, because they have a vested interest in doing it. But also they do it because it is almost unavoidable if they deal with a topic in which they themselves have a stake. I'm afraid that I will not be able to avoid completely this crisis-sermon style in what follows. I will, indeed, address myself to the topic of contemporary American religion mainly as a sociologist—and, contrary to many, I continue to adhere to the position that sociology is a value-free discipline. But I will not try to disguise the fact that I have strong personal commitments in the matter under discussion. Specifically, I'm a Lutheran, committed to a liberal Protestant understanding of the Christian tradition (and I should stress that the adjective liberal here does *not* refer to a political but to a theological position). Thus I'm far from indifferent to what is taking place on the American religious scene today and, especially toward the end (where this properly belongs in a crisis-sermon!), I will take the liberty of unapologetically discarding the pale mantle of sociological detachment.

Another point should be made at the outset: I will discuss mostly *Protestant* developments and will only deal briefly with what is occurring outside the Protestant community. This, however, is *not* simply due to my own Protestant affiliation. Rather, it is *sociologically* appropriate to make this emphasis. This is not only because American civilization has been crucially shaped by Protestantism and because the majority of Americans continue to be Protestants of one variety or another. It is also because the most dynamic phenomenon in the American religious situation is the massive upsurge of conservative Protestantism, to the extent that everything else that is happening must, I believe, be seen in relation to this central fact.

The Conservative Upsurge

Needless to say, the phenomenon has not gone unnoticed. At least since the mid-1970s (Jimmy Carter's campaign for the presidency was an important stimulus), commentators in the media and in academia have drawn attention to strange religious rumblings in that mysterious hinterland known as Middle America; by 1980—especially with the appearance of the so-called New Christian Right and its role in the first Reagan campaign—a good many people in what might be described as the secular provinces of the nation were in a state of near-panic about this development. Now, if one has one's social habitat in one of those provinces—say, one is a professor in Greater Boston or an upper-middle-class housewife in New Jersey—one may easily get the idea that suddenly, out of nowhere, this religious tidal wave arose in an essentially secularized America. Such an idea would be seriously mistaken. American society as a whole has *never* been very secularized, only certain areas (social even more than geographical areas) within it. Indeed, the most recent data on the religion of Americans strongly indicate that this society is at least as religious as it ever was and quite possibly more religious than ever before. I refer here to recent studies of American values undertaken by the Gallup organization and Connecticut Mutual Life and to the Middletown replication study, especially *All Faithful People*, by Theodore Caplow [1983] and his associates. If one looks at America in a cross-national perspective, it sticks out in an exceptional way indeed. By and large, throughout the world, there is empirical support for the thesis that modernization is positively correlated with secularization. Thus the highly modernized societies of Western Europe and Japan score highest on both objective and subjective measures of secularity ("objective" in the sense of religious activity, "subjective" as referring to the expressions of personal beliefs), with the Scandinavian countries standing out as paragons of secularized modernity. At the other pole are countries like India. America is the big exception. There is, indeed, a secularized sector, significantly located in the cultural centers of the society. But the rest of the country, no matter how modernized, continues to be furiously religious. This is not the place to speculate on why America has, as it were, been shielded from the secularizing effects of the modernization process (I happen to think that there are possible explanations of this in American history). But the fact must be registered. It is as if we had a little "Sweden" superimposed on a vast "India," and that image may already help us in understanding what is happening today. Nor, of course, did the evangelical upsurge of the 1970s occur ex nihilo. Conservative, evangelical Protestantism has always been an important presence in the United States, and in sections of the country it has been the predominant religious form for a long time (see Marsden, 1982; 1983). What one may observe today is, rather, an intense *activation* and a sort of nationalization of this particular religious community.

We are beginning now to have an increasingly clear picture of the contours of this evangelical resurgence (I refer, for example, to the excellent recent study, *American Evangelicalism*, by James Hunter [1983]). The most obvious fact here, of course, is the sheer growth in numbers. *All* the conservative Protestant churches are coming through with what one may call truly Japanese growth rates, while the liberal churches are declining or just about maintaining their membership. But there is more here than just numerical growth. Evangelicalism is becoming a

(21)

significant presence in parts of the country and among population groups in which it was previously marginal. Also, evangelicalism is becoming more self-assured and politically assertive on the national scene. Thus evangelicalism benefits both from conversion, that is, it is attracting people from other religious backgrounds, and from the social mobility of its original membership, that is, people from evangelical backgrounds are moving both geographically and into higher socioeconomic levels (Berger, 1981). The second development has a certain analogy to the assimilation of ethnic immigrants. Conservative Protestants, of course, are not immigrants and they are not exactly an ethnic group, but the manner in which they are now moving into the centers of the society is reminiscent of what happened earlier on to Catholics and Jews; in that limited sense, evangelicalism is being "Americanized," and this assimilation will change them as it will change the larger society.

Here, too, it is useful to look at all this in a cross-national perspective. In the contemporary world there are two massive, immensely powerful religious movements. One is conservative Islam, shaking up all the Muslim societies from Morocco to Indonesia. The other is conservative Protestantism, with an even wider geographical scope. It is sweeping across East Asia (with the notable exception of Japan), most dramatically in South Korea (which, if present trends continue, will have a Protestant majority early in the next century), but also in Taiwan and in the Chinese communities in Southeast Asia. Conservative Protestantism, often in syncretistic combination with indigenous folk religion, is in neck-to-neck competition with Islam in black Africa. And perhaps most surprising of all, it is growing rapidly in Latin America. Thus, for example, it is estimated that about 20 percent of the population of Guatemala is now Protestant. Neither the reasons for this nor its enormous social and political implications can be pursued here. But it is significant for the present topic if only because American evangelicals are very much aware of these foreign developments, and this awareness is probably related to their growing sense of being part of a historic change.

A word of caution here: A number of commentators (usually

hostile ones) have compared the Protestant and the Muslim versions of what they often call "fundamentalism" (usually a pejorative term). There may well be certain parallels, especially as regards the psychology of religion in play in both cases. But there are also decisive differences. The most important difference is this: conservative Muslims have an image of the ideal society that derives from the second half of the first millennium A.D.; the ideal imagery of conservative Protestants, by contrast, belongs squarely in the nineteenth century. Much more is involved here than a hiatus of a thousand years: The first imagery is premodern and, in many ways, antimodern; the ideals evoked by the Protestant imagination belong to precisely the period when Western society was going through its most intensive modernizing phase; it is by no means antimodern. Indeed, especially in the third world, a case can be made that this kind of Protestantism is uniquely suited to modernizing populations (or, if you will, Max Weber is being proven right from Seoul—which, incidentally, houses the largest Protestant congregation in the world—to Santiago de Chile). In any case, one should be careful before one understands conservative Protestantism in America as some sort of counter-modernizing movement, a label that fits much better some of the countercultural movements whose members are most appalled by the evangelical upsurge.

Any religious phenomenon touches on the deepest levels of the human spirit; one must be cautious if one tries to interpret the often wild stirrings of this spiritual realm by the arid methods of the social sciences. Still, I think that the social scientist can make some contributions to our understanding of the particular phnomenon at issue here. I suggest two interpretations, one more narrowly in terms of the sociology of religion, the other a broader sociological interpretation of the cultural dynamics of class conflict.

Secularization as a Theme

Looked at in sociology-of-religion terms, the conservative upsurge is a protest against secularization. As a faithful adherent of Max Weber, let me point out that this is not just an interpretation brought from the outside, but rather the way in which conservative Protestants interpret themselves and what they are about. Their opposition is to what they call "secular humanism"—not at all a bad term, if one divests it of its negative connotations in conservative rhetoric. Where, in what is still an intensely religious society, is this secularization to be found? In two places, I would suggest. One I have already mentioned: in the centers of elite culture. (The word center should be understood more in a social than a geographical sense, although there are physical concentrations of "secular humanists"—I should know; I live in what is probably the place of densest concentration.) Now, most Americans couldn't care less what happens in these circles—except for one simple but crucially important fact: These same circles have been quite successful in imposing their values on the rest of the population by way of the educational system, the communications media, and, last but not least, the law. This is why the Supreme Court decision banning prayer in the public schools was such a powerful trigger in activating the conservative protest. Richard Neuhaus, in the title of his recent book, has given a graphically descriptive name to the secular-humanist ideal for American society— *The Naked Public Square*—denuded, that is, of any religious symbolism (1984). Conservative Protestantism is a protest against this secularization of public life.

But there is also what, quite some time ago, Thomas Luckmann called "secularization from within," that is, the substitution of secular for religious contents within the mainline Protestant churches (1967). These secular contents, in the main, have been a theologically unappetizing mix of psychotherapy and politics (and the fact that the politics has been consistently left of center hasn't made the mélange anymore palatable to many Americans). Thus conservative Protestantism is also a reaction against secularization within mainline churches. One of the early interpretations of this phenomenon, Dean Kelley's book *Why Conservative Churches Are Growing* (1972), uses this line of argument. It is quite valid at least as a partial explanation. Most people (except, perhaps, in Cambridge, Massachusetts) go to church because they want to worship God and hear the age-old message about God's dealings with humanity; they *don't* go to church to receive psychotherapeutic advice or running commentaries on American foreign policy, especially if they dislike the advice and disagree with the commentaries. Thanks to religious liberty, these people have no reason to stay in churches where their religious needs are being systematically frustrated; logically enough, they go elsewhere.

Another earlier book about trends in religion, Jeffrey Hadden's *The Gathering Storm in the Churches* (1969), may also serve as an interesting benchmark for what has happened. Hadden based his argument on data from the 1960s which showed that mainline Protestant clergy were consistently more liberal (socially and politically, as well as theologically) than their congregations. He predicted that there would be increasing conflict between the clerical leadership and the laity, a "growing storm." Well, in retrospect, one can say that Hadden was both right and wrong. The gap betwen clergy and laity has continued, even deepened, and there have been various stormlets, if not storms, within the mainline churches. But the big conflict that he predicted has failed to materialize, at least to date. The reason is terribly simple: The lay people who were most annoyed didn't make a lot of fuss; they just quietly stole away, taking themselves (and, not unimportant, their financial support) *elsewhere*. All in all, what has happened here is a particularly striking verification of one of W.R. Inge's nastier dicta: "He who marries the spirit of the age soon finds himself a widower"; it holds important lessons for all religious liberals who believe that institutional survival depends on accommodation to the *Zeitgeist*.

The New Class

So far, so good (or so bad). There are broader sociological considerations, however, that can help us in understanding the phenomenon. They have to do with class. More specifically, they have to do with what some have called the rise of a "New Class" in the United States (and, incidentally, in other Western societies), a class best described as those people who make their living from the production and distribution of symbolic knowledge in the "teaching, caring, and communicating" industries. The conservative Protestant upsurge can then be seen as part of the rebellion against the cultural and political power of this class. Now, we are dealing here with a recent development (it didn't really start until after World War II); its dimensions and features are as yet less than clear; there is a limited data base for some of the sweeping statements—pro and con—that have been made about it (for example, by Irving Kristol on the con side, Alvin Gouldner on the pro side—interestingly, Kristol and Gouldner agreed on the empirical facts concerning the "New Class"—only what Kristol took to be bad news, Gouldner looked on as the best news in town [see Kristol, 1983; Kristol and Bell, eds., 1981; Gouldner, 1979; 1985]). Still, a number of statements can be made with some assurance.

American society today is in the midst of a *Kulturkampf,* a battle over a number of fairly clear issues. On both sides of the conflict there are clusters of values and opinions ranging from national policy to matters of personal life-style. One may mention here such issues as the use of military force in the foreign policy of the United States, the merits of American patriotism (not so much in the abstract, but as applied to specific national objectives), capitalism and the range of the welfare state, the environment, the problem of crime, and, last but emphatically not least, all the issues that have been raised by the feminist movement. Now, what is important to understand is that views on all these issues are not distributed randomly across the population. Far from it. They tend to cluster together and they tend to be correlated with socioeconomic status. They cluster: An individual opposed to U.S. policy in Central America is likely to be positively disposed to the feminist agenda; an individual opposed to abortion is likely to have pro-business attitudes; and so on. These clusterings may not have a logic that would be persuasive to, say, a philosopher from Outer Mongolia, but they are empirically real all the same. But these values and opinions also tend to correlate with class: Tell me an individual's occupation and income and I can make a reasonably intelligent guess where he or she will come out on these matters (of course, there will be cases about which I'll be wrong—there are always "class traitors"—but that is true of *all* statements about human society). In other words, the *Kulturkampf* has an important dimension of *Klassenkamp;* put differently, we are confronted here with a conflict between *class cultures.*

A central battleground is the abortion issue. It convincingly shows the class dynamics I have proposed. A recent sociological study of pro-life and pro-choice activists in California, Kristin Luker's *Abortion and the Politics of Motherhood* (1984), gives an excellent picture of the sharply divergent social characteristics of these two groups. The author, in her analysis, does not use the class categories to which I have referred, but her findings bear them out persuasively. Put simply: *Class* (*not* gender, *not* even religious affiliation) is the major predictor of an individual's stance on the abortion issues. (By the way, using conventional sociological categories, it would appear that the most pro-abortion grouping consists of upper-income white males and the most anti-abortion grouping, of lower-income black females.) On several of the other clusters enumerated before (for example, support for American military power, or lack of such support—or support or lack of support for a strong environmental policy, for harsher treatment of criminals, and for the Equal Rights Amendment), there are data indicating similar class cleavages.

All this is terribly important in understanding contemporary American society (and some similar constellations in Western Europe), especially recent American politics. I cannot go into this here. But the class-based *Kulturkampf* is the broader background for the phenomenon that is described in this essay. I would hypothesize that, as often before in history, religious symbols are used today as weapons in a class struggle. (I'm using a Marxist phrase here; I trust that it is clear that my analysis of the American class system has little to do with the way Marxists see it.) In other words, at least a portion of the people constituting the conservative Protestant upsurge are not only expressing themselves religiously, but are also engaged in

(27)

a protest against social and political developments that in themselves have nothing to do with religion. On both sides, religion, as so often before, serves to legitimate class interests.

A military analogy suggests itself here. The class armies are arrayed against each other in various societal battlefields. And on both sides there are the military chaplains, invoking divine blessing on their cause and assuring the troops that God is in their corner. This, so to speak, "chaplaincy" function is most evident in the most politicized church organizations—such as Jerry Falwell's Moral Majority on one side and the National Council of Churches on the other. Frequently, there are people in the middle or the battlelines are confused. All the same, if one looks at the public posture of mainline liberal Protestantism on the great majority of the issues in question, there is no doubt where these churches come out: Their social and political views are highly consonant with those of one camp—the one intended by the "New Class" designation—and ipso facto highly distasteful to the other camp. This has, indeed, blown up a big storm (visibly so during the 1984 presidential campaign). It is not quite the storm that Hadden predicted (1969), but it is much more serious than the latter. What Hadden saw was a storm in the relatively limited teacup of mainline Protestantism; the storm we are witnessing today threatens the symbolic unity of American society and, given the international position of the United States, has ramifications that reverberate far beyond its borders. In this American *Kulturkampf*, as in just about every other development within this country, much more is at stake than the future of a few domestic religious institutions. One example is the way in which the two Protestant camps line up in the matter of U.S. policy in the Middle East. But that, too, is another story that I cannot pursue here.

The Broader Religious Picture

American Protestantism is a vast social universe, and I do not for a moment pretend that the foregoing observations apply to all of it. Thus I have said nothing about the black churches, themselves a complex and variegated phenomenon, in which, as I see it, there is an interesting sociocultural tug-of-war at work. Theologically and in terms of their religious praxis, most black Protestants would have a natural affinity to the conservative upsurge—they (literally) march to the same music. At least since the civil rights movement, however, black clergy and black congregations have been active within a political milieu that is located on the other side of the aforementioned divide. I regret that I cannot go on about this important segment of the Protestant scene. Nor have I said anything about the Lutheran community, divided into three major denominations, two of which are about to merge with each other and (I suspect) to merge gradually into the liberal Protestant mainstream, in which they will probably lose their distinctive identity, while the third, the Missouri Synod (still containing more than 2 million members) stands by itself in splendid isolation both from the mainstream and from the evangelical turbulence. But then one cannot cover everything. Rather, let me, however briefly, make some observations about the three other principal players in the field—the Catholics, the Jews, and the Eastern Orthodox Christians.

Catholics, to begin with the obvious, are different from any other religious group in America in that they are members of a (still) tightly organized international system. To be sure, the system has become much looser since the 1960s, but it is still true (and will almost certainly continue to be true) that, in the end, Rome determines at least the outer limits of change. Given this fact, it is remarkable to what extent American Catholicism has begun to resemble the liberal Protestant mainstream. The great watershed, of course, was Vatican Council II. This assemblage (or, at any rate, its great majority) had no intention of starting a revolution; it wanted a reasonable and controlled aggiornamento—a prudent adjustment of the church to the demands of the times. What then happened may serve as a textbook example of Max Weber's doctrine of unintended consequences and of the political science theory which says that, if you open one window too many in an authoritarian system, all hell will break loose (the trouble with this theory is that, so far, it doesn't tell us just *which* window is the one too many).

The most visible changes brought about by Vatican II were

liturgical; I suspect that, given the importance of liturgy in the Roman tradition, these were crucial for everything else. From one day to the next, Latin was abolished and replaced by a rather tepid vernacular. This was supposed to make the liturgy more understandable to the laity, which perhaps it did; it also invited the sort of reflection about the meaning of words that leads to theological trouble. The congregation was now invited to participate more actively in the liturgical proceedings and (a terrible mistake, in my opinion) the priest was turned around, facing the congregation from behind the alter—thus powerfully suggesting that the object of worship was right here, within the community, rather than beyond it—a powerful symbol of secularization if there ever was one. Then various elements of folk piety (especially those directed to the Blessed Virgin and to the saints) were marginalized, if not proscribed. And (perhaps the worst mistake, sociologically speaking) the clergy were strongly encouraged to preach on all occasions—changing them overnight from ministrants of awesome mysteries to spouters of debatable opinions. All this has come to mean, in terms of actual social experience, that someone dropping into a Catholic service today may be there for a while before being sure that it *is* indeed a Catholic service and not a liturgically amplified Protestant one.

Be this as it may, as far as the topic under discussion is concerned, American Catholicism has become "Protestantized" to the point that the public statements of the American bishops are about as predictable as those of the bishops of the United Methodist Church and, with one or two—equally predictable—exceptions, pretty much identical in content. The central bureaucratic apparatus of American Catholicism has been captured by the same New Class types as inhabit the headquarters of the central Protestant organizations. Major portions of the religious orders, for sociological and psychological reasons that are perhaps not all that hard to surmise, have moved even further to the left than the central bureaucracy, serving as a shrinking but active assault force on behalf of these political causes. The results have been similar to some of those observed in the Protestant community—confusion and disaffection among the laity, financial drain (which is especially critical for the Catholic educational system), a precipitous decline in candidates for the priesthood. There are two important differences, however; there is not—and probably cannot be—a Catholic equivalent to the conservative upsurge (the so-called Charismatic movement, as far as I understand it, has a different character); and, given Catholic beliefs, it is much more difficult for Catholic lay people quietly to go elsewhere—for a Catholic, there is no elsewhere. These differences, along with the controls still exercised by Rome (especially under the present pope) over the wilder reaches of religiopolitical radicalism, may make the crisis more protracted and slow-burning than the Protestant one.

I cannot resist the temptation of making a sociological prediction here. The two recent and much-discussed statements by the Catholic bishops—the one on issues of war and peace and the one, still in draft form, on the economy—have illustrated clearly to what degree their location in the current *Kulturkampf* has become partisan. The bishops have now promised us another pastoral letter, this one on the status of women. I predict that, with two necessary exceptions—abortion and the ordination of women—they will wholeheartedly endorse the entire gamut of feminist causes. I also predict that they will particularly endorse what is becoming the feminist cause par excellence—to wit, comparable worth—which they will be able to show, with unassailable logic, to be consonant with the essentially anticapitalist doctrine of "economic rights" that they have already espoused. Sociology is an empirical discipline subject to falsification; I'm hereby laying at least one part of my interpretation of American Catholicism open to being falsified.

I'm much more of an outsider when it comes to American Judaism, but I will venture some observations, necessarily tentative ones. Secularization has been as much a force in the synagogue as it has been in the church in America. Perhaps its impact here has been mitigated by the often-remarked fact that Judaism is more concerned with orthopraxis than with orthodoxy—that is, with observance rather than belief—and thus may be less vulnerable to cognitive challenges. At the same

time, I tend to think that Jews have overestimated the importance of the difference when it comes to the inroads of secularization: As soon as individuals ask themselves *why* they
should observe this or that element of *halacha,* they find themselves in a cognitive process that is structurally similar to the
Christians' questioning this or that element of the creed. Here,
too, there have been various degrees of resistance and accommodation to modernity, which are fairly faithfully reflected by
the three major Jewish denominations. Indeed, the fact that
American Judaism has divided up into denominations (a Protestant category in a profound sense) indicates the extent to
which it has been assimilated into the American religious situation. But there is also the uniquely Jewish synthesis of religion
and ethnicity that sharply differentiates Judaism from any
Christian group and that has led American Jews to worry end-
lessly about the meaning of their "Jewish identity"—there is no
Christian analogy to this. Nor is there a Christian parallel to the
American Jewish relationship with the state of Israel and to the
interaction of Judaism and Zionism in the American Jewish
consciousness.

As far as the current *Kulturkampf* is concerned, there is a
particular dilemma for American Jews. This dilemma is social
rather than religious. At least since the New Deal, the political
proclivities of American Jews have tended toward the liberal
and the left-of-center positions of the spectrum. What is sociologically more significant, a disproportionate number of
Jews belong to the new knowledge class, and thus naturally
participate in its class culture and share its class interests. But
there are at least two important countervailing interests. One,
the direction, taken by liberal social policy since the invention
of affirmative action is sharply threatening to Jews precisely
because of their disproportionate place in (let us call it) the
"teaching, caring, and communicating" sectors of the labor
force. And two, commitment to the survival of the state of Israel
sharply limits what would otherwise be a natural affinity to the
quasi-pacifist and third-worldist positions of the New Class
camp. On this one I shall be prudent and refrain from making
any predictions.

I ought to say at least a word about Eastern Christian Orthodoxy, an interesting "sleeper" on the American religious scene. It is instructive to reflect on the statistical fact that there are almost exactly the same number of orthodox Christians as there are Jews in the United States. So far, the impact of orthodox Christianity on American culture has been minimal when compared with the Jewish influence. The reason for this is that until recently, orthodoxy has been encapsuled in the several ethnic subcultures—Greek, Russian, and so on. This is now changing. The most dramatic change has been the decisive de-ethnicizing of the largest Russian community, which has now become the Orthodox Church in America, with its liturgy in English, with no special links to any foreign country, and with both clergy and laity coming increasingly from nonorthodox ethnic backgrounds. Historically, this is the first time that a sizable body of orthodox Christians have become, as it were, players in a pluralistic field. It will be interesting to observe what effect this will have on them—and, even more interesting, what impact, if any, they will make on the overall American religious scene.

Prospects

What are the prospects? As far as the conservative Protestant resurgence itself is concerned, there is no reason to assume that it will soon abate—it is far too massive and powerful a phenomenon. As the evangelical community becomes more established and ipso facto more culturally respectable, it is inevitable that it will modify some of its more grating deviances from the majority consensus. In other words, in the long run Evangelicalism will also become "domesticated." But, as John Maynard Keynes observed, in the long run we'll all be dead: The long run in this instance means at least one generation, and a lot can happen in that time. One development that I expect to continue happening is the decline of the mainline Protestant churches, barring a reversal of direction that would be tantamount to a revolution— an unlikely event, I should think.

If my sociological interpretation has merit, the future of American religion will be strongly determined by the outcome of the current *Kulturkampf*—read *Klassenkampf*. Assuming that there are no catastrophic events at hand—such as major wars or an economic collapse, in which case all bets are off—I would predict an ongoing but indecisive continuation of these battles for a long time. Given the structure of an advanced modern society, it is unlikely that either side will achieve total victory. Each side will win some and will lose some; there will be political compromises; there may be some blurring of battlelines. If I were to make bets, I would bet that the New Class will win many of its social and cultural causes (such as those on the feminist agenda) but will lose more of its economic and foreign policy ones (such as those that would undermine capitalism or the international position of the United States). These changes and compromises would then be reflected accurately within the "chaplaincies" of the respective class armies.

Speaking sociologically, then, I cannot really conform to the crisis-sermon style. Neither American society nor American religion is quite "in crisis," if by that phrase one understands a situation in which cataclysmic change is about to occur or in which the very cohesion of the society is in peril. I must, therefore, confess that it is as a committed American Christian, and not as a sociologist, that I'm tempted to a crisis-sermon conclusion. I shall yield to the temptation. But I should emphasize that this conclusion is based on my personal beliefs and values; that is, it is not based on the empirical data as such and cannot be put in the form of falsifiable hypotheses or predictions.

I am a theological liberal, and therefore find the current conservative upsurge unacceptable in most of its religious content. At the same time, I emphatically reject the notion that theological liberalism implies a secularization of the Christian tradition. Thus, when I started to study American Protestantism in the late 1950s, I was appalled by what were then the secularizing contents—a celebration of middle-class morality and of the American way of life, increasingly admixed with pop psychotherapy as exemplified by the works of Norman Vincent Peale. As I see the world politically, both in this country and abroad, I find the current mixture of left liberal ideological agendas even less palatable. I'm appalled, as a Christian in

America, that the public postures of the major churches should increasingly be nothing but near-automatic reflexes of the class cultures to which their leaders belong or aspire. I don't think that chaplaincy in a class war is the proper function of Christian ministry to society. I'm particularly repelled by that peculiar form of false consciousness that, in mainline Protestantism and now in the Catholic community, perceives as a "prophetic mission" what is in fact a Pavlovian reaction to the class position of the alleged "prophets." At the risk of offending some Christian ears, I would venture a rephrasing of a New Testament proposition: *Do not call yourself a prophet if your hometown agrees with you.* The proper task of the church is to bear witness to the tradition in preaching and through the sacraments. Prophecy, in its terrifying biblical meaning, is a rare and desperate mandate. The normal social ministry of the church, in addition to ordinary *caritas*, is to mediate, to reconcile, to provide a neutral ground on which societal antagonists can meet as human beings. When political partisanship becomes a routine feature of the church's public role, the consequences are much more serious than divisiveness and confusion within the laity. The most serious consequence is that the church loses one of its defining marks, that of *catholicity*: It ceases to embrace all Christians, and this means that it ceases to be the church. (I leave it to others to draw out the implications, if any, for Judaism.)

If this were really a sermon, preached within my own Protestant community, it could only be a call to *metanoia*, to repentance and reform, to a turning away from the various secular idols that so many have worshiped in place of the God of Abraham, Isaac, and Jacob. But this is not a sermon. I have no authority to preach; faute de mieux, I will conclude as a sociologist. I see little likelihood for the sort of radical redirection that would change the character and the prospects of liberal Protestantism in America. Put differently, the "crisis" that I would like to see as a Christian is improbable in my perspective as a sociologist. But, even as a sociologist, I cannot quite suppress an intriguing thought. I have imagined a big research project in the sociology of religion in Europe around, say, the beginning of the sixteenth century—a band of Columbia- or Berkeley-trained sociologists, transported backward by time machine, interviewing a cross-national sample of people all over the continent, even amplifying the study with depth-interviews and participant observation: I have the consoling hunch that they would have failed to predict the Reformation.

2

Liberal Protestantism:
A Sociodemographic Perspective

William McKinney
Wade Clark Roof

Speculating about the future of religious groups and move-ments is not a new enterprise. Looking ahead 100 years from his vantage point of 1783, Yale president Ezra Stiles foresaw an American future divided about equally among Congrega-tionalists, Presbyterians, and Episcopalians. These were the "colonial big three" churches that he fully expected to domi-nate the culture into the distant future. At the time it seemed a reasonable prediction.

But Stiles' prediction was off—by some 19 million persons! In the century that followed, both the nation and these churches underwent important changes. Congregationalism struggled with the loss of its established status in New England and found it difficult to adapt to life on the frontier and to make inroads among immigrant groups of the nineteenth century. With its insistence on an educated clergy and penchant for doctrinal controversy, the Presbyterians faced their own diffi-culties on the frontier and eventual division into northern and southern branches at the time of the Civil War. The Episcopal Church languished in the Federal period as a result of loyalty to the British cause and a liturgical style and form of ecclesiastical organization that seemed ill-suited for the American frontier.

And new churches emerged—the Baptists, the Methodists, the Disciples—soon to outgrow the older established ones.

At present it is quite popular to predict the future course of liberal Protestantism. George Gallup Jr. and David Poling (1980:10) are pessimistic: "The Presbyterian, Episcopalian and United Church of Christ communions cannot long exist as viable church organizations nationally if the declines of the 1970s persist in the 1980s." Similarly, sociologists Jackson W. Carroll and Robert Wilson (1980:38), with more than a little bit of whimsy, have calculated that if the trends in membership and ordination that prevailed between 1950 and 1977 continue into the future, the Episcopal Church will reach the point of having one member per clergyperson in the year 2004. The Presbyterians will reach this point in 2012!

This concern for what Martin Marty has referred to as "representatives of the older establishment at the heart of what has come to be called the mainline of churches" (1979c:71) grows in part from the sharp membership declines of these churches since the 1960s. Between 1960 and 1980 the membership of the largest Presbyterian denominations declined nearly 900,000, the United Church of Christ more than 500,000, and the Episcopal church more than 480,000. Other demographics have likewise been striking, most notably declines in baptisms and church school enrollments (Kelley, 1972; Hoge and Roozen, 1979). Taken as a whole, the new demographics point to a changing institutional face for religion in the United States.

In this essay we look at the shifting membership base for liberal Protestantism in the United States. Our analysis is largely demographic and concerned with the factors affecting its growth and future shape as a religious community. The interpretation put forth builds on a larger project on the changing shape of American denominationalism.[1]

Although membership declines have been widely commented on, growth factors generally have been largely overlooked in analyses of the current plight of liberal Protestantism. The size of any religious group over time is dependent on two fundamental factors: its *natural growth* and its *net gains or losses from conversions*. Natural growth comes about as a result of a favorable ratio between birth and death rates within a group. Most churches are able to hold the loyalty of a majority of children born to members, and thus the higher the birth rate among members, the greater the likelihood of numerical growth. In contrast, conversion involves the addition or subtraction of members by means of willful choice. People join or leave on their own accord. A group with a sufficiently high birth rate can, within limits, lose substantial numbers of persons to other faith groups and still experience growth. At the same time a group with a low birth rate and a high death rate can attract disproportionate numbers of persons from other faiths and still decline over time. Both factors are important, and the size of a religious group over time is very much a product of its interaction.

Here we address the growth question by examining survey data on liberal Protestants. The data show the core constituency of this religious community to be aging at above-average rates, and a slowing of the "switching" into liberal Protestantism from other religious families. Our argument is that unless liberal Protestantism can improve its ability to attract newcomers from beyond the existing core constituency of persons born into its midst, it will face continuing difficulty in maintaining its current social position. We conclude with some comments about its future niche in the American religious mosaic and the direction we think best for it to follow.

Liberal Protestantism: The Problem of Definition

Protestantism's internal diversity presents major definitional challenges to sociologists of American religion. Even to define Protestantism for purposes of research is difficult enough. What does the term mean? In one sense Protestantism is a body of religious teachings, symbols, and ritual practices dating from the Reformation of the sixteenth century. In another sense it means the people affiliated with religious bodies: the 14 million persons listed on the rolls of the Southern Baptist Convention, the 9 million United Methodists, the 226 members of the Christian Nation Church, USA, and those who belong to the more than 1,000 other self-consciously "Protestant" religious groups

(39)

that populate the American religious landscape. In still another sense the term refers to the formal organizations that give religious values and convictions a public face; the churches themselves and their affiliated agencies.

With "liberal Protestantism" one faces a similar problem of definition. Is it to be understood as a body of theological assumptions and attitudes that crystallized in a particularly powerful way in the latter years of the nineteenth and early twentieth centuries? As people on the rolls of specific churches? As formal organizations, such as the National Council of Churches, whose theological and social stances are publicly regarded as in some sense "liberal"?

We use the term liberal Protestant in this essay to refer to persons who identify their "religious preference" as Episcopal, Presbyterian, or United Church of Christ (or one of the latter's predecessor bodies). By virtue of their history and cultural position, these three groups lie at the heart of the old historic Protestant mainline; they have long held to a mediating posture as custodians of the culture and concerned themselves with public and private faith. Generally, they are more liberal theologically, as well as socially and politically, than the more moderate and conservative Protestants.

Our rationale for treating liberal Protestantism as one of seven major "families" of American religion, and for including these three specific groups in the liberal Protestant family, are discussed at length elsewhere.[2] It is sufficient to note here that our groupings emphasize both religious and cultural traditions as they have developed historically in the United States and follow from an understanding of denominations as religious *subcultures*. Michael Novak (1975:321) captures such a view when he writes of Catholics, "To be a Catholic is not so much to belong to an organization as to belong to a people. It is, willynilly, even without having chosen it, to have a differentiated point of view and sensibility, to have participated in a certain historical way of life, to have become a different sort of person." To be a member of a religious family is to be exposed to a common thought world, a similar life-style and behavior pattern, an enduring heritage of religion and culture. From the

(40)

time of H. Richard Niebuhr (1929) down to the present, commentators on American religion have stressed the importance of viewing religious communities in this way.

Who Are the Liberal Protestants?

For a profile of liberal Protestants we rely on the General Social Survey, conducted from 1972 to 1984 by the National Opinion Research Center.[3] The eleven surveys conducted over this period, taken together, provide detailed demographic and attitudinal information on more than 17,000 Americans, including 1,482 we have classified as members of the Liberal Protestant family (786 Presbyterians, 439 Episcopalians, and 257 members of the United Church of Christ). Together these groups are 8.7 percent of the American adult population.[4]

Relative to the population as a whole, liberal Protestants are overly concentrated in the Northeast (31 percent) and underrepresented in the nation's largest cities (20 percent). They are more likely to be white (95 percent) and to be of British or German ancestry (33 and 20 percent, respectively). Liberal Protestants remain toward the top of the American status hierarchy: 27 percent have completed college and members average 1.4 more years of schooling than the "average" American; two thirds regard themselves as members of the "middle" or "upper" classes. An upper-middle class social base is evident despite a diminishing WASP hold on the culture.

Their loyalty to religious institutions is less impressive. They are less frequent worship attenders than are members of other groups: 39 percent attend services nearly every week or more often, 21 percent attend occasionally, and 37 percent attend services of worship less than once or twice a year. They are less likely to consider themselves "strong" members of their denomination (33 percent do so). Members are above-average, however, in their participation in church activities outside of worship (43 percent are members of church-related groups) and affirm slightly higher-than-average belief in life after death (82 percent). Institutional and group attachments are weak relative to other traditions; faith and commitment are more highly privatized.

(41)

Socially and politically, on most issues, members of the liberal Protestant family are indeed more "liberal" than the general public and to the "left" of other Protestants. They are generally tolerant of unpopular social groups, such as atheists and homosexuals, are supportive of racial justice and women's rights, and are unusually open to nontraditional understandings of personal morality. For example, a majority favors unrestricted access to abortion and is generally more accepting of moral and life-style diversity. Tolerance and pluralism as themes run deep within the tradition.

The "Graying" of Liberal Protestantism

None of these descriptions will be especially surprising to those who have followed public opinion polling data. The surveys document, however, the less well-known fact of the aging of liberal Protestantism's core constituency.

With an average age of 48.5 years for adults, liberal Protestants are 3.9 years older than the general public, 0.5 years older than Jews, 1.1 years older than moderate Protestants, 3.7 years older than black Protestants, 3.8 years older than conservative Protestants, 5.7 years older than Catholics, and 12.5 years older than those with no religious preference. Liberal Protestants are aging at a far more rapid rate than the general public and members of other religious families. This is shown rather dramatically in Table 2:1, which looks at the percentage distribution of religious group members by age.

Of persons age fifty-five or older at the time they were surveyed, 11.2 percent are liberal Protestants. The proportion drops to 9.3 percent for those thirty-five to fifty-four and to 6.6 percent for persons eighteen to thirty-four; the proportion of the youngest sample who are liberal Protestants is just over half that of the oldest group! The pattern for the moderate Protestant family is similar, while the black Protestant and conservative Protestant share of each age-group is about the same. As the age level goes down, the Catholic and no religious preference proportions go up. The figures make clear what is an indisputable fact: liberal Protestantism is "graying" disproportionately to other major

Percentage Distribution of Religious Families by Age

| | Age | | |
	18–34	35–54	55 +
Liberal Protestants	6.6	9.3	11.2
Moderate Protestants	20.9	24.5	30.2
Black Protestants	9.5	8.9	9.6
Conservative Protestants	15.3	16.7	15.7
Catholics	27.9	26.7	22.0
Jews	2.0	2.2	2.8
Others	6.2	5.9	5.2
No religious preference	11.5	5.7	3.3

religious groupings; the "mainline" of churches is becoming "oldline."

Of Deaths and Births

A factor of considerable importance to the growth and decline of religious groups, as suggested earlier, is the relationship between rates of births and deaths. Other things being equal, groups with a favorable ratio of births to deaths will experience growth, whereas groups with lower ratios will suffer decline. Is it plausible that low birth rates have contributed to the membership declines of the liberal Protestant denominations? Table 2:2 explores this possibility. It shows the number of children born per woman for the major religious families. Data are given for all women, for women age forty-five or older, and for women under age forty-five.

Table 2:2 does indeed show significant fertility differentials among the religious families. With an average of 1.97 children per woman, liberal Protestantism's births are below the replacement level of approximately 2.1. This is also true for Jews and for those with no religious preference. For liberal Protestant women age forty-five or older, the number of children born is also below average. Older liberal Protestant women, most of whom have completed their childbearing, report 0.85 fewer children than do conservative Protestant women, 0.81 fewer

Table 2:2

Average Births per Woman by Religious Family

	Births		
	Total	45 +	Under 45
Liberal Protestants	1.97	2.27	1.60
Moderate Protestants	2.27	2.67	1.80
Black Protestants	2.62	3.08	2.24
Conservative Protestants	2.54	3.12	2.01
Catholics	2.20	2.75	1.82
Jews	1.69	1.96	1.37
No religious preference	1.39	2.30	1.18
National	2.25	2.75	1.73

than do black Protestants, and 0.42 fewer than do moderate Protestants. The average number of births for liberal Protestant women under age forty-five (1.60) is below average as well and lower than the average for the other Protestant families.[5]

Thus we see that the number of births is an important factor in the equation of natural growth. Also important is the number of deaths. We cannot estimate the impact of religious death rate differentials with poll data, but it is generally known that liberal Protestant churches draw their numbers from those sectors of the society with the greatest longevity. We suspect that these differentials have an impact on rates of growth but cannot estimate the extent of the impact. But given the number of older persons who are members of these groups, one can anticipate high death rates in the foreseeable future.

For sure, the low fertility of liberal Protestantism has had a significant effect on the low rates of growth of its churches. Consider the fact that in 1980 there were 7,784,334 persons on the rolls of the three major liberal Protestant denominations. Assuming one half of these members to be women (a conservative estimate given the fact that women outnumber men in all three churches), an increase in the liberal Protestant birth rate to the national level (2.25) projects to an increase of more than 1 million liberal Protestants; an increase to the birth levels of conservative Protestant women represents an increase of more than 2.2 million. Imagine, if the birth rates were different, how our assessment of the churches' future might be different. The topic of this book might well be changed from whether liberal Protestantism has an American future to how it is to deal with its continuing numerical success.

Liberal Protestantism and Switching

A second major source of religious group members is conversion: persons "switching" from one tradition to another (or from the ranks of the "unchurched"). Historically, liberal Protestantism has benefited from an "upward movement"—switching out of the conservative and into the more liberal churches. Religious mobility occurred along with social and economic mobility. But as the traditional "social sources" of religious belonging lose some of their influence on the ways individuals express their religious commitments and values, is it possible that liberal Protestantism suffers disproportionately from religious switching? Do more people switch out of liberal Protestantism to other groups than switch in from other families?

Fortunately, the General Social Survey allows us to look at this question. Individuals are asked not only their current religious preference and denomination, but also the religious tradition and denomination in which they were raised. Overall, liberal Protestants are about average in their rates of switching. Of persons raised in this family, 64 percent continue to identify with a liberal Protestant denomination.[6]

Table 2:3 summarizes the switching patterns, or movement of members into and out of the liberal Protestant family. The sample uses as its base the 1,264 persons who were raised as liberal Protestants. To that total it adds persons raised in another family who have *switched in* (e.g., 269 moderate Protestants, 74 conservative Protestants, 55 Catholics, etc.). The 269 moderate Protestants who switched into liberal Protestantism represent a gain of 21.3 percent to the base of the persons who were raised in this family. Similarly, the table shows the number of persons raised as liberal Protestants who *switched out* to other families; for example, 170 are now moderate Protestants and 101 have no religious preference. The 170 moderate Protestants represent a loss of 13.5 percent, those switching to

(45)

Table 2:3
Switching to and from the Liberal Protestant Family
(Base N = 1264)

		Mod. Prot.	Black Prot.	Cons. Prot.	Catholic	Jews	None	Total
Switchers In	(N)	269	12	74	55	1	27	438
	(%)	21.3	0.9	5.9	4.4	0.1	2.1	34.6
Switchers Out	(N)	170	13	62	66	2	101	414
	(%)	−13.4	−1.0	−4.9	−5.2	−0.2	−8.0	32.8
Net Gain/Loss	(N)	99	−1	12	−11	−1	−74	24
	(%)	7.9	−0.1	1.0	−0.8	−0.1	−5.9	1.9

no preference a loss of 8 percent. Finally, the table shows the *net* result of the interfamily switching. In the liberal-moderate Protestant exchange, liberal Protestantism is ahead 7.9 percent. In the exchange with no religious preference it is behind 5.9 percent.

Overall, liberal Protestantism benefits from religious switching. In the movement from one religious family to another, it enjoys a net gain of 1.9 percent. Table 2:3 gives no evidence of movement from liberal Protestantism to more conservative religious groups; liberal Protestantism actually gains in the exchanges with moderate and conservative Protestantism. Its principal competition appears not to be the more conservative religious families, but dropping out of religion altogether; the problem is one of people leaving for a more diffuse secular mode of values and identity.[7]

It is tempting to conclude the investigation at this point with the suggestion that the current plight of liberal Protestantism is essentially demographic; that its members' low fertility rates contribute to membership declines but that these are offset at least in part by slight gains through religious switching. To stop here would be a mistake, however. There is good reason to expect age differentials in religious switching. Table 2:4 looks at overall switching patterns for both younger and older persons raised as liberal Protestants. Because the number of cases is reduced, the table shows only switching to and from other religious families and no religious preference.

Table 2:4 suggests two main differences between earlier and later generations of liberal Protestants that may have significant bearing on the future. First, movement into liberal Protestantism from other religious groups has slowed. For the older generation, movement into the tradition was a major source of new members: the net gain is fully 20.2 percent. For those under age forty-five what was a gain in the exchange between liberal Protestantism and other religious families turns to a *loss* of 0.9 percent. This may suggest a slowing in what has been regarded as "traditional" switching in the direction of upward social mobility. Second, there seems to be an acceleration of movement among the later generation of liberal Protestants into no religious preference. For the older generation this exchange resulted in a net loss of 3.1 percent; for the younger, it is 8.7 percent. The losses to nonaffiliation among the young point to a serious institutional problem for these churches in holding on to their members. Compared with the other major religious families, the liberal churches fare quite poorly in retaining members.

Table 2:4
Liberal Protestant Switching for Younger and Older Groups

		Other Religious Families	No Religious Preference	Total
Under Age 45				
Switchers In	(N)	154	18	172
	(%)	24.3	2.2	27.1
Switchers Out	(N)	−159	−73	−232
	(%)	−25.0	−11.5	−36.5
Net Change	(N)	−6	−55	−60
	(%)	−0.9	−8.7	−9.4
Age 45 +				
Switchers In	(N)	277	9	286
	(%)	44.6	1.5	46.1
Switchers Out	(N)	−152	−28	−180
	(%)	−24.5	−4.5	−29.0
Net Change	(N)	125	−19	106
	(%)	20.2	−3.1	17.1

Summing Up: The Shape of Liberal Protestantism's American Future

Let us review what we have uncovered in this brief sociodemographic overview of liberal Protestantism. First, this family of denominations is below average in its rate of natural growth. Its members have fewer children than do members of other religious families, and thus a smaller number of persons "born into" its tradition. It is reasonable, given the age of liberal Protestant members, to expect above-average death rates in the years ahead. Second, its fertility rates, like those of other groups, appear to be declining. Younger members report fewer children than older members and fewer children than members of other families. In addition, there are proportionately fewer liberal Protestants of childbearing age, and these members are having fewer children. Third, while liberal Protestantism has benefited in the past from interdenominational switching, its competitive advantage seems to have diminished in recent years. In the past this religious community was able to offset its low fertility rates through its appeal to persons raised in other traditions. This seems no longer to be the case; its younger members are more inclined to drop out of religious participation altogether and conservative Protestant groups are doing a more effective job of retaining the loyalties of persons raised in their tradition.

Taken together, this profile suggests that liberal Protestantism faces real challenges, many of them beyond the control of religious leaders. For example, there is relatively little that can be done to affect rates of natural growth.[8] The demographic base for these churches is weak and may indeed get weaker unless they can recruit more young adults in the childbearing years.

Is liberal Protestantism, therefore, faced with an inevitable condition of further membership losses and a steadily diminished social role? We think not. Its future will depend in large part on creative responses to three important challenges.

First, the future shape of liberal Protestantism will depend on its ability to counter the secular drift that has had a profound impact on its traditional constituencies. The movement to no religious preference (and to lower rates of participation among those who continue to identify with religious traditions) is one of the significant religious changes of our time. It reflects the long-term rise of religious individualism—what Ernst Troeltsch (1931:2:796) called "mysticism," or the "secret religion of the educated classes." The notion that religion is, in essence, a private issue, a matter of an individual's working out his or her religious commitment independent of religious tradition and community, has wide acceptance in American life. In its emphasis on individual responsibility in matters of faith and morality, liberal Protestantism has contributed to this rise of religious individualism; it has not emphasized to the same degree what is a complementary emphasis in the Reformed and Anglican traditions—the gathered community of believers in which faith is shaped and nurtured, and whose members share a sense of responsibility and accountability to one another and to the world of which it is a part. Here we concur with the main thrust, if not the details, of Dean Kelley's argument in *Why Conservative Churches Are Growing*. Liberal Protestantism needs to recapture a sense of community of faith as it relates to personal faith and commitment.

Second—and here we disagree with Kelley (or perhaps more accurately, with those who have taken his book to be a call for a more "conservative" stance in matters of faith and morality)—liberal Protestantism needs to hold firm in its commitment to the values that have informed its recent history: to intergroup toleration, to the responsibility of Christians for social and economic justice, and to a continuing renewal of public life. We say this not only because we are personally committed to these values and see them as ill-represented in much of the public debate of the 1980's, but also because these values retain significant support among those who are the principal prospective members of the liberal Protestant churches. If, as we argue in the larger work on which this essay draws, the lines among Protestant religious families on moral and ethical issues are being drawn more sharply, liberal Protestantism's future may well lie not in a move toward the theological and ideological center, but in its being more self-consciously "liberal." The tradition's "competition," as noted earlier, is not the more con-

(49)

servative religious groups, but the drift to the ranks of the "unchurched," whose numbers include the most liberal segments of the population.

Third, liberal Protestantism's future requires a clearer sense of its new public role. These churches, as Martin Marty has suggested, have long occupied a position at the heart of the mainline. Their members retain economic, cultural, and political influence far out of proportion to their numbers, both in local communities and in the nation as a whole. Constructive dialogue with the culture and concern for the public good are essential to the survival of the tradition. But as the data presented here demonstrate, liberal Protestants can no longer sit back and wait passively for people to come and join them. The values that have informed this tradition are no longer part of the taken-for-granted fabric of American life; people are not attracted automatically to churches simply because they symbolize membership in an "establishment."

The liberal Protestant churches have in no sense been relegated to the margins of American society, but neither do they retain their place at the center. This development is something new for these groups, and its full impact may not be evident for several generations. They seem destined to have more of a minority voice in a pluralistic religious and secular context, yet the possibility that they will become silent or lose their distinctive identity is not likely. How the churches accept and deal with their new situation is crucial—not only for their own future, but for the future of the nation itself.

3

The Extravasation of the Sacred and the Crisis in Liberal Protestantism

Phillip E. Hammond

Although secularization is a major term in the social scientific study of religion—and has been from the beginning—knowledge of just how it occurs is less certain than the belief that it does occur. People do not *create* the sacred, but *encounter* it; likewise, it seems, we can more readily encounter the result of secularization than the process itself.

How holy things escape from their "proper vessels" is puzzling indeed; the extravasation of the sacred is not easy to understand. (See, for example, Hammond, 1985, for a number of illustrations.)

Yet understand it we must if the current crisis in liberal Protestantism is, in turn, to be understood. At least that is the assumption I operate with here. The puzzle I address is this: How did the great denominations of the American past, the churches that once dominated American culture, lose their custodial position? How was it, so to speak, that the sacred was let out of its "proper" vessels?

The ultimate answer is to be found in Protestant theology itself, denying as it does that the church is a necessary (i.e., proper) vessel for all that is holy. Salvation, Protestantism asserts, is a matter between people and God, requiring no sacrament, no priest, and thus no church. At most the church can be

(51)

a gathering of like believers, but one shared belief will be the conviction that persons come together to glorify God, not to conform to ecclesiastical demands. To varying degrees therefore, Protestants have been suspicious of ritual, authority, pomp, and costume. The church may ultimately be a *tool* of the sacred, but it is not the *vessel* of the sacred.

Such Protestant conviction is at least the theoretical explanation for the extravasation of the sacred; Protestants, on principle, have been reluctant to exalt their churches. In actuality, however, Protestant churches, no less than Catholic, have enjoyed a sanctified status. Their leaders have often been charismatic, their spaces regarded as holy, their rules believed to be God-ordained. Put briefly, membership in a Protestant church has oftentimes been seen to carry the same sacred obligation as membership in the Roman Catholic Church. Protestants never went so far as to *say* that outside the church there is no salvation, but many Protestants certainly behaved as if they believed it. Informal establishment status has thus been as eagerly claimed by Protestant churches as formal establishment status has been eschewed.

Informal establishment status is precisely what a number of Protestant denominations—those we now call liberal—enjoyed in America, at least until late in the nineteenth century. Even after that time, after the experience Robert T. Handy (1984) calls "the second disestablishment," certain Protestant denominations continued their custodial relationship with American culture, and thus came to be regarded as "mainstream," or "mainline," churches. Well into the twentieth century, for example, most public school teachers were presumed to be members of one or another of these denominations. Higher education modeled itself after a few universities historically tied to these denominations. (For instance, William Bowen, president of Princeton University since 1970, is the first Princeton president who is neither a Presbyterian clergyman nor the son of one.) And all three branches of the federal government were disproportionately in the hands of persons who claimed affiliation with these denominations.

Talcott Parsons had special insight into this subtly maintained custodial relationship. The family, he allowed, was a key to understanding how, despite decreasing formal status, liberal Protestantism diffused outward and remained influential. Families played a critical role in the transmission of these values, of course, but in addition "it is to be taken for granted that the overwhelming majority will accept the religious affiliations of their parents. . . . [Even] if some should shift to another denomination it is not to be taken too tragically since the new affiliation will in most cases be included in the deeper moral community" (1963:61). Only in the event of a radical reorganization of society would churches generally—and liberal Protestant churches specifically—relinquish their custodial relationship with the central (Protestant) values, Parsons believed. As long as these values were spreading throughout the social structure, so to speak, and as long as each generation continued to "inherit" the religious affiliations of the parents, then church membership would be a major way by which Americans identified with their society, and liberal Protestantism would continue to have special custody of America's central values.

It is in the nature of these values that their holders would welcome the "liberal Protestantization" of Judaism and Catholicism, and it was Will Herberg's (1955) view—obviously shared by Parsons—that being Protestant, Catholic, or Jew in America was merely a set of alternative ways to be "American," of declaring one's attachment to society's core values.

Toward the end of this essay I shall return to this relationship of church-family-values. It is enough for now to say that while the theological warrant for a greatly reduced role for churches can be traced to the Reformation itself, this reduction has not, until recently, been particularly visible. The extravasation of the sacred has perhaps been occurring over a long period of time, but many of the consequences of this process are only now becoming noticeable. So dramatic are these consequences now, however, that Roof and McKinney (1986) see fit to call the present a time of "third disestablishment"—a truly significant alteration in the relationship of liberal Protestantism and American culture.

How are we to understand the situation?

Getting to the Present

During the years from approximately 1890 to 1920, the American Protestantism that had enjoyed near-establishment status for a century confronted the forces of modernity and responded in basically two ways. One of these responses attempted to hold firm—on doctrine especially perhaps, but also on ethic, church polity, worship, and its understanding of religious experience. It was "defensive," to use Peter Berger's term, in its approach to culture (1969:153ff.). The other response was prepared to accommodate to culture, especially those sectors of the culture most caught up in social change.

The first response led to conservative Protestantism, which, for all the differences to be found within it because of selective emphasis—some defending biblical inerrancy, others the paramountcy of the Holy Spirit, yet others dispensationalism—had as a central feature a resolve *not* to adjust to the changing culture's standards, but to hold on to standards that it regarded as its own. Evangelicals were, and are, a major component of this conservative response, so much so in fact that the labels evangelicalism and conservative Protestantism are often used interchangeably today.

The second response led to liberal Protestantism, which, for all its differences, had as a central feature precisely the willingness to adapt its standards of truth, value, and justice to standards drawn from beyond its own traditions.

Conservative Protestantism thus elected, for the most part, not to engage the culture at large, but to ignore it where discrepancy existed, whereas liberal Protestantism became liberal primarily in order to remain in relationship with culture. Estimates now suggest that many church members remained conservative in outlook in almost all denominations, but most of the large church bodies at the turn of the century—Methodist, northern Baptist, Presbyterian, Lutheran, Congregational, Episcopal, Disciples—were "captured" by those of the liberal persuasion. Their leaders, colleges, seminaries, publications, and a great many of their clergy toed the liberal line. They accommodated by their concern for social ministry, their willingness to cooperate across denominational lines, and their openness to "higher criticism" of the Bible. Sometimes, then, liberal Protestantism is known as Social Gospel, ecumenical, or modernist Protestantism.

Liberal Protestantism, in seeking to stay culturally engaged by responding to the forces of modernity, thus began a radically redefined relationship with American culture. Moreover, this radical redefinition may have represented—and may represent yet—the only relationship possible for any religion in the religiously plural situation if it seeks cultural engagement. If true, this means that not only will today's evangelicalism be unable to recapture the cultural role once played by Protestantism-turned-liberal, but so also will liberal Protestantism be unable to recapture its own former role. Put another way, the hegemony gained by liberal religion over conservative religion after the turn of the century was a hegemony won at the cost of greatly altering religion's place in society. Put yet a third way, the second disestablishment led inexorably to the third disestablishment.

Motivation vs. Adjudication

Part of this story is well known and is argued most forcefully by Peter Berger (1969): Pluralization of religion leads to the privatization of all religions, which means that, however important religion might be in the private lives of individuals, the mutual interchange of persons drawn from different religions tends to downplay, if not exclude, their religions. To understand how this happens, we need to distinguish religion at the motivational level from religion at the adjudicatory level, and this part of the story is not so well known.

Modernity and religious pluralism may tend, empirically, to diminish the role played by religion in the mental process of individuals, especially to the degree that they encounter and acknowledge religious claims conflicting with their own. But this is not necessarily the case. Mere knowledge that others are religiously different does not automatically weaken one's own religion. People may still be powerfully motivated by their spiritual outlook, and indeed it would be surprising if, in a society as devout as America, one did not frequently run into such people. In addition, numerous insulating techniques—from isolated communities to separate schools—help to protect religion at the motivational level.

At the adjudicatory level a different picture emerges as the implications of religious pluralism become clearer. For example, person A claims that her religious convictions not only permit, but may even dictate abortion under some circumstances, while person B claims that her religious convictions prohibit abortion not only for herself, but for all persons. More commonly perhaps, A makes a claim based on religious convictions, but B—who does not hold such religious convictions—rejects the claims. For example, Hindu parents insist on vegetarian meals for their children in the American public school cafeteria, while other parents—having no religious scruples about meat—disapprove of such an adjustment. The question is, how do these persons adjudicate their differences, assuming their mutual desire to remain in the same society?

In a certain sense one side inevitably "wins" and the other "loses." Abortion will or will not be allowed; vegetarian meals will or will not be served. If religious pluralism is to be maintained, the winning side will not—in winning—have its religious convictions vindicated, and the losing side will not—in losing—have its religious convictions discredited. Rather, religious convictions on both sides will, at this adjudicatory level, be held in abeyance—however important we might recognize them to be at the motivational level. Not to hold religious convictions in abeyance at the adjudicatory level is to establish one religion over another, something explicitly prohibited in the U.S. Constitution and implicitly unacceptable in all modern nations that are also religiously plural.

On what basis, then, are such cases adjudicated? The answer is on the basis of "principles" (variously labeled legal, ethical, or moral). In a functioning system, such principles must meet two distinguishing qualifications: (1) The principles must be abstract, that is, applicable not just to the case at hand, but to other cases as well. People need to be able to discern from principles invoked in one case how similar cases—including those in which entirely different religious convictions may be involved—would be decided. (2) The second qualification is that, since such principles cannot be articulated in the religious language peculiar to either contending party, they can be articulated only in language *common* to the contending parties—which, as society gains in religious pluralism, is language increasingly devoid of religious references and therefore oftentimes called "secular humanism."

Now this set of circumstances happens to be relatively easy to perceive in the legal setting (see Hammond, 1984, for illustration), but it is no less operative in any social setting where persons of diverse religious backgrounds interact. Religion may yet be important at the motivational private level, but it inevitably recedes in importance at the adjudicatory level. The "public square," as Richard Neuhaus (1984) says, becomes "naked."

Social circumstances, chiefly immigration, forced "established" Protestantism after the Civil War to recognize the fact of religious pluralism. Even if individual Protestants remained as convinced as ever of their singular hold on religious truth, they were destined—because of pluralism—to see a decline.

I am by default, however, describing chiefly what was the liberal Protestant view of things, not the evangelical view. To a significant degree, conservative Protestants "withdrew" from cultural engagement, which minimized their need to recognize their altered relationship to it. Liberal Protestants, however, ever eager to maintain their embrace of that culture—even if it were religiously plural—set themselves up for the rude awakening they now experience.

Waking Up to the Rude Reality

That account brings us to the present—and to the contrasting situations of liberal and conservative Protestantism. One is dispirited, the other optimistic, but neither is quite aware of what its future can be. In the case of evangelicalism, the ordeal of modernity, especially the full import of pluralism, has yet to be squarely faced. When it is, there is every reason to assume that a domestication process will occur not unlike the process that gave rise to liberal Protestantism. Indeed, ample evidence suggests such process is already underway, especially among

the politicized evangelicals who are sincerely trying to influence American culture; their only choice, so to speak, is to
compromise at the adjudicatory level with those who share
their political aims but not their religious motives. In the process, religious language is bound to recede, and so, in an adjudicatory sense, will their religion.

But if evangelical Protestants are slow in realizing that their
religious motives are not also coins of the realm at the adjudicatory level, liberal Protestants have yet to realize the full
meaning for them of the pluralistic game they have for decades
been playing. Unlike their conservative brethren—whose loss
to liberals early in this century left them both culturally
powerless and, until recently, culturally disengaged, and thus
unconcerned about being culturally powerless—liberal Protestants have remained culturally engaged but not fully aware of
their cultural powerlessness. The extravasation of the sacred
has gone largely unnoticed. The reason, put simply, is that the
culture toward which Protestantism is powerless has only
slowly lost its Protestant appearance. That slowness camou-
flaged—especially perhaps for liberal Protestants themselves—
the altered relationship they had had with culture since the
turn of the century. American culture, to put it another way,
remained "Protestant" far longer than the American population.

Three Examples

Three examples of the rude awakening Protestantism now
experiences can be cited, all three deserving fuller treatment
than can be given here. Although drawn from quite different
sectors of church life, each exemplifies the process of extravasation—the seeping out of the sacred from the vessel of the
church:

• Even after the second disestablishment, mainline Protestant
churches continued their foreign missions designed to "Chris-
tianize" diverse peoples. Granted, in accommodating to external standards of what constitutes worthy mission work, Bible-
reading, hymn-singing, and personal witnessing diminished as
concern for education, public health, and crop yield increased.
But the motivation of missionaries was not called into ques-

tion—by themselves or others—by this transition; they were still Christians doing Christian deeds. When, therefore, alternate means of doing foreign missions came into existence through such structures as Crossroads Africa or the American Friends Service, Christian ideals were not being forsaken, but the close links between church and Christian motivation were. These programs were able to recruit people inspired by the goal of insect control or crop fertilization. As long as expertise, enthusiasm, and physical stamina were present, what did spiritual maturity and wisdom—let alone doctrinal orthodoxy—matter?

Even so, the loss of the sacred from foreign mission-sponsoring churches did not get starkly revealed until the Peace Corps, modeled after Crossroads Africa, became the major channel for youthful expertise, enthusiasm, and stamina. The church, it could now be seen, had lost control of any "sacredness" in foreign missions. The link may still have been there in some volunteers' motives, but it was not there at the adjudicatory level; the church no longer chose either mission or missionary, for example. Extravasation of the sacred had taken place in foreign missions.

• A similar process occurred in the cure of souls. Part of the accommodation made during the second disestablishment was the adjustment from "curate" to welfare worker and pastoral counselor. Recognizing that agencies other than churches were trying to deliver mental health care and social services, more and more denominations added social welfare and counseling techniques to their seminary training.

But just as, say, the Methodists who built the hospital had to recognize that there is no such thing as a Christian (let alone Methodist) appendectomy, so did churches offering free meals or psychological advice come to realize that the "Christian" cure of souls was an elusive concept indeed. That personnel may be motivated by Christian charity might still be true, but who was to care? And how would they know? The models of practice were now imported from non-Christian contexts, as were the standards for judging the success of those models.

As long as churches nonetheless remained major vehicles by

which such services were delivered, the loss of the sacred in the cure of souls was not widely noticed. As competing government and "private" agencies grew popular, not only was the line separating church-delivered services from secular services growing increasingly hazy, but so also did it make decreasing difference whether the practitioner was Christianly motivated, and therefore even Christian. Extravasation of the sacred had taken place in the cure of souls.

• A third example is found in the Protestant ministry to higher education. Before the second disestablishment, of course, higher education generally was part of the Protestant establishment. Even the first of the great public universities were disproportionately administered and staffed by clergy or the sons of clergy. And the private colleges, most of which were founded by mainline Protestant denominations, regarded moral philosophy, frequent chapel, and religious study as natural parts of their undertaking.

The nearly automatic link between higher education and Protestantism was broken by the turn of the century, and chapel services diminished, became voluntary, or disappeared altogether. No longer did the school day begin with a moral exhortation from the clergyman-president. Many more subjects were added to the curriculum, as preparation for the ministry, for example, became a minor goal at best of a college education.

By no means did Protestantism's custodial relationship with higher education disappear, however. For one thing, until after World War II and the rapid expansion of higher education, church-related colleges continued to play a dominant leadership role. For another, "the church followed its students," to use the title of an influential book chronicling these events (Shedd, 1938). If the campus was no longer a surrogate parish, then the parish would move to the campus. As a result, the extravasation of the sacred in higher education—occurring as public sponsorship replaced church sponsorship—was hardly noticed. By offering social activities, counseling, opportunities for witness and discussion, as well as worship and fellowship, Protestantism continued to play a vital role in college and university.

In due time, however, many of the functions initiated by the Protestant ministry to higher education were taken over by higher education itself: counseling, off-campus housing service, social and political forum, etc. Because of the second disestablishment, so to speak, Protestantism could do nothing about such takeover, even if it had wanted to. But the realization that such takeover had occurred came as part of the third disestablishment, and campus pastors were largely left with having to invent programs, few of which could be advertised as compulsory, compelling, or sacred; that aspect of campus ministry had already escaped. (See Hammond, 1966.)

The Link Is Broken

Not only do liberal Protestant college students stay away in droves from campus ministerial programs; many also see no reason even to identify themselves by religious preference, thus preventing "their" church from following them by way of the campus ministry. Increasing numbers, moreover, have no church preference to declare because their parents have no church affiliation. In other words, the assumption that Talcott Parsons could make two decades ago ("it is to be taken for granted that the overwhelming majority will accept the religious affiliations of their parents") is now a dubious assumption indeed. Tables 3:1 and 3:2 present the evidence.

Several observations are worth making in Table 3:1. First, among Protestants in the twentieth century, deviation by children from parental religious affiliation has routinely been high—roughly a third. Second, Catholics and Jews, although

Table 3:1
The Proportion, by Year of Birth, of
Protestants, Catholics, and Jews (Age 18 +)
Who Do Not Share Their Parents' Religious Affiliation[1]

Year of Birth

Parental Affiliation:	1931 or Earlier	1932–46	1947 and Since
Protestant	35 (2,361)	37 (1,239)	33 (1,090)
Catholic	13 (1,122)	17 (764)	22 (827)
Jewish	10 (135)	16 (56)	25 (57)

Table 3:2

The Proportion, by Year of Birth, of Those Who,
Having Defected from Parental Religion,
Have Departed Religious Affiliation Altogether

Year of Birth

Parental Affiliation:	1931 or Earlier	1932–1946	1947 and Since
Protestant (all denom.)	6 (1,138)	21 (500)	34 (400)
Methodist	6 (301)	10 (127)	30 (123)
Lutheran	7 (125)	23 (66)	41 (59)
Presbyterian	7 (107)	15 (79)	35 (20)
Episcopal	13 (39)	38 (29)	47 (17)
White Baptist	8 (253)	13 (153)	31 (104)
Black Baptist	12 (60)	26 (46)	38 (40)
Catholic	26 (146)	44 (130)	55 (182)
Jewish	50 (14)	67 (9)	64 (14)

experiencing lower rates of intergenerational differences in religious affiliation than do Protestants, are nonetheless seeing significant increases through time.

The third observation is, properly speaking, only speculation in Table 3:1, but it finds convincing confirmation in Table 3:2. It is that, while the higher Protestant rates in Table 3:1 have been owing, as Parsons assumed, to the fact of denominational switching within Protestantism, *this is decreasingly true.* Rather, difference between generations in religious affiliations is coming to mean not denominational switching, but defection altogether. Moreover, such defection—not uncommon among Catholics and Jews throughout this century—is becoming common indeed among liberal Protestants.

Table 3:1 shows that a third of the Protestants deviate from parental denomination, but Table 3:2 shows that, while at an earlier time only 6 percent of these dropped out altogether, more recently the percentage is 34. Moreover, this pattern obtains in all the liberal denominations for which sufficient data are available. (Catholics and Jews who deviate from parental religion are even more likely than Protestants to defect altogether, but the proportion who deviate to begin with is smaller.)

The point made forcefully by Will Herberg, and analyzed by Parsons—that church affiliation is a common way to identify oneself as an American, and is thus a common expression of commitment to core values that in America are institutionalized in liberal Protestant churches—must now be questioned. At the very least it can be said that churches are decreasingly the means of expressing membership in the national community. Just as likely also perhaps, core values have so eroded or changed that they no longer resemble "liberal Protestant" values, and thus liberal Protestant churches no longer embody them.

The consequence, of course, is the loss by liberal Protestant churches of their custodianship of American culture, a process, I have been arguing, set in motion by the turn of the century but the products of which came as a clear shock only after defection rates skyrocketed after the 1960s. One message is obvious: increasing numbers of Americans find their identities and maintain their communities without church affiliation generally, without liberal Protestant affiliation specifically.

Conclusion

Does this loss of custodianship represent a crisis for liberal Protestantism? It most certainly does if liberal Protestant churches continue in the assumption that they automatically create, maintain, and express the national community—and thereby are the chief purveyors of the sacred in America. If that possibility once were true, it is decreasingly so today. Protestantism's very tolerance in accepting the conditions of religious pluralism meant that its link to the national community, and thus its grip on the sacred, was loosening.

But optimism might be in order to the degree that other kinds of "community" can be developed in and around churches. If community no longer depends on theological conviction, it is still the case that conviction emerges out of community. Emile Durkheim was right on this particular point—religion grows out of experience with the sacred, which in turn grows out of intimate relationships with others.

Modernity brought about considerable discontinuity in intimate relationships, not just between generations, but between populations divided along all kinds of lines. Moreover, *awareness* of this discontinuity has itself become a mark of modernity, so that different experiences of the sacred not only exist, but are widely known to exist. Churches, then, as embodiments of religion expressing the sacred, find their task increasingly problematic. The sacred has been extravasated, being discovered instead in institutional settings sometimes far removed from churches.

Discovering alternative communities and building on them thus becomes the key to liberal Protestantism's continued presence. This is the lesson, for example, of the "homogeneous unit" line of reasoning now dominating the church growth literature. But the larger question is whether all manner of such communities can be discovered, absorbed, and served. In a sense, this is the question addressed throughout all the essays of this volume.

4

Past Imperfect: History and the Prospect for Liberalism

William R. Hutchison

Although the term liberal Protestantism carries several mean-ings, and is thus more than a little troublesome, the choice of that label enables one to begin with an upbeat answer: Does liberal Protestantism—as a species of thought, faith, and social commitment—have a future? I believe religious liberalism, thus understood, is doing rather well and does assuredly have a future.

If one had been asked, instead, about the prospects for a certain set of denominations usually called the mainline churches, such an emphatic response might not be possible. The mainline churches ("oldline," as some have suggested, is probably the better term), while they won't pass away, will predictably continue to experience losses in "market share" within the American religious economy. As populations shift, as overall church adherence expands, and as religious forces rearrange themselves, these bastions of an earlier, heavily Northern and Eastern, Establishment will "decline" further from the amazing degree of domination they enjoyed in the first part of the twentieth century. They have been undergoing a process of that sort, at the rate of 4 or 5 percent in most decades, since the 1920s. This process probably will continue for the foreseeable future.

But this loss of institutional hegemony should not be equated too readily with a weakening in the various forms of liberal impulse—theological, ecumenical, social, political. The spirit of liberalism, like other spirits we are told about, bloweth where it listeth. A famous and often-married actress was asked, during one of her seasons of respite between husbands, whether she would do it all again. She replied that she would—but with different people. Liberalism, like evangelicalism or most other important isms, will perdure, but there's no reason to suppose that it must express itself always and forever through the institutional forms within which it flourished in the past.

Some will want to dispute or qualify my contention that liberalism persists, and will persist, through changing embodiments. Many, both liberals and others, are convinced that the impulse itself is enervated and has little prospect of making further contributions to our religious and cultural life. Yet most of those same observers, when pressed for an opinion as to where the vital juices are running in contemporary American religion, will call our attention not only to born-again conservative evangelicalism, but also to movements and tendencies that stand in a direct line of succession to the liberal traditions.

To prefer the label "postmodern" for liberation theologies, as Harvey Cox does, may be legitimate and useful. And the fact that moderates and dissidents among the Southern Baptists or Missouri Synod Lutherans have not called themselves liberals is understandable. But such impulses, along with the broader currents of social Christianity and critical biblical scholarship that have been running within the new evangelicalism since the 1950s, surely owe a great deal—just how much scarcely matters—to historic liberalism. With such major centers of the new evangelicalism as Fuller Seminary now showing a good deal more affinity to neoorthodoxy than to fundamentalism (Sheppard, 1977), surely we must be cautious both about assuming flatly a "decline" of classic liberalism and about implying a one-to-one relation between the liberal ideologies, whatever their current condition, and the oldline denominational structures.

If the fate of liberalism and the fate of certain denominations are two different issues, they are both important issues. I shall try to address both of them, especially at those points where they intersect. I intend to confine myself to the three points that preachers traditionally allow themselves (more aptly, perhaps, the three wishes that fairy-tale characters are always granted just before they are turned back into frogs). I wish, first of all, that one might avoid the statistical traps that lie in the path if one relies too much on changing church membership figures— in this case the figures that are supposed to show drastic decline and weakening in oldline Protestantism since the 1960s. Second, I wish one would forego the equally perilous nostalgia trips that transport one to an earlier—and I think mythical— America of serene moral and religious consensus. Finally, I shall single out, as the most neglected (although not necessarily most important) desideratum for liberal thinking and strategy, something I would like to call a positive theology of pluralism.

Before considering these three points I will state, as fairly as I can in a few sentences, what seem to be the most common reasons for questioning the survivability of liberal Protestantism. The usual assertions are (1) that this kind of religion is today on the defensive; (2) that the defensive posture is occasioned by the flourishing of "conservative churches" (although the alleged liberal enervation is also seen in more autonomous terms); (3) that the growth in religious conservatism and conservative churches is itself the result of widespread reaction against "secular humanist" values and against those who hold such values; (4) that our society as a whole has been experiencing a breakdown in moral consensus, a loss of moral coherence somehow connected with a decline in oldline Protestant dominance; and (5) that some or all of these happenings have been quite sudden, so that the early 1960s can be taken as a kind of benchmark—as a time before the fall.

Avoiding the Statistical Traps

One might phrase the survivability question more poignantly as:"Whatever Happened to the Old Main Line?" or, "Tell Me How Long the Train's Been Gone." The answer in much current commentary would seem to be: "Not long at all. You just missed it." But that answer is wrong or misleading—and in such a way as to skew projections for the future. We need, at this juncture, not so much to be "saved from the Sixties" (in Steven Tipton's wonderful phrase) as to be saved from the sixties statistics.

Those who point with alarm to a precipitate decline of the oldline churches and a sudden thriving of conservative ones are not, of course, referring only to numbers. Yet some specific analyses, and countless casual assertions, have taken the apparently shifting figures for membership and attendance, especially since 1965, as signaling a grossly and suddenly changed situation. Such inferences have been prompted especially by the fact that a few oldline denominations in these years have shown negative growth. Although decline in absolute numbers does not give a qualitatively different signal from the declines against population growth that we had seen quite regularly in earlier statistics, minus signs are admittedly eye-catching and scary.

, The first problem here is that, minus signs or not, the fluctuating growth rates for the oldline churches (quite healthy growth during the postwar revival; decline during the 1970s; some recovery in the first half of the eighties) tell us little if they are not compared, and compared over a number of decades, with the growth rates for the conservative churches. I would go further: in the absence of such historical controls, we are lured into just the kind of dubious suppositions—for example, about allegedly increased defections from oldline to conservative— that have plagued recent discussions.

I cannot claim to have attempted an exhaustive quantitative study. Given my skepticism, perhaps natural in a Quaker, about correlations between quantities and vitalities, I am unlikely to do that. But if one looks only at the most accessible figures for religious groups from 1920 to 1985, the prima facie case for a recently increased "movement" from oldline to conservative churches is simply not there. If you wish to contrast an alleged liberal disarray, since the sixties, with evangelical purposiveness and consensus, that's fine, and it can perhaps be argued on other grounds. But the idea that the statistics of church adherence (even *before* we consider the enormous changes and varieties within evangelicalism) will support such a contrast is faulty. Indeed, in historical perspective the figures for membership and attendance could easily be used to argue that the so-called conservative churches have been growing less spectacularly over the past twenty years than in the period from 1920 to 1965.

Will Herberg tried to tell us in the mid-fifties that, despite a conventional wisdom to the contrary, conservative churches had been booming since the Scopes trial; and at a rate roughly three times that of the oldline churches. Those observations were rephrased by Pitney Van Dusen and others, at the end of the decade, as admonitions to the liberal churches that they had better take account of "third force Christianity." The point was regularly confirmed and reiterated as scholars like Joel Carpenter studied the very-much-alive fundamentalism of the second quarter century. Yet too many of our analysts have now, seemingly, forgotten about those earlier realities.

One frequently cited bar graph has been used to suggest, for the decade 1965–75, a severe diminution of seven mainline Protestant bodies by contrast both with their gains in the preceding ten years and with the continuing growth of selected conservative churches (Carroll et al., 1979:15). The gap in growth rates for 1965–75, as shown on that graph, is more than twenty-nine percentage points (an average loss in the oldline denominations of 8.9 percent against average gains among the conservatives of 20.5 percent). This is indeed a substantial difference, but it does not approach the difference in growth rates recorded for the same religious groups in the 1930s, when the discrepancy amounted to sixty-two percentage points. It is smaller than the gap discernible in the 1920s, and only slightly larger than those for the forties and fifties. (See *Yearbooks of the American and Canadian Churches,* 1920–1984.)[1]

One can grasp a little better what such percentage-point differences mean by noting that between 1920 and 1960, the conservative churches represented in this particular sample experienced an average growth of well over 400 percent, while their oldline competitors were able to show, on average, a forty-year increase of 78.4 percent. It is common to explain such vast differences by speculating that conservative churches must surely have begun with smaller numbers. That would apply in some cases; in others, such as the Southern Baptists and the Missouri Synod Lutherans, it would not. (The Southern Baptist Convention, which increased by 334 percent, began at a figure larger than any oldline body save the northern Methodists.) In those instances, moreover, in which a small membership base is a factor before 1965, it usually is afterward as well.

A good many such corrections and variables could, in any case, be accepted without much affecting the main point: if differing growth rates were really a matter of people marching from one kind of church to the other, recent liberal net losses would appear somewhat less alarming than the Great Trek we would need to posit for some earlier periods. By extension, if we were to take changes in church population as indicating in any significant degree how people react to liberal tendencies in the oldline churches and the ecumenical movement, we might find ourselves trapped into concluding (mirabile dictu!) that liberal policies have been acting to stem an earlier flow from liberal churches to conservative ones.

The differences between American Baptist and Southern Baptist growth rates have been considerably smaller in 1960–85 than they were in 1935–60. Are we to suppose that the liberalism of the American Baptists has been keeping potential defectors in the fold? An absurd suggestion, to be sure; but not much more absurd than the conclusions induced by overinterpretation of the oldline churches' faltering and sometimes negative membership statistics after the early sixties. Not only were these churches leveling off from the heady gains of the postwar revival era (the main Presbyterian bodies from 1940 to 1960 had gained adherents at more than twice the rate of the preceding twenty years), just as important, even more than before, they were "losing" members and potential members because the regions in which they were strongest were "losing" population. The South, since 1960, has grown by 45 percent, while the Northeast has expanded by a modest 11 percent. And if the population "moving" to fast-growth regions have not clamored for Congregational churches, that is at least partly because the churches already there—in rank defiance of our stereotypes—are not bound to be different from those they have left behind.

The data for the ecumenical organizations of the older Northern Establishment tell much the same story: diminution in "share of market" has been the rule, never the exception. As American Protestantism tripled in size between 1920 and 1985, realigning its elements in what were natural and healthy ways, the percentage of Protestants belonging to member churches of the Federal, or later National, Council of Churches—bodies not adhered to by Southern Baptists, Mormons, or Missouri Synod Lutherans—decreased gradually but with great regularity. Figure 4:1 shows, for those years, FCC/NCC membership as a percentage of the total constituency of non-Roman Catholic Christian churches.

One sees by this measure, as by others, that for the oldline churches it was the higher growth rates of the 1950s that were unusual, not the relatively lower ones that set in after the early sixties. The immediate postwar period was, for the oldline establishment, a brief shining moment that is not a particularly good benchmark for subsequent "decline."

Many of us, it may be recalled, were not so sure that the crowding of the suburban churches in the fifties had constituted a shining moment in the first place. When the statistics leveled off in 1963, and Time magazine announced that the great postrevival was over, church leaders were quoted as "thankfully saying 'Amen.'" Bishop John Wesley Lord and a

Figure 4:1

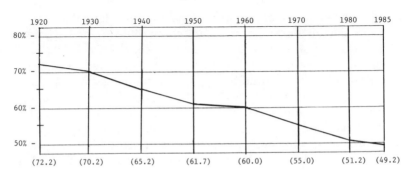

dozen others told reporters that now the churches could get back to real religion. In what one cleric called the "boom of numbers and dollars and buildings," too many suburban parishioners had been recruited, as Bishop Lord remarked, "who had been starched and ironed before they were washed." Although the churchly commentators of that moment might be suspected of putting a good face on things, their reactions were, on the whole, consistent with the reservations most of them had voiced throughout the revival. On this ground, too, we should think twice before taking the years around 1960 as a standard against which the current vitality or impotence of the churches is to be measured.

My plea is not that we abandon statistical criteria, but that we use the recent statistics with far more caution. More particularly, social scientific analyses have usually been too casual about one essential kind of "control"—the historical kind. Are the liberal churches declining? Well—to use an old rejoinder—compared with what? The seriously researched comparison has been not to past rearrangements of the religious landscape, but to concurrent growth in "fringe" and conservative religion.

Even those much-exploited comparisons, as I've suggested, too often treat evangelicalism as though we were living in 1955 rather than in 1985. In what senses, exactly, are the no-longer-tiny Evangelicals for Social Action unmentionable in relation to "liberal Protestantism"? Aside from the abortion issue, not many. Is the thriving, 40,000-member Peacemaker organization among the Southern Baptists not to be placed, in our analyses, somewhere near Clergy and Laity Concerned? In more individual terms, do we really mean to allow the Methodist family from Dayton that joins the Baptists in Houston to become a statistic of political or ideological change? Such migrants may or may not belong in a discussion even of theological change.

When, on the oldline-liberal side of the ledger, we speak of such things as withdrawal from foreign missions or from sponsorship of higher education, we might refer also to the phenomenal growth of religious studies (not predominantly under conservative sponsorship) in public and private higher education and to the manyfold increase in overseas agencies doing very much what liberal Protestants did in the heyday of foreign missions. When we find that youthful defections from religious affiliation were significant in the mainline losses of the seventies (Roof and Hadaway, 1979), surely it is relevant to inquire whether or not that has been the case in the past; we should consult some of the numerous studies and plaints on that subject—beginning perhaps with Washington Gladden's Columbus, Ohio, survey of exactly a century ago: *The Young Men and the Churches: Why Some of Them Are Outside, and Why They Ought to Come In*. When trying to glimpse the future, on this same point, we might take seriously Robert Wuthnow's warning, in 1976, that "predictions about religious trends based on data from the past decade . . . are likely to be highly misleading" (862). Wuthnow proposed that "as successive age strata mature . . . there may well be a return to more traditional religious commitments" (862). We should, further, consider the degree to which the suburban church boom after 1945 was affected by the return of lost sheep (trailing their little lambs) from the late thirties.

On many fronts we must monitor the indicators and figures already appearing for the 1980s. In matters of some significance, such as congressional "representation" of religious groups, the enormous and disproportionate visibility of the oldline bodies continues (in 1984, sixty-seven Episcopalians, one Pentecostal); the "losses" have been to Roman Catholic and Jewish representation, not noticeably to right-wing or even "evangelical" Protestantism (Menendez, 1983; *Christianity Today*, 1985). Even in the membership sweepstakes it appears that the NCC bodies may do reasonably well in the 1980s. Of the six oldline churches (the Presbyterians having now amalgamated) whose negative figures for the 1970s were discussed earlier, none has decreased at the same rate in the 1980–85 reports (covering 1978 to 1983). Three have declined at substantially lesser rates. Two have virtually held firm. One (the American Baptists) has grown.[2]

I am willing, in fact, to hazard a prediction about the trendier media reports and worried conference papers of 1990. We may be in for titles like "Mainline Protestantism: Why Is It Growing?" or "Yuppies, Late Marriage, and the Sunday School Boom," or even "The Suburban Captivity of the Churches."

Foregoing the Nostalgia Trip

In 1611, a year now considered—with the King James Version and all—a pretty good year for Christendom, John Donne complained that "new philosophy casts all in doubt. . . . 'Tis all in pieces, all coherence gone. . . . Prince, subject, Father, Son, are things forgot." Assumptions about moral and general declension usually play well in poetry and homiletics—Donne's two genres—and as witticism. (An old codger is supposed to have lamented that "your modern thunderstorm don't clear the air.") But such assumptions usually make for poor history. And bad history, I think we would agree, can lead to dubious prognostication.

The "decline" of liberal Protestantism to which many are pointing—some with satisfaction, others with dismay—is frequently linked, especially by the dismayed, to a purported loss of moral coherence in American society. If expending my second wish at this point, I would ask only for a change of wording: for "loss of coherence" I should like to substitute "lack of coherence." Our society certainly falls tragically short of coherent response to its own stated ideals, to say nothing of more transcendent ones. And the notion that these ideals were once far better realized gives them, of course, a kind of imprimatur from our ancestors. But such imaginings also provide handy and well-known tools for reaction. One appropriate response for the religious liberal, as for the social scientist, is to inquire very closely just what sort of past we are being asked to return to.

None of us admits to nostalgia when important matters are at stake. Even the New Religious Right would balk at Grant Wacker's characterization of their thought as a Norman Rockwell view of American history (1984). Yet a great many of our diagnosticians, to the left as much as on the right, do allow elements of nostalgia to creep in. It does not take much attentiveness, at any rate, to find behind many analyses and prescriptions an *idee fixe* that prepluralist America was morally

(74)

more coherent, more "together," more effectual than recent and current America.

While these implied contrasts between a moral past and an amoral present can be documented in certain respects, as general propositions they are ill-founded and, to be frank, downright wild. The anthropologist Mary Douglas puts part of the case as follows:

> Reflection shows that the evidence for old-time sanctity comes from suspect sources such as hagiography, panegyrics and sermons. If we were to read even that biased evidence more critically, we would notice the professionals upbraiding the mass of ordinary people for lack of faith, as if the gift of which, we are told, modernity has deprived us was always rather the exception.

Douglas adds, with respect to the equally common assumption that people of past ages were spiritually and (hence) generally fulfilled, that she can see "no evidence that there is more unhappiness and mental disturbance now than in those famous ages of faith. How can anyone possibly say? The evidence is weak, the arguments weaker" (Douglas, 1983:29; see also Robinson, 1985).

Most cultural and religious historians would want to second Douglas. In the case before us, the idea that America under mainline Protestant hegemony was, on balance, more coherent morally than today's society may have been assumed in a traditional history that focused on those who exercised hegemony. But few interpretations in political or cultural history, and almost none in social history, have implied such a favorable view of the American past. And for at least a generation, broadened purviews in religious and intellectual history have made such views distinctly obsolete in those fields. Robert Handy, writing in 1971 of "a Christian America," juxtaposed in his subtitle "Protestant hopes" and "historical realities." His interpretation was, if anything, a trifle more celebratory than most.

But the opposite tendency persists, and not without respectable sponsorship. Peter Berger, while he deplores any reliance on "dubious historical warrants" or "fanatical reiterations of this or that erstwhile certitude," nonetheless insists that society today

(75)

suffers not just from insufficient moral coherence, but from a loss of such coherence—a declension. With moral pluralism "becoming increasingly prevalent," Berger wrote recently, it is now not difficult or farfetched to imagine statements such as "My moral preference is for the use of arson in labor disputes," or "I happen to be a rapist," or "I'm into spying for the Soviet Union." Would anyone in the past have uttered such sentiments, or implied them in their actions? (Berger, 1983:18)

Most historians would have to reply sadly that, whatever may have been the case in other societies, Americans in the past have been quite prone to act out all those sentiments; they have, moreover, been more ready than most to articulate them—and in something like the phraseology Berger imagines. Richard Slotkin's *Regeneration Through Violence* (1973) is only the most noteworthy contribution to a small library of studies depicting a moral preference for violence in the American past. Our literature and thought forms have been replete with moral justifications or excuses for arson, rape (on and off the plantation), and—as the advertisers would put it—much, much more. Slotkin, without carrying his analysis beyond 1860, records the use and justification of violence as a mode of initiation, self-creation, and love; as a mode of progress, self-transcendence, and regeneration; and, however incredibly, as a mode of reconciliation and of relation to God.

But surely, you may say, those anarchists of the past who expressed moral preference for the use of arson in labor disputes were denounced roundly by their contemporaries; and that is certainly true. It is also true today. But let me concede such points. If we were to do that, if we were to concede the relative benignity of the railroad strike of 1877 (in which arson was a preferred method) or of the Harlan County troubles in the 1930s, I'm afraid we would still have to talk about expressed moral preferences, in the American past, for burning convents, burning villages and cities, and burning Negroes.

If either Protestantism or the moral directorship of society at large has recently displayed divided counsels regarding war, injustice, poverty and industrial organization, I see in our past more seriously and acutely divided counsels. The moral directorship of the past was perhaps more effective than any consensus of today in the realm of personal morality; but even that is far from clear, given the bitter divisions in the nineteenth century over temperance, chastity, sabbatarianism, and a dozen other moral issues. If we, in addition, consider the degree to which moral directorship was or was not effective—if we estimate conservatively the actual crime rates, actual poverty, actual incidence of corruption and allowance of corruption—it is not clear that what we are seeing today can be called the loss of a former moral coherence.

We are talking about a past American society that, for example, either approved lynchings, or did nothing about them, or was morally confused about them. While the movement from such a society to that of the civil rights revolution may not prove any theories of inexorable moral progress, it also does not prove, or even permit, a theory of moral declension. Henry Adams believed that the development of American politics from Washington to Grant disproved the law of evolution. He had a point; and if we then ask about the "progress" from Grant to Nixon, we would have to acknowledge something like stasis in our political morality. Yet the moral development from a society that largely approved of Grant—or of Boss Tweed, or of Warren Harding's friends—to the one that condemned Nixon and Watergate may reflect something better than stasis.

I am not urging a triumphalist or even progressivist view—triumphalism being not at all preferable to nostalgia. I am suggesting that the search for solutions to our moral disarray is needlessly confused, even if it is helpfully dramatized, by fantasies concerning moral decline. More particularly, our consideration of the fate or future of religious liberalism is skewed from the start by unproved and, in most cases, unprovable assumptions about the past effectuality of institutional Protestantism.

Exploiting the Positive Theology of Pluralism

Another of Will Herberg's observations that might help us now was that Protestants in America, as of the 1950s, were suffering from the rather sudden onset of "psychological minority" feelings—a sense of relative deprivation in relation to the power and dominance they had enjoyed in the past (1955:250–51).The oldline denominations today, jolted by the minus signs of the seventies, are in a similar way struggling to adjust to long-term developments, this time within institutional Protestant-ism, that have come belatedly to their notice. Once we have attained a calmer and historically deeper sense of what has been happening—once we move beyond both panic and pan-egyrics—it should be possible to discern more clearly the future roles of these churches and of the religious forms of liberalism.

Peter Berger, in an aperçu that I admire very much, has predicted that secular humanism in America, having failed to achieve the sort of success many had expected or feared, will be forced to accept a kind of denominational status (1983:22). The oldline Protestant denominations, oddly enough, may also have to accept denominational status. That, severally or together, they will ever regain the cultural dominance of yesteryear is, as the British say, simply not on. Those who hope that a few of the more egregious prime-time preachers will be replaced by liber-als (or even by evangelicals) are in for a long wait; I'm afraid it is accurate, even if elitist, to expect that event to occur several days after *Dallas* is bumped by *Masterpiece Theatre*. But the liberal churches do—both severally and together—stand for reasonably distinctive traditions or emphases. To own, refur-bish, and spiritually invigorate these distinctive features seems somewhat more important to the future of liberal Protestantism than the efforts, understandable though they are, to reach broader constituencies or to do something about the inadequate liberal birthrate.

I mean, obviously, to support those who think of the future usefulness of these bodies, and of their federative structures, in "gathered-church" more than in "churchly" terms (at that juncture I agree with Kelley [1972]. To put this concretely, let me offer just one example. A common explanation for unim-pressive mainline growth rates has been that monies for church building have so often gone instead for work in the ghettos, or to Angola or perhaps Nicaragua. Now until Congregationalists tithe like Adventists (another long wait), the funds for doing what one would like in both these fields of endeavor are going to be limited. I believe that the liberal churches and ecumenical bodies, faced with such choices, should maintain much the same kind of balance—or imbalance, if you like—that in recent years has brought them under criticism. That is a personal preference, but at this point I am offering it also as a guess about the sources and shape of liberal Protestantism's "American future."

In thus embracing a status that will be closer to "sectarian" than these churches are accustomed to, I would hope that liberal Protestantism might become less timid and less grudging in its commitment to religious pluralism—or, better, in its religious commitment to pluralism.

Despite the historic American and Protestant credentials of church-state separation and other elements in the pluralist tradition, some may find it a peculiar idea that mainline Protestants should go out of their way to defend that tradition theologically—especially if they are in search of a future. Isn't this, when all is said, something the churches should leave to the Anti-Defamation League (ADL) and the American Civil Liberties Union (ACLU)? Doesn't "pluralism" connote a fragmentation that liberal Protestants, whether or not they must accept it, don't have to like or defend?

The answer should be "No" to each of those queries. "Pluralism" will endorse moral fragmentation only so far as we allow it to do so. The term pluralism, I take it, means not simply "diversity" (although it is sometimes used that way), but more especially the acceptance, or even celebration, of diversity. It is a value term, not just a descriptive one. As such, it becomes an ally of fragmentation and moral anarchy only to the extent that we leave its defense to the fragmenters and moral anarchists. And my impression (as a non-theologian venturing beyond his competence and willing to be corrected) is that, despite ample encouragements from theologians in the liberal and neo-orthodox traditions, what we are calling liberal Protestantism has not exploited those resources within its own tradition that justify or even demand a positive theology on this point. Pluralism, if not religious freedom, has been too often allowed to appear as something the religious interests concede to political necessity.

Bodies like the ADL and the ACLU, far from endorsing moral anarchy, have mounted positive rationales for pluralism from the perspective of libertarian and other traditions. To these, liberal Protestantism ought to be adding its own potentially powerful voice. In other contexts, such as that of social action, we may want liberals to be more assertive about convictions that divide them from others; to be willing, for example, to call a social policy unchristian that they think is unchristian. But liberal Protestants have also been too timid about owning and expressing the biblical and theological warrants for their—or anyone else's—speaking out in just that initially divisive way.

In an address several years ago at Harvard, Eugene Borowitz of Hebrew Union College argued eloquently for what I would call the first step toward a firmer religious affirmation of pluralism and laid the groundwork for a further step that I consider equally important. Borowitz suggested that, in the interest of pluralism itself and of those whom he called the "partially enfranchised of our society," liberals of all types must speak more strongly about the *compatibility* of the demand for an open, pluralistic society with steadfastness in the strongest kind of personal and group convictions.

To the partially enfranchised, Borowitz said, the danger in the current conservatism is "that under the guise of ending ethical anarchy, America will grow more repressive." The problem, he said, develops when those who properly seek to reclaim ethical absolutes begin to insist that the truth they have found is all the truth anyone needs. Is that step inevitable? Is there no way, he asks, to hold an "ultimate" strong enough to ground and guide us, without then forcing our versions of truth on those who vigorously disagree with us? Borowitz answers that there has to be another way, since

> we cannot be asked to accept the principle that, affirming the one God, we deny the virtues of pluralism. For myself, I would rather run the risks of the occasional abuse of freedom than face the profanation of God and the degradation of people that religious persecution and intolerance create. Our generation now needs to

learn how to proclaim the truth of faith and liberty simultaneously.

Borowitz in that speech based the argument for pluralism on what he called "a profound theological modesty."

> Though I know enough about transcendent truth to base my life on it, I also realize that it expresses and manifests itself in ways far more complex than I can fully understand. . . . For all my personal conviction, I must bow to your right to make up your own mind. My spirit and my intellect tell me that my understanding of the ultimate is the best that anyone has—but that does not imply that those who disagree with me are necessarily in error and have no spiritual right to what I perceive as their religious folly.

As had often been done before (although rarely so well), Borowitz linked humility before God to democratic ideology.

> Against the old logic and the old theologies, we now assert the religious virtue of approaching the truth pluralistically. Transcendence without fanaticism, pluralism without permissiveness, the moral courage of the old faiths with modern democracy's respect for differences—America should have taught us that. We, who seek to bind up her spiritual wounds, need to be true to what this blessed nation has given her successive generations. (1982:272–73)

Although this, as it stands, constitutes an important base for revitalized moral consensus, one further step is required. It is a move that I'm sure Borowitz would agree to, since it is at least prefigured in his own argument. Why should one be "modest" theologically? Not out of timidity, but because humans are less than God. Why must pluralism be maintained? Not just because of political or social necessity, but because the denial of pluralism means a "profanation of God and degradation of people."

If we pursue the defense of pluralism only to the point of professing theological modesty and democratic necessity, there is the distinct chance that we shall still be talking about toleration. And that would not be enough. Toleration says, "I know I am right, but you are welcome to use the Club. On weeknights. Please use the back entrance." Pluralism says, "I believe firmly that I am right; but only God is God, and only God knows who is right."

In thus explaining and championing religious pluralism on affirmative theological grounds rather than on negative or concessionary ones, liberal Protestants could make one of the more important of their distinctive contributions to the moral coherence and consensus that our sprawling society needs but has found it difficult to maintain. Much else—in the realms, for example, of piety, of doctrine, and of social zeal—can be seen as vital to the revivification of a distinctive liberal witness. But surely the theistic rationale for pluralism, in distinctive Protestant forms, deserves central attention. A liberal Protestant pluralism unconscious of its own grounding in the radical otherness of God and in an uncompromising respect for persons will continue to be vulnerable to charges of timidity—of not knowing what we are about, or at least of being too skittish about asserting the spiritual and theological grounds of what we are about.

A historian, to be sure, must feel some diffidence in offering such confident, perhaps judgmental assertions about a project that must be carried out by others—by theologians. Yet the contributors to this book were asked—as, mostly, historians and sociologists—what liberal Protestantism must do to be saved. I can only say, as one historian of the liberal Protestant phenomenon, that I see the need for a bolder, more explicit theistic rationale for pluralism as perhaps the greatest unattended need of the moment. At the point where this, along with other assertions of a positive liberal theology, meets the secular demands and human needs of a diverse society and world—at that point of convergence—we would also discover a liberal Protestantism conscious of its own strength and conscious of its capacity to promote the healing of our social order.

PART

II

HISTORICAL

ANALYSES

5

Our Country: One Century Later

Edwin S. Gaustad

When in 1885 Josiah Strong analyzed America's present situation and its future possibilities, he showed himself to be a most astute observer. He also demonstrated his desire to have as much factual data at his disposal as possible. His book was to be no mere homily, no simple call to repentance, but a hardheaded analysis of what was good and promising about the country as well as what was bad and frightening. Because he saw the time and the place as pregnant with wondrous possibility, he all the more expressed the deepest concern lest those wonders of the future somehow become horrors. "There are certain great focal points of history": for example, the incarnation, the Reformation, and now the "closing years of the nineteenth century" in America.

For grand dreams to become true, one must avoid present perils of major magnitude. Seven such perils Josiah Strong described at length in 1885, giving an entire chapter to each: immigration, Romanism, Mormonism, intemperance, socialism, wealth, and the city. (In the 1891 edition of *Our Country*, Strong added an eighth peril: Religion and the Public Schools.) Each peril threatened the future prospects of both the nation and its religion: that is, Protestantism. Although the entire country was in danger of fatal infection, that danger was greatest in the American West. Like Lyman Beecher, a half century earlier, Strong saw the West as presenting the greatest challenge and the greatest opportunity to "pure, spiritual Christianity." The challenge must be faced; the opportunity must not be lost. The harshness with which Mormonism is treated can be attributed in part to the deep anxiety created by an interloper who seemed capable of not only disturbing, but perhaps destroying that pervading Protestant dream for the West.

Why was Strong's book so enormously popular? *Our Country* sold 175,000 copies within a thirty-year period, and portions of the book were printed separately or excerpted in newspapers and magazines.[1] The book went through new editions and reprintings, the most recent by Harvard University Press in 1963. What responsive chords did it touch? First, the future of civilization rests with America. "The world's sceptre passed from Persia to Greece, from Greece to Italy, from Italy to Great Britain" and now it is passing from Great Britain to America (1963:29). Moreover, within America, it is passing from the East to the West, where the national character and the country's destiny will be determined. Second, Strong identified the enemies who sought to thwart this destiny, and he did so in language that was vigorous, concrete, and emotionally stirring. Third, his own confidence could not fail to be contagious: God and history were on America's side, God and history will prevail. No spiritual malaise here, no theological hesitation, no academic weighing of all the alternatives that concludes with the safe (if wholly unsatisfying) call for more research. Strong's trumpet blew no uncertain notes.

Its Strengths

What are the enduring strengths of this volume published 100 years ago? Wherein do we find Strong's brand of Protestantism still looking good? In the first place, Strong never lets go of the transcendent dimension: his trust is more in God than it is in humans. This is the basic problem, according to Strong, with socialism. It wants to deal with suffering but not with sin; it wants to promote the "brotherhood of man" but thinks it possible to do this without attention to the "fatherhood of God." Therefore, despite the high moral purposes of some socialists, despite even their sometimes sacrificial character, the movement will not succeed, even in its own terms. God is in history and over history; God's possession of all that human beings preside over as mere stewards must be ever acknowledged. It may be charged that Strong's rhetoric is more transcendent than his social and economic reality. This might be argued particularly when, in exclaiming the virtues of stewardship, he demonstrates a keen interest in raising more money for home missions. But on the whole, he seems buoyed by a faith that can and will move mountains, by a power that vastly exceeds the feeble muscles of humankind.

Second, Strong seems motivated by a lively sense of justice and fair play, this being true whether or not the particular issue in question has clear biblical or theological command. Such "modern" ideas as the liberty of individuals and the priority of the people over against government were sure signs of progress and deserved the approbation of all humankind. In that regard, the abolition of slavery was an altogether appropriate application of the general principle of individual freedom; so also the progress being made in the elevation of women and the "enhanced valuation of human life" in general. The number of crimes for which capital punishment was deemed the appropriate penalty had been radically reduced, notably in England. So many "amazing changes" have taken place in the nineteenth century "that if we reckon time by its results, twenty years of this century may outmeasure a millennium of olden time" (6).

But progress in justice and liberty does, from time to time, require our helping hand. It is a tribute to Strong's moral sense that in the midst of a chapter attacking socialism, he provides many powerful criticisms of capitalism. The best way to defeat socialism is to make capitalism more just, to instill it with its own sense of fair play. Socialism has a passion for equality, some of which goes well beyond the demands of common sense or the realities of human nature. But when inequalities "become practically hereditary" and the gulf between rich and poor grows ever wider, then we are confronted with inequalities of class that "are both unrepublican and dangerous" (94). The effect of industrialization has been to do just this: separate the classes more widely and harden the lines as well as the antipathies between them. In Massachusetts, for example, in 1883 nearly thirty thousand children under sixteen years of age were employed in the factories. In the average working man's family, moreover, about one third of the income had to come from the wives/mothers and children for the family to survive. Such is the lot of the employed. Industrialization, however, has produced great numbers of the unemployed, persons who, on the whole, furnish "ready recruits to the criminal, intemperate, socialistic, and revolutionary classes" (98). Capital and labor are arrayed against each other, with the unemployed prepared to make war against both. This not only violates justice, but it also threatens to destroy democracy—as de Tocqueville warned.[2]

The author's strictures against capitalism are so strong that, if read out of context, they would appear to be an argument on behalf of socialism. Of course they are not, but the tone of voice is not softened thereby. What was developing in America in the 1880s, Strong declared, was a feudalism far worse than that of the Middle Ages. In "modern and republican feudalism" the lords simultaneously have more power and less responsibility than their counterparts of earlier centuries. "The capitalist can arbitrarily raise the price of necessaries, can prevent men's working, but has no responsibility, meanwhile, as to their starving. Here is 'taxation without representation' with a vengeance" (106). These "money kings," Strong explained in a separate chapter on "Wealth," were open invitations to despotism: they have tenure for life, there is no rotation in office, there is no system of checks and balances. Why, Cornelius Vanderbilt alone has more wealth than the assessed value "of the aggregate property, real and personal, of four great states of the Union" (124). Monopolies and trusts, cartels and combines, price-fixing, and the prevailing "congestion of wealth" violates our religion, divides our peoples, and destroys our land.

Already the youngest nation in the world is well on its way to becoming the richest nation in the world, Josiah Strong correctly prophesied in 1885. Sounding like the old English Whigs, Strong pointed to the corrupting power of wealth, the brutalizing force of materialism, the destructive effect of luxury and idleness. Great accumulations of wealth are destructive of the political good health of the nation as they are of the social health. The ballot box is corrupted, while the highest offices go not to men of wisdom and virtue, but to men of wealth and therefore of power. No reform, moral or political, can be undertaken if it threatens the wealthy. Every enterprise, however immoral or undemocratic, can be justified on the sole ground that it is a money-maker. "Ever since greed of gold sold the Christ and raffled for his garments, it has crucified every form of virtue between thieves" (118). Christianity itself is threatened by the tendency to translate everything into monetary terms, to value only that which can be cashed in. Our materialism outruns our idealism, as we forget that wealth is only a ministry to enlarge life, not life a ministry to enlarge wealth. "The means of self-gratification should not outgrow the power of self-control" (120). All America is endangered by the gospel of greed, but the American West especially so, since nineteen out of twenty going west go with the intention of getting rich. In fact, everybody in the West is motivated by money—everyone except the invalid and the home missionary (126).

Third, an enduring strength of *Our Country* is its effort to engage in hardheaded analysis, to accumulate and interpret the data, to opt for realism over sentimentalism. When dealing with the "peril of intemperance," for example, Strong details the growth in the number of saloons, in the consumption of liquor, in the power of the alcohol industry. Alcoholism increases as the pace of life quickens, as modern industry and the modern city bring people into proximity, and as tensions and frustrations mount. "The American people are rapidly becoming the most nervous, the most highly organized, in the world, if, indeed, they are not already such" (73). Moreover, people "of nervous organization" are both more likely to use alcohol to excess and more likely to suffer severest effects therefrom. In a nine-year period (from 1868 to 1877) the population of the United States increased less than 10 percent, but the increase in the consumption of liquor was 37 percent. Official government reports, Strong noted, show that per capita consumption of alcohol was four gallons in 1840, but twelve gallons in 1883. And the production of malt liquor in America went from about

1.5 million barrels in 1863 to nearly 19 million a mere two decades later. If the situation is bad in the nation as a whole, it is even worse in the West. By counting the number of saloons per voter, Strong demonstrates—at least to his own satisfaction—that "the people in the western third of the United States are two and one-half times as intemperate as those in the eastern two-thirds" (77–78).

If the statistics of consumption and production are frightening, even more so are the data regarding the growing power of the liquor industry. Liquor bosses threaten to boycott businesses that do not cooperate with them; they organize for the express purpose of influencing legislation in their behalf, resorting to bribery if there appears to be no other way of exercising their will. Rum runs our cities: "In 1883, of the twenty-four aldermen of the city of New York, ten were liquor-dealers and two others, including the President of the Board, were ex-rumsellers." Strong quotes *The New York Times* in its deploring of the great municipal evil "which gives the saloon-keepers more power over government than is possessed by all the religious and educational institutions in the city" (84). The "Liquor Power" dominates the city; soon the cities will dominate the country. What, then, will become of the republic and of its thoroughly corrupted, hopelessly besotted citizenry? (See Rorabaugh, 1979.)

In subsequent chapters, this Congregational missionary and liberal Protestant reveals how intemperance and urbanization are closely related, how huge personal fortunes and the rising interest in socialism interact. The city is the locus of all the "perils," except for Mormonism, and that peril serves to aggravate the vulnerability of the American West to all the others. Demographic trends are analyzed, comparisons with European nations are drawn, denominational as well as governmental statistics are assembled, the leading and latest authorities are quoted—all this with a view to making his case as convincing and valid as possible. Neither homily nor jeremiad, *Our Country* endeavors to gather and assess the "social statistics" relevant to the progress or the peril of the nation.

Its Weaknesses

What were the limitations of both book and author? In what ways is liberal Protestantism ill served, or in what ways do its limitations stand in sharp relief? Very much a product of its time, Strong's book is filled with an optimism that is often naive, short-term, or misplaced. Like Ezra Stiles a century before him and many statisticians a century after, Josiah Strong is prepared to follow any line on the graph to infinity. He makes little allowance for the vagaries of history and the unpredictability of humanity. He had difficulty, as do we all, in distinguishing between the ageless and the quickly aged. "The three great civilizing instrumentalities," Strong writes, "are Christianity, the press and steam" (69). The first civilizes humankind morally, the second mentally, and the third materially: The steam engine has "annihilated . . . nine-tenths of space." When the present seems so bountiful and the future so promising, then Strong can only see himself and other Americans standing at the very fulcrum of world history. This moment, now, is the decisive one, the most critical in nineteen hundred years of civilization. In addition to ethnocentrism, we have here a chronocentrism that grants a sense of unlimited power and virtual control of the future. The stuff with which we create that future appears infinitely malleable, ever tractable, and always capable of being improved.

The future is bright with promise, especially so if we can remove certain dark spots from the present. In delineating these dusky perils, Strong reveals his limitations as nativist, as jingoist, and as racist. His nativism corresponded closely with the post-Civil War burst of European immigration. Ever the data-gatherer, Strong cites the Tenth Census (1880) as his authority for asserting that already 15 million foreigners dwell in the United States. Given the continuing rapid flow of new arrivals (about 800,000 a year), the number of foreigners by 1900 will have increased to well over 40 million. "So immense a foreign element must have a profound influence on our national life and character," Strong writes (40) and then proceeds to explicate those influences in the realm of both morals and politics. Morally, the typical European immigrant is of inferior quality; his "moral and religious training has been meager or false" and some are actually ex-convicts. All the support of law and custom and community, moreover, is left behind by the immigrant. We know, even among native-born Americans, that piety many times "will not bear transportation." "Very many church-members, when they go west, seem to think they have left their Christian obligations with the church-membership in the East" (41). In fact, a surprising number obviously labor under the impression that "the Ten Commandments are not binding west of the Missouri." We cannot expect, therefore, more from the immigrant from afar than is demonstrated by our own migrants at home. The sad result, nonetheless, is that immigrants form a widely disproportionate number of our offenders against both moral and criminal law. In New England, where foreigners constitute 20 percent of the population, they commit 75 percent of the crime. The sabbath is profaned, chiefly by foreigners, and the liquor trade is promoted, chiefly by foreigners.

Politically, immigration is dividing the nation into "little Germanies here, little Scandinavias there, and little Irelands yonder" (45). We have an Irish vote, a German vote, a Roman Catholic vote, a Mormon vote, a liquor vote, and who knows what besides. A republic, resting on the foundation of good local government across the land, cannot endure with this sort of division introduced by unchecked immigration. If all were properly educated and assimilated, if all were Americanized, then the prospects would be different. But this does not happen, partly because the numbers are too large and the pace too swift. Left to their own devices in our "rabble-ruled cities," the knots of immigrants fall victim to demagoguery rather than become participants in democracy. So great is this flood of humanity now becoming that the question before us is this: Shall the immigrants foreignize us, and shall we be able to Americanize them?

Religiously, the picture is even more disturbing. For this enormous increase is changing the nation from a Protestant to a Roman Catholic one. And that is to change more than denominations alone. In the West, moreover, Mormonism grows chiefly by immigration, changing the promise of freedom and liberty there to a reality of authoritarianism and fraud. Catholicism unravels the very fabric of the nation as it treats liberty of conscience as "a most pestilential error" and freedom of religion as a right belonging solely to the "true faith." Finding in the Syllabus of Errors (1864) of Pius IX a treasure trove of useful items, Strong proceeds to show how the Roman Catholic Church opposes free speech, a free press, and free public education. Wherever the Catholic Church has held full sway, education is totally under Rome's control; education has also in such places been limited to the elite, Rome's preference being to keep the great mass of the people in "besotted ignorance." To support this assertion, Strong affirms that in Italy 73 percent of the population is illiterate, in Spain it is 80 percent, and in Mexico, 93 percent. The highest obedience of the Catholic living in America is not, and cannot be, to the United States, but must be to an infallible pope living in a foreign country. Under such circumstances, pledges of allegiance are worth little and Constitutional guarantees are scarcely secure. "Manifestly," Strong concludes, "there is an irreconcilable difference between papal principles and the fundamental principles of our free institutions" (53). This fact triggers great alarm when we look at the rapid growth of the Catholic Church in America, far more rapid than the growth of Protestantism or of the population in general. From 1850 to 1880, population increased by 116 percent, Protestant church membership by 185 percent, Catholic population by 294 percent. Such evidence as we have suggests that, since 1880, the Catholic increase has been even more rapid. Moreover, Rome "with characteristic foresight" is concentrating on conquering the western territories and states, knowing that this region will ultimately control all America. One must especially watch out for the Jesuits. "When the Jesuits were driven out of Berlin, they declared that they would plant themselves in the western territories of America. And they are there today with empires in their brains" (58).

The West is also, of course, by 1885 the seat of the Mormon empire. Americans, Strong wrote, are more likely to recognize

Mormonism as a disgrace than as a danger. It is both. Everyone worries about polygamy "as the most striking feature of the Mormon monster," but polygamy is on its way out, while Mormonism is not. The real strength of this new religion lies not in its sexual aberration, but in its ecclesiastical despotism. Actually, the despotism is much more than just ecclesiastical: it is political, social, industrial, territorial. Mormonism is not a church, it is a state. Over that state is a man "who is prophet, priest, king and pope, all in one—a pope, too, who is not one whit less infallible than he who wears the tiara" (61). Like Catholicism, Mormonism must be taken seriously because it is growing so rapidly. Strong had only to quote Mormon leaders who confidently predicted that the Saints would soon dominate the entire West. "We will then hold the balance of power, and will dictate to the country. In time, our principles, which are of sacred origin, will spread throughout the United States" (63, quoting Bishop Lunt). Much of this growth, as previously noted, was by foreign immigration. Sending out between two hundred and four hundred missionaries a year, according to Strong's calculation, this church imported a steadily increasing number of converts from abroad. Large families, great wealth, much industriousness, tight centralized control, and enormous room for expansion—all of this did not bode well for the American future.

"And what are we going to do about it?" Outlawing polygamy, while clearly a step in the right direction, will probably not impede the growth of Mormonism. The powerful priesthood together with the ever increasing number of infallible revelations will keep this church strong. "Mormon despotism . . . has its roots in the superstition of the people; and this Congress cannot legislate away." Hope lies only in better education and pure Christianity, in other words in greater support for and effectiveness by the American Home Missionary Society. The foreigner in general, the Catholic and the Mormon in particular, threaten to deny America its true destiny, to turn it away from its proper heritage, to trample underground the "faith of our fathers."

To so great an extent, the destiny of America is the destiny of the world. If Strong is a jingoist for "our country," he is even more of one for the American West. Every peril is even more perilous in the West. Socialism is off to a faster start in the West because class distinctions are greater there: "The West has today more millionaires and more tramps than the whole country had a few years since" (111). Wealth has greater corrupting power in the West, in part because it comes so quickly and goes so fast; in the East, settlers started out more or less on an even basis, and so strongly engrained were the necessary habits of thrift and economy that these virtues endure even where external conditions no longer demand them. But in the West the land rush, the gambling bonanza, the mining strikes, the illusion of a golden bounty almost within reach—these make the race for wealth "peculiarly eager" (126). Cities, too, will be an ever greater factor west of the Mississippi, partly because so little land is arable. Mining and manufacturing populations will be responsible for the creation of great urban centers, so much so that the majority of large cities will some day be in the West. With respect to immigration, Strong found little reassurance in the datum that "seventy-five per cent of it is pouring into the formative West" (45). This was the section of the country most likely to be "foreignized" rather than "Americanized." And, as we have seen, intemperance is likely to be far worse there as indeed is the growth of a religion other than evangelical Protestantism.

But if the West has more perils, it also has more promises: more land, more opportunity, more impact in shaping the future of the nation. "The unrivaled resources of the West together with the unequaled enterprise of her citizens are a sure prophecy of superior wealth" (27). As many have known for ages, the movement of populations is to the West. And as George Berkeley wrote, "the course of empire westward takes it away." The acme of this whole imperial shift is our own "mighty West, there to remain, for there is no further West; beyond is the Orient" (29). And no one ever wrote that the course of empire led to the inscrutable Orient.

Strong was also a racist, not in his hatred for those of other races, but in his unbounded pride in his own: "the Anglo-

Saxon race." The most impassioned writing of the book is to be found in chapter XIII, entitled "The Anglo-Saxon and the World's Future." The Greeks brought beauty to the world, the Romans, law; the Egyptians brought the "seminal idea of life," while the Hebrews stressed purity. The Anglo-Saxons have made two contributions: the love of liberty and a "pure spiritual Christianity" (160). Christianity in its purest form has spread where Anglo-Saxons dwell. Fortunately for the world, the Anglo-Saxons are also a great missionary race. So this kind of Christianity has spread to North America; now, in 1885, "it is chiefly to the English and American peoples that we must look for the evangelization of the world" (161). Even more fortunately, demographics are not wholly on the side of Mormons and Roman Catholics. In 1700 there were only about 6 million Anglo-Saxons, in 1800 more than 20 million, and in 1880 nearly 100 million. ("I use the term somewhat broadly," Strong explained, "to include all English speaking peoples.") By the year 2000 it is not unreasonable to assume that "this race will outnumber all the other civilized races of the world" (165). But it is far more than a matter of mere numbers: "I look forward to what the world has never yet seen united in the same race: viz., the greatest numbers and the highest civilization."

The future of the race is also the future of America. England will by the year 2000 account for no more than one twentieth of the Anglo-Saxon population. America, however, only sparsely settled at present, will a century from now have a population of a half billion—and it will still have room for more! It will inevitably become the home of Anglo-Saxon power, and "we may reasonably expect" that it will also be the home of the highest type of Anglo-Saxon civilization (168). Accepting Darwin and enjoying Spencer, Josiah Strong agreed that the evolving Anglo-Saxon race would be even finer a hundred years hence. Americans, Herbert Spencer had declared, can look forward to a time "when they will have produced a civilization grander than any the world has known" (172). Grander because more evolved; grander because of the dedication to civil liberty and pure Christianity; grander, in addition, because Anglo-Saxons had a genius for making money as well as for colonizing; and grander because of the race's "intense and persistent energy." The world is about to enter on a new stage of its history wherein "this race of unequaled energy, with all the majesty of numbers and the might of wealth behind it . . . will spread itself over the earth" (175). With his social Darwinism clearly showing, Josiah Strong argued that inferior races will not need to be conquered in some great war of extermination: the sheer vitality of the Anglo-Saxon will make it supreme. At that point, nothing can save the inferior races "but a ready and pliant assimilation." Some may object that this is unfair, even cruel. But think again: "What if it should be God's plan to people the world with better and finer material?" (175).

It appears, in any case, as though this has been the way that history has always operated. Aryans supplanted the Finns, Russians the Tartars, and now Anglo-Saxons the aborigines of North America, Australia, and New Zealand. "It would seem as if these inferior tribes were only precursors of a superior race, voices crying in the wilderness: 'Prepare ye the way of the Lord!' " All-conquering Anglo-Saxons would turn out to be all-destroying as well, were it not for the saving grace of the Christian religion. Christianity is the salt that prevents the speedy decay of Anglo-Saxon civilization; it curbs the lust for power and cures those diseases that all civilization appears destined to carry with it. Just as the English language is spreading around the world, "gathering up into itself the best thought of all the ages," so Christianity will become the one truly world religion. This epochal event will transpire partly because of "the out-populating power of Christian stock" (quoting Horace Bushnell) and partly because of the ability of the Anglo-Saxon race to adjust to all environs and climes. "In my own mind," Strong concludes, "there is no doubt that the Anglo-Saxon is to exercise the commanding influence in the world's future" (177–79).

The final limitation of *Our Country* requires only brief comment because it is such a familiar phenomenon found all around us and within us. We fail to be consistent, we fail even to perceive our absurd inconsistencies. "Christianity is the solvent of all race antipathies," Strong wrote (210). Yet his racism runs rampant. Out of love for the Roman Catholic and the Mormon, Strong would obliterate Roman Catholicism and the Church of Jesus Christ of the Latter-Day Saints. Strong has a worldwide vision, a genuine universalism, but it is grounded in a particularism and parochialism as limited as that of the citizen who has never raised his eyes beyond his own backyard. Josiah Strong honors the transcendent above all else, denouncing the "Mammonism" and materialism that he sees growing around him. Yet his God is all too immanent, and his confidence in the processes and institutions within this world all too serene.

Lessons for Our Time

So what are the lessons for our time? In what ways do Strong and his popular book assist us in answering the question, Does liberal Protestantism have an American future? One can see in this liberal Protestant of a century ago one who thought he had the helm of history in his grasp, but who in fact was being driven by the forces of nineteenth-century Europe and America. He was tied to race, to place, to time, to wealth, to politics, to education, and to sectarian loyalty to a degree that he could hardly detect. By seeing what he could not see, is there any chance that we can see what we do not see? It is, of course, enormously difficult to measure the tides if one is at the same time riding those tides. As noted in chapter 6 of this book, the decline in the number of liberal missionaries, compared with the rise of conservative ones, is to be seen not as a failure, but as a success in the training of native clergy in third world countries. It is hard to perceive the cultural trends if one has in fact become a cultural trend. This is the peculiar vulnerability, the special peril of that Protestantism which sees itself as in steady dialogue with the world rather than as withdrawn from or antagonistic to the world. Is there any way to distance ourselves from the age in which—inevitably it would appear—we live and move and have our being? Is there any way to live, as we were long ago advised to do (not by a liberal Protestant) "under the aspect of eternity"?

In 1985 we have a religious situation that differs drastically from Strong's in 1885. Protestant liberalism is now on the defensive, not on the move. It is found to be both timid and intimidated, neither bold nor prepared to go forth into battle shielded by the whole armor of God. Strong saw the Anglo-Saxon population as expanding explosively; now, one hears much about the declining birth rate and the loss of what few youth liberal Protestants manage to produce. Strong spoke to and from a confident community; in the late twentieth century, community has apparently collapsed and some deem denominations to be irrelevant. While Strong did not explicitly discuss worship, his "practice of the presence of God" is readily apparent. Worship wins little favorable attention in most analyses of weaknesses in today's mainstream Protestantism. In 1885, Protestants saw themselves as proud partners in America's destiny; in 1985 they see themselves charged with "social control," elitism, and a white Anglo-Saxon mentality that contributed to America's difficulties all around the world.

Protestantism in 1985 still retains that sense of justice that Strong manifested a century earlier, however. It still embraces history rather than attempting some escape from its lessons and its hard limits. Liberal Protestantism also became even more a student of society and of politics than Strong had been, facing and probing the complexities in preference to shouting slogans and reciting smooth simplicities. A century later than the time of Strong's first book, much has been changed, but by no means all.

Consider for a moment Strong's "perils," or his enemies list. These were immigration, Romanism, Mormonism, intemperance, socialism, wealth, and the city. Opinions will vary as to how "dated" some or all of the items on this list may be. It is safe to say, however, that our own "perils" in 1985 would constitute a rather different list. The question, though, is not how our list in 1985 might differ from one drawn up in 1885. Rather, it is how "dated," how short-sighted or myopic our 1985 list will appear one hundred years from now. The liberal Protestant's enemies list in America takes many forms, but on somebody's political list will surely be the not-so-new radical Christian right; on somebody's cultural list, the revivalist, the healer, and the charismatic; on somebody's theological list, the dispensationalist and the erring inerrants. All of these "enemies," I strongly suspect, are such because of our own cultural conditioning and will appear strangely irrelevant or perhaps even embarrassing one century hence. Today's battles may be real; they are something less than eternal.

So, too, Josiah Strong looked around him and found those agencies then in existence to be the very best that could be devised, and to be wholly adequate to the enormous task at hand. Strong did not seem interested in questioning the qualifications or the capacity of either Congregationalism or the American Home Missionary Society. A mere century later, questions about both abound. Because of decline in membership or money or "influence," mainline Protestant denominations in 1985 are not as sanguine or unquestioning as Strong. Yet they are hardly any more inventive, any more searching for entirely new institutional or organizational forms by which other enormous tasks (e.g., avoiding nuclear war) might be most effectively discharged. The Consultation on Church Union, should that turn out to be a truly new form, drags on and on to the weariness of participants and disillusion of observers. The National Council of Churches digs in; should it self-destruct? The move from sect to denomination to church is amply documented; should the move now be from church to denomination to sect? (It is becoming that in several areas of American religion but rarely within liberal Protestantism.) How much of our institutional profile in 1986 will appear, from the perspective of a later century, to have been a coral reef monument to vitality and vision once contained therein but no longer present?

Strong's ebullient optimism is easy to detect and even easier, a tough century later, to dismiss. His demographics went awry, his anthropology was askew, and his rhetorical extravangances were in the genre of promotional literature. We can explain his bouncy confidence in terms of Darwin, Spencer, *Zeitgeist*, Manifest Destiny, Main Street "boosterism," and the newness of the land. From all these illnesses, liberal Protestants no longer suffer. On the graph of human history, Josiah Strong rode the curved line of optimism much too far. On the same graph, however, his descendants stand in danger of riding the curved line of pessimism much too far. William R. Hutchison, among others, warns against both the statistical and nostalgic traps that idealize a former time and demoralize our own time. For either the optimists of 1885 or the pessimists of 1985, immanence obscures transcendence as an earth-bound timetable is substituted for a heaven-free one. When we are optimists the world's purposes and power become God's; when we are pessimists the world's perversions and weaknesses become God's. In both instances the temporal supplants the eternal, as God is reduced to running for office, endorsing a party, filling a church, meeting a deadline. And genuine religious fellowship, as Donald Miller notes in chapter 12, is reduced to a series of committee meetings concerned with trivialities.

The fault of much pietism is that it sought to save the soul apart from the world. The fault of much liberalism is that it sought to save the world apart from the soul. In recent years the "new evangelicals" have done more to redress their imbalance than have the "old liberals." The task is not to become more strict, but to become more satisfying and fulfilling; to make people no less than nations whole. Liberal Protestantism cannot undertake that task, of course, as long as its own health is so much in question. Until theology becomes once more an energizing source, until corporate worship is revived, until transcendence is believably affirmed, the spiritually hungry are unlikely to be fed—at least by us (see Gaustad, 1983).

6

Overseas Mission: Failure of Nerve or Change in Strategy?

Michael Burdick

For the past two decades, mainline Protestant denominations have experienced a decline in membership, church school enrollment, and missionary personnel. Concomitantly, evangelical and conservative denominations have flourished. In the wake of these numerical shifts, sociological analyses and prescriptive pontifications abound on the future of "oldline" Protestantism in America. Liberal Protestantism is said to suffer from malaise. A "failure of nerve" is seen to be evident by scholars and church leaders in the religion's loss of direction and purpose. No longer does the liberal Protestant establishment set the national social agenda; instead, evangelicals have come of age politically and are now vying to be the moral conscience of the nation.

Scholars, whether liberal or conservative, stress a primary relationship between church and mission. That is, the viability of a religious tradition is often characterized by its missionary activity. Robert T. Handy, writing in regard to the 1920s, states: "One sensitive indicator of a religion's vitality is its missionary program" (1971:432). Martin Marty argues that, likewise, during the twenties, there occurred a "failure of nerve" in foreign missions because "notable Protestants . . . were less sure of their manifest destiny to bring the whole world under Protestant Anglo-Saxon imperial domain" (1970:236). This "failure of nerve" theme, applicable to the problems arising from the modernist-fundamentalist controversy, continues to inform contemporary interpretations of missions. Phillip Hammond states, for example, that "American mainline denominations had lost their conviction that as Christians they had much to offer" (1983:288).

Has there really been a liberal Protestant failure of nerve? Or is there a way to view recent developments that moderates this statistically based assertion? I suggest that there is, and I cite, in particular, what has happened with Protestant missionary efforts in the post-World War II era. The change in missionary strategy in this period had more to do with the geopolitics of the period than with a failure of nerve. Liberal Protestantism confronted the rise of fledgling independent nations freed from their colonial legacies and adopted strategies accordingly. These strategies accord with the historical liberal Protestant approach to the world, and they can be seen as indicative of strength rather than of weakness. Instead of interpreting the decline of missionary personnel as a loss of nerve to "reduce the world in the name of Christ to the faith and culture of the superior west" (Marty, 1970:244), the change in strategy can in fact be seen to be a strong moral position consonant with the times and with the liberal paradigm of mainline Protestant denominations; thus the decline in numbers is not indicative of a "failure of nerve," but of a change in strategy in response to what has happened in the third world.

Evidence for a "failure of nerve" interpretation by scholars is readily proffered. For example, the dramatic numerical decline since World War II of National Council of Churches-Division of Overseas Ministries (NCC-DOM)-affiliated personnel is startling and seems to conclusively prove such a position. Yet in a recent statistical analysis of NCC-DOM personnel, the study indicates that the 65 percent drop of personnel would have been only 29 percent if there was not the defection of thirty-three mission-sending agencies who transferred out of NCC-DOM affiliation since 1952 (Coote, 1982:74). This withdrawal was the culmination of a long-standing uneasiness with the liberal theology and social activism associated with the National Council of Churches.

Conservative and evangelical agencies are currently dominating the mission field in a 10:1 ratio. Apart from the 35,000 personnel already in the field, 123 new mission-sending agencies were established in the 1970s. There is tremendous growth and flexibility as Protestant churches respond to the evangelistic and humanitarian concerns in the world today. However, the historical legacy of Protestant missions, combined with the changing geopolitical situation and the distinctive paradigmatic developments of the modernist-fundamentalist controversy, illumines the real nature and orientation of the missionary enterprise as the twentieth century draws to a close. This history provides the necessary context for understanding Protestant missions today.

The Halcyon Period

Two thousand years of Western civilization are characterized by a distinctive fusion of Christianity and political power. Hence Christian missions became inextricably linked to their sending nation and culture. Western colonialism, in its territorial expansion, offered a protective environment for missionaries. Although not always friendly, this relationship between religion and power was mutually beneficial.

The five decades after the Civil War, labeled the Protestant Era of America, mark a unique moment in the sociopolitical history of the United States; it was a time of vast expansion and consolidation of wealth and territory. As Ted Ward states: "The spiritual zeal and moral convictions [of Protestants] were founded in the entrepreneurial wealth, colonial expansion, a vast but reachable globe, controllable others, and paternal perceptions of other cultures" (1982:2). Political pressures emerged for the annexation of new territories in Texas, the Caribbean, Hawaii, and, eventually, the Far East. A new spirit of Christianity, fused with a sense of national manifest destiny, pervaded the churches.

Christian missions mirrored the national mood. America's sense of self was one of being "an elect nation, divinely chosen for a unique role in the world" (Hogg, 1977:367). Confidence and optimism marked the American mood as the nineteenth century gave way to the twentieth. In this time for great enterprises, the student volunteer movement generated much enthusiasm with the slogan "The evangelization of the world in this generation." The sending of missionaries flourished between 1890 and 1915. Mission agencies also reflected the national preoccupation with business efficiency and planning. The desire for organizational efficiency led to the incorporation of mission agencies into ecclesiastical structures. This shift to denominational guidance did not result from a profound theological conviction that the church exists for mission, but from pressures of practical administration and organization (Forman, 1982:54). The vigor and success of this earlier period of American missionary activity set the stage for later changes in mission strategy as the third world nations struggled for their political, economic, and cultural viability and independence.

Apart from the enthusiasm for economic expansion and world missions, the emergence of modernism at the turn of the century carried with it seeds of later disruption and dissension within the mission movement. The question of salvation for non-Christians, as one example, brought on a "bruising battle," fought in mission circles, that continues today. Nascent modernism's embrace of biblical criticism, Social Gospel, and continental theology was staunchly rejected by fundamentalist groups. Premillennialism, in reaction, became widespread among mission thinkers; they opposed efforts for structural changes in society, since Christ was coming before any real change could take place. Yet this pessimism actually inspired evangelistic efforts, as Timothy Weber noted: "Despite their views on the dismal future of the world, pre-millennialists were enthusiastic supporters of evengelical foreign missions. . . .Others experienced a new desire to bring the gospel to a dying world in its final slide toward inevitable doom" (1979:67).

(105)

The "Two-Party" System

The modernist-fundamentalist controversy evolved into a "two-party" system that reified competing world views (Marty, 1970). George Marsden (1982) uses Thomas Kuhn's theory of paradigm shifts to illustrate the nature and problems of the "two-party" system. Marsden notes that in order to establish an orthodox world view, one must affirm set theories as normative and authoritative. The fundamentalist world view, on the one hand, was undergirded by a Baconian model of common sense. The modernist position, on the other hand, was willing to see perception as an interpretative process. Both models limited the theories that could be derived from the perceived facts, and each side was deeply entrenched in the inviolability of its position.

In reaction to the emerging modernist position, conservative Protestants of varying theological persuasions could come to an agreement that truth was unchanging and that personal experience verified commonsense interpretations of the Bible. Fundamentalists refused to compromise with modernists on theological or doctrinal issues, especially since the latter "denied the fixed character of supernaturally guaranteed truth" (Marsden, 1982:215). Theological consensus developed for conservative Protestants along lines of rationality, morality, and experience, creating an increasingly reactionary Protestant religion.

In contrast, the modernity paradigm had three characteristic features. First, there was a conscious adaptation of religious ideas to modern culture and thought. Theologians sought to reinterpret Christianity given the new developments in science, sociology, and psychology. Second, the immanence of God in human nature and cultural development provided a tacit blessing to the technological and humanitarian advancements of Western society, especially as it was exported to underdeveloped nations. Finally, with great optimism, modernists assumed that society has headed for a kingdom of God here on earth (Hutchison, 1976). These three features affected the nature and strategies of Protestant missions, which sought not only to fulfill the gospel mandate of the evangelization of the world, but also to embody the vision of realizing the kingdom of God on earth through the technological achievements of Western society.

By 1920 the Protestant foreign missionary enterprise had felt the effects of the modernist-fundamentalist controversy. The two competing parties offered different orientations toward the nature and objectives of world missions. In light of this historical development, I use "evangelical" and "ecumenical" as sufficiently inclusive terms delineating the respective paradigms.

The Evangelical Paradigm

The evangelical mission paradigm has a scriptural basis for its theoretical and pragmatic objective—the evangelization of the world. In addition to this objective, evangelicals affirm the theological conviction that no person can be saved outside of a personal conversion experience with Jesus as the Christ of God. This paradigm describes a three-tiered world and a humanity utterly lost without the saving grace of Jesus Christ, who will one day return for the final judgment of the world.

The evangelical paradigm is exemplified in the 1980 Thailand Statement issued by the Consultation on World Evangelism (CWE): "As His witnesses He has commanded us to proclaim the good news in the power of the Holy Spirit to every person of every culture and nation, and to summon them to repent, to believe and to follow Him." This document also illustrates the orientation of this paradigm toward political and humanitarian problems. In response to the thousands of refugees pouring into Thailand, the CWE participants denounced the injustices and sufferings caused by the political turmoil, and they resolved themselves actively to work on behalf of refugees throughout the world. More important, they rejoiced in the opportunity for evangelism: "We thank him [God] also that growing numbers of them, uprooted from their ancestral homes and cultural inheritance, are finding in Jesus Christ a new security and a new life" (Thailand Statement, 1981:30).

The Ecumenical Paradigm

The ecumenical mission paradigm is notably characterized by a relativistic theological temperament that sees dialogue, mutual respect, and humanitarian concerns as essential components in the worldwide mission of the church. The ecumenical movement sees such dialogue as a means to seek a greater understanding of other people's respective national, cultural, and religious traditions. Liberal Protestantism is, in particular, noted for its de-emphasis on the otherworldly dimension of Christianity and its primary focus on the humanistic dimension of love and social service.

In 1973 the World Council of Churches' Commission on World Mission and Evangelism (CWME), a group representative of the ecumenical position, interpreted their conference theme, "Salvation," as liberation from economic injustice, political oppression, social alienation, and personal despair. Their position also reflects the increasing participation of third world Christians in the ecumenical structures of the Protestant churches. The ecumenical emphasis sees suffering and injustices by way of a biblical perspective that calls on the church to discern and to denounce structural sin on a national and international level. This corporate emphasis is not to deny the personal element in the ecumenical paradigm, but to delineate the theological and ethical priorities inherent within it. A statement issued by the 1980 CWME conference illustrates their global priorities:

> We meet under clouds of nuclear threat and annihilation. Our world is deeply wounded by the oppressions inflicted by the powerful upon the powerless. These oppressions are found in our economic, political, racial, sexual, and religious life. Our world, so proud of human achievements, is full of people suffering from hunger, poverty, and injustice. People are wasted. (World Council of Churches, 1981:29)

The ecumenical mission orientation generated severe criticisms from both evangelical and their own constituencies. One evangelical missiologist stated that the ecumenicals do not see "any validity in attempts to convert persons to the Christian faith"

(Copeland, 1973:416). Such accusations and bitter polarization exemplify the differences and hostility between the two paradigms. Evangelicals are fervent for the uniqueness of the Christian message; ecumenicals are committed to the universality of the gospel of love and the ethical imperative for social justice and basic human dignity. Both positions are logical expressions of the respective paradigms.

Differing Strategies

Objectives for the two paradigms resulted in differing strategies for mission. As the protective umbrella of church-state relations was removed in the third world, the church faced an identity crisis. In fact, it is still disengaging itself from "a kind of missionary outreach that is felt to be paternalistic, domineering and insensitive" (Braaten, 1976:70). The vestiges of neo-colonialism and "Yankee imperialism" accost the missionary who faces a different environment, one of national self-determination, revival of indigenous cultures, and dormant religious faiths. Third world churches are continuing this independence process by seeking self-government, self-support, and self-propagation, and hence are dictating new parameters for American missions abroad.

Evangelical critics are concerned that young third world churches will align themselves with national or revolutionary ideologies that are contrary to first world interests and will thereby limit further missionary activity in those countries. These critics argue that the young churches run the risk of being "co-opted, of losing freedom and independence and degenerating into a religious mouthpiece for official policy" (Scherer, 1982:8). The role of the church in the third world is an awkward and tenuous one as it seeks to maintain fidelity to its understanding of the gospel in the wake of emerging nationhood.

The concerns of the global Protestant church affect North American mission strategies and objectives. Both evangelicals and ecumenicals are in partnership with the younger third world churches and are sensitive to their nationalistic, anti-colonial impulses and the need for the continual training of indigenous leadership. But the form of partnership is different for the two groups. The ecumenical partnership takes the form of interchurch aid, allowing the third world Christians to dictate their needs and priorities for personnel and financial resources. The evangelicals, however, are in partnership with their third world counterparts for the goal of completing the task of reaching the unreached.

The traditional missionary format has ended with the emergence of the global Protestant church. For ecumenicals, the failure of an earlier optimism, the realization of an implicitly cultural and religious imperialism, the growing dissatisfaction of third world Christians, and a relativistic theological temperament have caused a continual reassessment of the nature and purpose of the mission of the church. Evangelical missions, however, are flourishing in the wake of the ecumenical recession—seemingly impervious to this multiplicity of factors.

Third World Christianity

In order to understand the matrix of global missions, consideration must be given to the prevailing position of third world Christianity. Third world Christians, in general, identify with both the evangelical spirit and theology and the ecumenical commitment to social justice. But there is significant frustration among third world Christian leaders concerning the continual domination of their people by the missionary resources and personnel of the first world churches. This frustration found a formal voice when the Rev. John Gatu, general secretary of the Presbyterian Church in East Africa, called for a mission moratorium in the early 1970s.

When Gatu called for the moratorium, anti-Western feelings were strong, and mission agencies experienced considerable challenges at home and abroad. Reeling from the impact of Vietnam and sensing their complicity in the cultural and economic imperialism generated by the United States, mission agencies were further challenged in 1973 at the CWME conference in Bangkok, Thailand. Gatu demanded a cessation of all sending and receiving of monies and personnel from the West. Reaffirmed at the 1974 All Africa Conference of Churches, the moratorium call was a means to free third world churches from

(110)

a continuing dependence on and domination by foreign countries, a dependency that inhibited the growth and maturation of many churches in Asia, Africa, and Latin America.

Gatu asked for a five-year moratorium in order for each side to rethink and reformulate its future relations with the other side. As long as the existing situation continued, it would perpetuate the relationship between weak and strong and the domination of the younger churches by the strong first world leadership and financial resources. The missionary had become a symbol of the universality of Western imperialism; hence the change in structures was needed. The moratorium would allow younger churches to struggle with their independence and develop the necessary indigenous resources and leadership firmly to establish a sense of identity that was both consistent and plausible for their nation and culture. Gatu asserted that "true selfhood might be better achieved through a period of independence, rather than by gradual modification of existing patterns. Thus the moratorium would be a dynamic process leading to a true partnership and interdependence" (Moratorium, 1973: 275).

Third world Christians were outspoken in their hostility toward Western missions. Father Paul Verghese, a Syrian Orthodox priest and a former associate general secretary of the World Council of Churches, denounced the "economic imperialism" of mission boards and relief agencies, which stifled the growth and maturity of younger churches. In a vehement summation of foreign missions, he stated that "the mission of the church is the greatest enemy of the gospel" (1970:1118). Jose Miguez Bonino, a leading Protestant Latin-American theologian, likewise argued for the necessity of "younger churches hav[ing] to learn the discipline of freedom, to accept and to refuse, to place resources at the service of a mission rather than to have mission patterned by resources" (1974:43).

North American Response

North American response to the moratorium request was indicative of the two paradigms. The evangelicals' response illustrates the identification of the gospel with American values and the evangelical certitude for world mission. Demonstrating both the theological insistence for continued American mission activities and the intransigence of the evangelicals' position, Wade T. Coggins, executive secretary for the Evangelical Foreign Mission Association, declared that "evangelization is a continuous process in which every country has to be confronted with the claims of Jesus Christ." The gospel imperative for evangelism must not be relinquished (1974:9).

Addressing the ecumenical position, Coggins illustrated the polarity of the two paradigms: "For those who do not have an acute conviction of the lostness of man, and of the uniqueness of Christ it seems to be no problem to ignore the vast unevangelized multitudes." More significant, he portrayed the discrepancies between ecumenical leadership and their constituencies: "This call has proved attractive to some larger denominational missions that are already in trouble because lay revolt against their radical political adventures has dried up a large part of their missionary resources" (1974:8). Coggins' perspective vividly portrays the disparities between the two paradigms and the tension with third world Christianity.

The remarks of Gerald Anderson, a leading evangelical missiologist, also reflect the differences between the North American evangelical paradigm and the emerging consciousness of a third world Christianity. He commends the moratorium call, noting how it is representative of the churches' vitality and maturity. But he reminds the first world churches that their first priority is still faithfulness and accountability to the gospel mandate for world missions. Interdependence is a necessary dimension for the global church, and hence third world self-sufficiency becomes a threat to this dynamic.

Anderson is concerned that the domestication of the churches in their respective cultures would result in a syncretism of tribal religion and Christianity. To abandon the missionary task would only insulate the local churches and encourage this development. The "foreign missionary presence in the life of any church should serve as a particular reminder of the 'alien' nature of the gospel to every nation and culture" (1974:44).

The positions of Coggins and Anderson are telling examples of the evangelical mission paradigm. Their interpretation of Christianity and third world ecclesiology represents a cultural and religious superiority; such convictions empower evangelical missions to flourish at an unprecedented rate.

The ecumenical response to the moratorium call was virtually nonexistent; one can assume that the ecumenicals either ignored the call or had no difficulties with it.

The Paradigms Contrasted

Each paradigm starts with radically different assumptions from the other. Hence ecumenicals and evangelicals perceive the world and their responsibilities for it in seemingly irreconcilable ways. The ecumenicals no longer view the world as a mission field. The openness and tolerance of their world view now require respect for and dialogue with other world religions. The gospel becomes the basis or subject by which they see and engage the world, promoting a radical vision for social justice. For evangelicals the gospel is not only the subject, but also the object that must be preached to those who have never heard it. The two paradigms are often in conflict with each other and in tension with third world Christianity. This presents an intricate problem for denominational leadership and mission-sending agencies: How does one remain faithful to one's tradition and still be responsive to the demands of an ever-changing world?

The truth is that there are enormous humanitarian needs in many parts of the third world. Ecumenical missions take the form of interchurch aid, allowing the indigenous leaders to dictate the necessary personnel and resources needed for their particular circumstances. American mission executives perceive this as representative of the church's success in its historic evangelism. A major concern now, however, for ecumenical mission executives is for their agencies to continue this vision of the mission of the church in face of increasingly hostile attacks from critics on the homefront.

Conclusion

The current malaise characterizing mainline Protestantism does not necessarily indicate that a "failure of nerve" accounts for the decline of ecumenical mission personnel. Changing strategies to accommodate the needs of younger churches help to account for the decline in mission personnel. The earlier period of mainline Protestant missions, coupled with the fever of Christianizing America, flourished along with the national *zeitgeist* of economic and territorial expansion. The enthusiasm began to wane by the late 1920s, and the decline has continued to the present. As the geopolitical situation since World War II has dramatically changed, it has contributed to the reassessment of missionary priorities. More important, the voices of third world Christians are now being heard, especially within the forum of the World Council of Churches. These new conditions affect the direction and strategies of mission agencies.

The very nature of the liberal paradigm gave rise to a new moral conviction compatible with the "signs of the times." New strategies evolved as the success of earlier missionary efforts led to the transition from mission to church throughout the world. These strategies are consonant with changing social, religious, and political realities. Hence to judge the ecumenical paradigm by the indices of another (i.e., evangelical) or by its earlier historical counterpart is inappropriate and misleading. Apart from the present difficulties of liberal Protestantism in America—its inability to maintain denominational membership levels and exercise a compelling theology for the times—ecumenical missions must continue their vision of the gospel in action as one sure sign of the vitality of the liberal paradigm.

7

Campus Ministry and the Liberal Protestant Dilemma

D. Keith Naylor

The question of liberal Protestantism's future gains urgency from the recent past. The past twenty years have been full of tumult for liberal Protestant churches, reflecting the social, cultural, political, economic, and religious tumult of the American nation. The "weight" of liberal Protestantism, its number of adherents, its influence on the social fabric, its theological pathfinding and ability to articulate a rallying vision have all seemed in decline. A chorus of clergy, laity, and scholars, along with nonliberals and non-Protestants, now wonders whether the massive upheaval of the recent past represents an assault on liberal Protestantism that puts the very future of this historic religious tradition in jeopardy.

This essay looks at the liberal Protestant campus ministry in public universities as an expression of the dilemma of liberal Protestantism, and as a possible indicator of its future. Attention is given to the birth of campus ministry into the world of modernity and its lifelong attempt to survive and flourish in the modern, and increasingly secular, world. A summary of a recent survey of denominational and theological journal articles on campus ministry from 1965 to 1983 is included to show the relation of this ministry to liberal Protestant churches. An assessment of that time period for campus ministry follows, including comments from interviews with active campus

ministers, and some speculation about the viability and shape
of the future of liberal Protestantism.[1]

Liberal Protestantism and Higher Education

One might say that Protestants so loved the world that they
gave it higher education. At least in America, the first colleges
were founded and sponsored by the churches, primarily to
train ministers. Long after many of these colleges became independent, privately endowed universities, they were still led by
presidents who were ordained ministers (Van Dusen, 1951:43).
Higher education in the early years was a potent thrust of the
Protestant establishment, a way to extend and perpetuate Protestant thinking in the upper echelons of the society, while
serving as a vehicle of upward mobility for the masses. Following on Robert T. Handy's understanding of the "first disestablishment" (1984; see chapters 1, 2)—the formal separation of
church and state—higher education in America can be seen as a
strong remnant of the colonial religious establishment. Higher
education was on the front lines of the "fight for a Christian
America." Under these circumstances, Protestant churches
needed no special ministry on campus, for their own ministry
was embodied in the charter, personnel, and curricula of colleges and universities.

The last half of the nineteenth century brought vast expansion and change to higher education. Increased immigration
resulted in a greater ethnic and religious diversity. More conve-
nient travel allowed students to "go away" to school, where
they were taught by an expanded faculty that was increasingly
unordained (Hammond, 1966:4). New disciplines were being
developed based on recent discoveries. New explorations of the
natural, social, and psychological terrain generated new data
that were re-forming the content of higher education.

Taken as a whole, these changes amounted to the development of a new institution in America—the modern public university. This new modern public university was essentially
secular, having moved out of the sphere of influence of Protestant churches and having organized itself around the new modern data. Glenn A. Olds has noted commonalities in the Latin

word roots of religion and the university. Religion comes from *religāre*, meaning "to bind together," and university comes from *unus* and *versum*, meaning "to turn into one." Both terms speak to our "deep need to unify life and thought around some ultimate principle, object of loyalty, or subject of faith" (1964:229). However, it seemed that the "deep need" of the new modern university was not to unify, but to diversify. It was this new form of higher education that, in our century, became dominant, overtaking the church-related schools. It was this form of higher education that Martin E. Marty referred to as the "paradigm of modernity" and an "intensification of the experience of modernity" (1981:56). For Marty, modernity means "ever increasing differentiation, specificity, universalization, uprooting" (58). The university embodied the forces of modernity at work in the larger society, and as such presented a challenge to the churches. For the churches still operated around "coherence in Christ," still sought "to bind together," or perhaps more accurately, still presumed that people were bound together, or could be bound together, on its terms.

Campus Ministry as a Response

Campus ministry was born as a response by Protestant churches to the new modern university. It was a way of introducing or emphasizing religion in the academic setting. With typical Protestant industriousness, churches began, early in the 1900s to make ad hoc arrangements for campus ministry. Colleges and universities were generally receptive to the establishment of these ministries (Hammond, 1966:5), reflecting the apparent lack of rancor between the two institutions. This is in keeping with the apparent early enthusiasm of the liberal Protestant leadership concerning modernity. The challenge of modernity was seen as an opportunity, not as a burden. Peter Berger notes that "modernity multiplies choices" (1979:28), and these new-century Protestants, emerging from Victorian restriction, were apparently eager for choices. Only later did they begin to be troubled by Berger's further perception that in multiplying choices, modernity "concomitantly reduces the scope of what is experienced as destiny" (23).

The birth of campus ministry out of the courtship of religion and modernity can be used to exemplify the weakness and strength of liberal Protestantism. The weakness is shown by the fact that the very rise of the modern public university signaled a loss of Protestant influence in higher education. The university carried its secularity as a banner. The continuing process of secularization, "in which religion loses its hold on the level both of institutions and of human consciousness" (Berger, 1979:24), was the hallmark of this new institution. A specialized ministry to the university community, however welcomed or successful, represented, at best, an accommodation, an arrangement in which liberal Protestant terms were no longer paramount. Given the critical way in which higher education shapes human consciousness, and given the historical importance of education to Protestants (buttressed by Reformation theology), such a loss is substantial.

The strength of liberal Protestantism is shown by the placement of campus ministry within the secular university. Liberal Protestants "took on" modernity, decided to wrestle with it, to probe it to learn its benefits and its dangers. The campus ministry encountered modernity on its own turf. If the campus ministry was among the first to show enthusiasm for modernity, it was also among the first to sense that the challenge of modernity was massive, persistent, and not altogether benign for liberal Protestantism. It has been well documented that the crisis of modernity in the 1920s divided Protestants into liberal and fundamental camps, giving us the nomenclature that remains problematic to this day. William Hutchison (1976:256–87) shows how Gresham Machen's *Christianity and Liberalism* and Shailor Mathews' *Faith of Modernism,* among others, helped to draw the lines for battle. While the churches battled one another over the immanence of God, the divinity of Jesus, the authority of the scripture, and other sharp differences (often brought on by discoveries within the modern university), campus ministry was preparing people to live in the modern world. Such preparation was not always intentional and was sometimes imposed by circumstance; nevertheless, it occurred. Of

(118)

course, the early style of campus ministry was really a youth fellowship, a wholesome bonding, but the fellowship took place within the context of intensified modernity. What one learned in the laboratory, the classroom, on field trips, through contact with peers of different religious and cultural backgrounds, the questions, the doubts, the wonder, the shock, the restlessness, all this, so characteristic of the academic/intellectual life, was brought to the campus ministry. However awkward, tentative, or amateurish, the campus ministry responded within the arena of the university, seeking, to be sure, to bring a word of God but recognizing the university as a representation of the secularization of the whole society. Outside of campus ministry, some liberals and fundamentalists alike were so entrenched in their battle with each other that they were slow to recognize the emerging secular realities.

Campus Ministry Growing and Changing

The campus ministry accepted its marginality within the secular university. Often there were no religion or religious studies courses on campus (a legacy of disestablishment and modern secularity), and the campus ministry was a "voice crying in the wilderness." But the wilderness became a testing ground for campus ministry. Increasingly, and especially after mid-century, the campus ministry became innovative. It linked students with social service projects to serve and broaden their own social perspectives. It sponsored lectures and exhibits to probe the relation of religion to the sciences, social sciences, and arts. This ministry sought out neglected members of the university community, such as spouses of graduate students and faculty. It created communities in which students could express their religious commitment by living together and studying together, wrestling with the theological implications of what they were learning and how they were shaping their careers. Campus ministry was uniquely aware of the varieties of religious faith and experience and helped to develop a healthy respect for that variety. Campus ministry promoted encounter among religious traditions—much of the impetus for ecumenism among liberal Protestants in the 1960s was the result of ecumenical work by campus ministry in the 1950s. Many universities were (and are still) less racially segregated than the churches, and campus ministry's involvement in issues of race served as a model for later church involvement. Close contact by campus ministers with international students drew them to worldwide concerns of war and peace, hunger, arms limitation, and national independence movements.

To be sure, this was a ministry on the margins. No pretense was made that campus ministry was at or near the center of the university's purpose or activity. Numbers were generally small. No one would mistake the campus minister for the major power broker on campus. But the impact of campus ministry on the university was often substantial. Several campus ministers who began their work on public university campuses in the 1950s observe that universities often used campus ministry as a model and for consultation to identify student needs. Counseling centers for personal, sexual, and career counseling (and later draft counseling) grew indirectly out of the campus ministry, as did student affairs/student activities offices. [2] This represents a recognition on the part of the secular university of the value of campus ministry. Such recognition was not forthcoming from many other places.

Recognized or not, campus ministers continued their important work, gradually changing from campus ministry as Christian fellowship to ministry as Christian presence or witness and finally, in the 1960s, to what could be called campus ministry as social involvement and critique. These changes in the style of campus ministry were made in response to changes in society, the churches, and the university. Writing in the 1960s, Paul Schrading summarizes the changed conditions:

> The denominational era is clearly passed. No longer can churches hope to support campus ministers as agents to keep students safe for the church. That safety is too clearly lost in the pre-collegiate experience of most students. The current campus ministry experience is more to renew in people a motivation for a meaningful faith than to sustain a faith-experience during the college years. (1970:471)

A Baptist chaplain described the focus of the new campus ministry as follows:

> We feel . . . that the best thing we can do is simply expose students to the kinds of things a university is meant for—challenges and opportunities to expand their religious knowledge even outside the church, meaningful experience in worship, or in study. In other words, we should contribute to their religious life rather than to their church life. You would find within the majority of campus ministers on this campus the view that the church must lose itself in order to find itself. (Hammond, 1966:48)

These words from campus ministers themselves show their awareness of the effects of secularity on the student population and their desire to address that secularity through their ministry. Campus ministers operated at the margins of the secular university, but with growing skill they searched its terrain and moved accordingly.

Campus Ministry and the Churches: Marginal Contact?

In what way was the campus ministry the churches' ministry? Has the persistent contact with the university secularized the campus ministry? Has campus ministry become less religious, less Protestant? As shown earlier, campus ministry was begun as a ministry of service to people and their needs in the name of God. Campus ministers were "called and installed" by denominations that wanted to "place men of faith, intelligence, imagination and zeal" on campus.[3] These ministries were funded by liberal Protestant churches, but there is little evidence to show that the churches treated the campus ministry with anything other than token acknowledgment. This was due in part to the centrality of the congregational ministry, the priority of support for church-related colleges, and the relatively low percentage of parishioners who attended public universities.

This token treatment was corroborated by a recent survey of liberal Protestant denominational publications with articles on campus ministry. The survey aimed to see what the churches had to say and hear about campus ministry during the tumultuous years, 1965 to 1983. The publications chosen for the survey were those that were likely to have substantial readership among the laity, that is, the popular press, as opposed to the professional press. The journals chosen were *Mission/The American Baptist*, *The Methodist Story/The Interpreter*, *Presbyterian Life/A.D.*, *World Call/The Disciple* (Disciples of Christ), and *The United Church Herald/A.D.* (The fact that each publication changed names during this time period is in keeping with the tenor of the times.) Each denomination represented by a journal has historic ties to higher education, sponsoring colleges and universities across the nation. The journals represent a mixture of weekly, biweekly, monthly publication dates.

Over the eighteen-year period, seventy articles on campus ministry appeared in these five publications, many of them only a paragraph long. The majority of these articles concerned ministry at church-related colleges and contained appeals for financial support. Campus ministry in public universities was virtually ignored. Little discussion of the churches' role in campus ministry occurred, in contrast with repeated discussions of the churches' role in civil rights, the Vietnam conflict, church union, sexual morality, family relations, and so on. In comparison with other issues, the writing on campus ministry in these publications can be characterized as "an absence observed." Even when a potentially controversial aspect of campus ministry was covered, such as its growing ecumenicity, church publications reported without encouragement or discouragement. The survey was extended to liberal Protestant theological journals of the same period. These journals are aimed at scholars and clergy and tend to treat topics in greater depth (sometimes devoting whole issues to one topic). Over the eighteen-year period, fifty-two articles on campus ministry were found in nineteen journals. (These journals were published quarterly or biannually.) It was interesting to note that campus ministers were much more likely to write articles in the scholarly journals than in the denominational ones, hinting at the distance between campus ministers and the churches. The infrequent attention to campus ministry shown in the survey reflects the lack of awareness by church people of the dynamism of either campus ministry or of higher education. The historic liberal Protestant enthusiasm for higher education did not translate into knowledge of the details of modern university life nor into sustained interest in campus ministry. Of interest is that fact that this information gap occurred at a time when much social unrest and change was centered at the university.

The survey of what the churches said or heard about campus ministry suggests a breach between the two groups, or perhaps more accurately, a breach between campus *ministers* and the churches. Phillip E. Hammond and Robert E. Mitchell (1965) showed that campus ministers differed from their parish counterparts in being more critical of their denominations and in having greater affinity for the National Council of Churches and the World Council of Churches. They were better educated, read more liberal publications, and more regularly engaged in ecumenical contact. Such differences, along with others, probably accounted for some of the distance of campus ministers and campus ministries from the churches. But while the operation of the campus ministry at the margins of the university has been understood and accepted for some time, the marginalization of campus ministry in relation to the churches was a far more problematic concern. For these were not just operators, but ministers, charged with carrying the churches' word and sacrament, charged with articulating its theology and heralding its Savior.

There is much evidence to suggest that by the 1960s the campus ministry was increasingly marginalized in relation to liberal Protestant churches. This marginalization signaled a religious crisis. As campus ministers lost touch with the deep wellsprings of their religious and spiritual communities, they were increasingly at the mercy of the secular university. Cut off from those who "called and installed" them, these ministers began to experience Berger's notion that modernity "reduces the scope of what is experienced as destiny." That is to say, they were becoming unsure of direction, becoming lost. One campus minister at a large prestigious public university in the 1960s put it this way: "We ministered to the students, to the graduate students, to the faculty and staff, widening the circle and losing people all along the way. Then we ministered to the 'structures of the university,' whatever that means, and we were lost."[4] This same anguish, stemming largely from loss of communal religious experience, was later to be mirrored in the experience of the liberal Protestant churches. As campus ministers were found at the margins of churches, so were the churches found at the margins of their own religious and spiritual heritage that could best sustain them. The full churches of the 1950s did not lead to full hearts in the 1960s. Even a casual observer could tell that it was not a high time of faith. The communal "experience of the holy," at the least, was endangered. Just as campus ministers moved toward the center of the university (rather than the center of the church), expanding political alliances with student groups, establishing alternative courses, participating in various social movements and demonstrations, so did the churches move more into the world of the secular. Both the campus ministry and the churches modified their own terms of involvement with the wider culture. Changes in clerical dress and in liturgical music were but small signs of this modification. One was likely to hear ministers speak in their quest for "relevance" more in sociological and psychological terms than in religious terms. Relevance itself became a goal. But it was being demanded and defined by a largely unchurched, or "exchurched," generation.

This downplaying of religious distinctiveness amounted to a great loss for campus ministry and for the churches. It happened at a critical time. Higher education was to the 1960s what high technology is to the 1980s—the major growth industry. College and university enrollments were growing, new schools were being established, experimental curricula being introduced. The post-World War II babies were coming of age and the public was ready to support their education. A building boom hit the campuses to match the baby boom generation. Higher education was available to a greater diversity of the population than ever before. But in this dynamic setting too often the word of the campus ministry was indistinct from the variety of social critiques available on most campuses. It may be said that campus ministry had in its own tradition the ultimate social critique, the prophetic voice that addresses the social setting in terms of the judgments of God, but this voice, this "thus saith the Lord," was all too often weak or muffled or mute. To use Berger's terminology again, the campus ministers, the most explicit and persistent "bargainers with modernity," found that their currency was weak, and they lost out in the deal. This loss of opportunity to reach a large, idealistic, impressionable generation of educated people in the name of churches and their God resulted largely from the marginalization of campus ministry and church relations. Cut off from churches, campus ministry could not pool and strengthen its religious resources. Weakened in identity, it was easily ignored.

New Realities

All was not lost for campus ministry, however. Campus ministry went to extremes and lost its balance, but important insights were gained into the modern secular university, and thus the modern secular world. These insights may not be unique to campus ministry, but the proximity of campus ministry to the university, that "paradigm of modernity," gives them a clarity and intensity that must be noticed. Briefly stated, the campus ministry, through its involvement in the campus upheavals of the 1960s, had an intensive, detailed, hands-on experience of something akin to what Berger calls "the crisis of secularity" (1983).

The university is one of the major arenas in which this "crisis of secularity" is evident. By its very nature the university is, in the words of Langdon Gilkey (1969), "the arena of free discussion and free inquiry, a place where society's creed, myths, and beliefs, are tolerated only if and when they are subjected to radical question." Gilkey continues:

It projects, therefore, an essentially disenchanted world, a world where every affirmation becomes an hypothesis, every moral involvement—except that to free inquiry itself—a tentative proposal. Inherited mythologies, parochial passions, party loyalties, power, self-interest, greed, and violence alike are alien to its urbane tone of intelligence and its sole goal of understanding objectively. (109)

The campus ministry had addressed itself to this community of objective inquiry over the years, had established itself there, had endeavored to make a good case for religion there. But as Gilkey went on to point out, this view of the university was not accepted by "the majority of the sensitive and intelligent youths" of the late 1960s (109). These youths were the students to whom campus ministry has had to address itself in the 1960s and since. They are the students who

> see the university's claim to objectivity and its dispassionate disengagement from the moral issues of the social and political life around it, as what Freud would call a rationalizaton, a kind of, so to say, "secular supernaturalism"—a secular excuse for abdicating its own creative moral role in the struggle for a sane and just society. (110)

Students with this view were the radicals, perhaps a minority, but their argument with the university was a significant argument with modernity itself. In hearing this argument, and in sharing it, campus ministry recognized, at the least, an opening for the plausibility of religion among those most fully exposed to the secularizing thrust of modernity. This new opportunity for religion prompted a reassessment of religion by campus ministry itself. Seemingly lost in all the public upheaval was the fact that the campus ministry, in its alignment with student movements, helped to issue a serious moral challenge inside the temple of modernity and secularity. Campus ministry acquired critical, detailed firsthand knowledge of the vulnerability of the beast.

The moral challenge issued by the campus ministry to the university, while serious, was limited. The university goes marching on. Secularity goes marching on. But campus ministry marches on in a changed manner, seasoned, lean, and better fit for the future in a secular world.

Out of campus ministry's struggle with the modern secular university in a time of crisis has come a new clarity concerning purpose and place. Campus ministry has developed closer ties with the churches, restoring among the ministers a sense of common religious purpose and connectedness. Local church members are often active on campus ministry boards and carry positive views back to the parish. The decrease in denominational funding has forced campus ministry to be creative in its programming, often cosponsoring activities with various campus groups. Such cosponsorship builds ties to various groups that were not part of the liberal Protestant constituency and is "cost-effective." But if campus ministry has learned well how the university bureaucracy operates, and its benefits, it has been careful not to imitate its style. Increased attention has been given to the religious nature of ministry, with worship again becoming a pivotal act. This worship has been informed by its new participants, sometimes ethnic minority students and more often women. The entry of women into the professional ranks of the campus ministry and the exploration of feminine spirituality may hold the greatest promise for the vitality of the liberal Protestant campus ministry into the next century. Several campus ministers report that the rise in appeal of evangelical and fundamentalist campus ministry has promoted religon "in general" on campus and has benefited the liberals. Some have begun to work jointly with these groups in addition to the usual liberal ecumenical arrangements.[5]

Current issues of interest to college students, such as hunger relief, U.S. policy in Central America, and apartheid in South Africa, have been addressed by campus ministry for years, and campus ministers are being sought after for their knowledge and their views. Campus ministry in the mid-1980s, with its focus on community-building, peace-making, and justice-seeking, remains at the margins of the secular university, but it seems to have gained a large measure of credibility with sensitive and intelligent youths of our time.

It is generally accepted that the decline in liberal Protestant churches is evident in the fact that a significant number of those coming to maturity in the past twenty years have rejected them. Many of these young people have attended public universities where, for whatever reasons, they remained untouched by the appeal of campus ministry. Many of them have clustered around high-technology university towns; some have actually returned to the university as professors, administrators, or consultants. Few have shown signs of abandoning the search for meaning that sometimes brought them notoriety. In fact, as they attempt to form families and raise children in the face of the rapid change that is their inheritance, such searching takes on greater intensity. How ironic it would be if through some joint effort, based on some shared lessons learned, and using some spiritual appeal to those nearly overwhelmed by materialism, liberal Protestant campus ministry and churches could now attract those whom they lost before.

What of the future of liberal Protestantism in a secular world? Surely liberal Protestants ought to look at campus ministry as one of their strengths. Surely the lessons of vitality at the margins, the lessons of connectedness and of scale will be useful. Surely liberal Protestants will recall the ancient story of the small band of the committed who altered history and be inspired by it.

8

Self-fulfillment and Culture Crisis: America's Search for Soul in the 1960s and 1970s

Patrick J. Mahaffey

There is widespread agreement among sociologists and cultural historians which suggests that the past two decades represent a fundamental crisis or turning point in American culture. This essay analyzes the nature of this crisis in relation to the shift of values reflected in the new self-fulfillment ethos. This ethos has been described by some as the triumph of the therapeutic or the expression of a cultural narcissism; others interpret this therapeutic sensibility in salvific terms and celebrate its emergence as a cultural revolution that promises to revitalize American democracy.

The ambiguity of this ethic poses special challenges to liberal Protestant churches. They must find ways to address the needs of their members in the desacralized context of the modern world. In particular, they must address the spiritual form of the quest for fulfillment. This deeper impulse, evident in the revival of interest in spirituality and contemplation, expresses a search for the rediscovery of soul in cultural and religious life. It is this "lost dimension" of experience that the churches must address if they hope to revitalize themselves as well as our fragmented and disenchanted culture.

The Search for Self-fulfillment

Daniel Yankelovich has analyzed a major shift in values within American culture in his recent book (1982) on changing social mores. In the 1950s Americans lived in accordance with a giving/getting compact that was built historically on a foundation of self-sacrifice. The rules or shared values of this ethic included hard work, loyalty, and the suppression of impulses toward personal fulfillment in order to meet the needs and expectations of others. What people got in return was a good job, a nice home, a loyal family, respect from friends, a sense of achievement, and the pride of citizenship.

In the 1960s and 1970s a major cultural revolution replaced the previous ethic of self-denial with an ethic of self-fulfillment. The sacrifices entailed in the older ethic were called into question as an affluent society rendered them unnecessary. Accordingly, the ethic was modified to meet the needs and values of the self as self-restraint gave way to the individual's right for self-expression. The ethical sense of obligation to others gave way to an alternative concept of duty: duty to oneself. This new ethic presses for the freedom of the individual to express impulses and desires that people were previously accustomed to suppress. Its slogan, "do your own thing," expresses the language of self-interest understood as private fulfillment.

Yankelovich is critical of the misleading metaphysics that underlie the psychology of the search for self-fulfillment. The premise is that the self, in Maslow's language, is a hierarchy of needs. But this idea, argues Yankelovich, involves the mischievous notion of a private self that stands apart from culture and history and makes a choice in a vacuum. It further presupposes that we move up the hierarchy of needs on an escalator of increasing affluence. This, he observes, is a peculiarly self-congratulatory philosophy of a materialistic age.

The solution to the social dilemmas of this situation requires that Americans overcome the "self-fulfillment contradiction." The individual is not fulfilled by becoming a freestanding machine for fulfilling needs. Indeed, many of the "needs" of individuals in a consumer society such as our own are better understood as "desires." And desires are, of course, infinite. Thus anyone trapped in the fallacy that the self is a failure to the extent that all of one's desires (or "needs") are not satisfied has set herself or himself up for frustration.

The search for self-fulfillment represents the beginning of a new story in American life. It introduces important new meanings into our culture that revolve around the struggle to lessen the influence of the instrumental forces in our lives and heighten the sacred/expressive elements. However, the replacement of the old giving/getting compact with a duty-to-self ethic has proved nearly fatal, for nothing has subverted self-fulfillment more thoroughly than self-indulgence. Nevertheless, Yankelovich believes that Americans are starting to formulate new rules that will serve as the basis of a new social ethic that will substitute for both self-denial and duty to self.

A similar analysis has been made by Peter Clecak. Clecak argues that the quest for fulfillment was the central energizing thrust of American culture in the sixties and seventies. Both decades constitute a single, uncompleted chapter of the American enterprise. This quest is defined as the "pursuit of a free, gratified, unalienated self within one or more communities of valued others" (1983:6). The main effect of this quest is shown in the substantial extension of many facilitating conditions for fulfillment of the self: enhanced cultural options, rising economic, personal, and political rights. In sum, these changes permitted a significant number of Americans to discover a satisfactory synthesis of the main elements of fulfillment: salvation and a piece of social justice.

The notion of self-fulfillment understood as salvation requires clarification. According to Clecak, it must be linked to both personal liberty and social justice. The sense of the former was expanded through dissent. Dissent challenged the "structure of advantage" and extended the principle of personal liberty to citizens in all categories. Furthermore, it led to the conviction that all individuals must have a piece of social justice and the cultural space to pursue disparate images of salvation.

The quest for fulfillment during the sixties and seventies was a multifaceted search conducted by diverse elements of the population. Thus the postwar ideological shape of liberalism was challenged through dissent and gave rise to a new ideological pluralism. Clecak emphasizes the fact that every group and every ideological tendency experienced fragmentary losses, reversals, and disappointments as well as fitful gains. Consequently, no group realized its particular vision of social justice. The structure of advantage was both ameliorated and enlarged. Yet, while the definitions and ratios of salvation and social justice were in constant flux, these shifts formed part of the overall direction toward the progressive democratization of personhood in America.

The therapeutic manifestations of the quest were linked by several common themes. These include an accent on personal experience; the wish for a communty of affective, touching selves; and a light regard for authority, doctrine, and received institutions. These links, according to Clecak, are more significant than any ideological or doctrinal differences for understanding the main thrust of American culture in both decades; they call attention to the growing therapeutic dimension of salvation and to the salvific aspect of all therapies.

The therapeutic form of the quest was articulated primarily in personal, sexual, and psychological terms rather than in the language of social theory, politics, or theology. Nevertheless, metaphors of individual salvation figured importantly in expressly therapeutic conceptions of the self. This style of salvation may be understood as a secularization of the ancient Pelagian doctrine that individuals, although aided by God's grace, are the chief agents and beneficiaries of their own salvation. The modern-day therapeutic quest centers on salvation of the self from guilt and the most debilitating aspects of alienation. Moreover, a high percentage of those seeking therapeutic modes of fulfillment focused exclusively on the unused possibilities of this life rather than on the prospect of a life after death. Thus physical well-being, sexual amplitude, emotional intensity, and mental wholeness were sought as ends in themselves.

While Clecak does not wish to defend extreme manifestations of the therapeutic quest, his overall evaluation is clearly affirmative.

> The therapeutic quest was not simply a diffuse cultural thrust that gained force at the expense of various modes of authority and species of political involvement. It was rather a mode of personal and cultural activity that enhanced the psychological options of millions of Americans, and, to one degree or another, their public options as well. (147)

He is aware that critics such as Christopher Lasch do not share his optimistic assessment. Yet, when the critical dust settles, he believes that we shall see that the quest for personal fulfillment was culturally salutary with long-term significance for the American future.

Religion and the Therapeutic Sensibility

Clecak called attention to the growing therapeutic dimension of salvation and the salvific aspect of all therapies. A review of the literature concerned with the relationship between psychiatry and religion appears to substantiate this observation. It also reflects the new ideological pluralism and cultural syncretism that results from the breakdown of the traditional socioreligious ethos.

Personal mental health and well-being have become a national industry. Books on self-help, personal guidance, and pop psychology abound in bookstores and supermarket racks and on best-seller lists. Psychiatry, in this context, has lost its exclusive franchise on the mental health market. In short, mental health has become a more egalitarian and democratic enterprise. More significant, the mental health enterprises are no longer separate from religious enterprises in the common culture. The new alliances between psychiatry and religion are not a synthesis with the conventional "civil religion" or socioreligious ethos. Rather, there is a blending of mental health with particularistic religious orientations. Some of these blends are conservative in tone, whereas others appear in liberal garb; other blends take on hues that may be described as humanistic, pietistic, avant-garde, Eastern, and so on. This range of idio-syncratic blends reflects the new pattern of pluralism in American society. And the significance of this change is the loss of any synthesizing and superordinate belief system that can evoke commitment and integration (see Pattison, 1978a:9–11).

The pastoral counseling movement represents an example of the relationship between liberal churches and secular therapies. The American Association of Pastoral Counselors, founded in 1961, gave rise to the expansion of pastoral counseling ministries. A national study of the members of this association was conducted in 1977. The study revealed a major move away from the development of counseling ministries within the pastoral role and church context. In fact, the majority of the members surveyed favored a fee-for-service model based on the individual fifty-minutes psychoanalytical model of private psychotherapy. In addition, most of these members disliked pastoral and parish activities and tended to be personally uninvolved in church-related activities. These pastoral counselors were primarily liberal in their theology and nonnormative in their psychotherapy. "In other words, the pastoral counselor has deserted his religious background just like the psychiatric counselor, and has joined the new synthesis of psychiatry and religion as a fellow psychotherapist" (Pattison, 1978a:17–18).

What is the import of this kind of "synthesis"? It is often said that psychiatrists are the priests of our time. Implicit in this view is the assumption that psychiatrists have displaced the clergy as the custodians of everyday life problems. Andrew Abbott has argued that this assumption rests on insufficient foundations. It would be more accurate to say that psychiatrists invented the modern version of the everyday life problem. The pastoral counseling movement, from this perspective, is the clergy's involvement in that social problem as psychiatrically defined. The major thinkers of this movement came to view religion as a means to personal happiness rather than as a meaning system in itself. Therefore, the clergy's involvement in this social problem has implied a decline in clergy involvement with religion (1983:139). Abbott summarizes the implications:

If psychiatrists are the priests of our time, it is not because they have displaced the clergy from practice with the individual problems of life, but rather because they (and others) have persuaded the culture that personal realization is indeed the ultimate end of life. In the functional sense of defining ultimate meaning and order, the psychiatrists may indeed be our true religious officials. (141)

The history of pastoral care in America has been described as a Protestant journey from salvation to self-realization (Holifield, 1983:356). In the last phase of this journey, since mid-century, pastoral theologians have been especially interested in the relation between theology and psychology. This relation, however, tended to become a reduction of the former to the latter. "In an era of religious doubt within individuals and self-doubt within religious institutions . . . the temptation to allow the psychological language to overwhelm or define the religious tradition has often been irresistible" (355).

Most of the writers about pastoral care have come to recognize that self-realization cannot be equated with the ideals of spiritual growth inherent in the religious tradition. Yet this recognition poses questions concerning identity. What distinguishes pastoral counselors from secular therapists? What is distinctive about "pastoral" counseling?

E. Brooks Holifield shows that theologians have not found easy answers to these questions. Nevertheless, as pastoral counselors and theologians continue their search for distinctive identity, they may discover how the Christian vision of salvation might well enhance the cultural ideal of self-realization and may even define, once again, the church's understanding of the cure of souls.

The tendency of pastoral counselors to view religion as a means to personal happiness rather than as a meaning system in itself may account for their lack of involvement in the spiritual form of the quest for fulfillment. Morton Kelsey has observed that there is a lack of individuals within the church engaged in the ministry that serves this quest. He links the need for more spiritual directors within the church to the decline in its authority. College youth, in particular, demand experience as well as reason (doctrinal teachings). But herein lies the problem. Little emphasis has been given to spirituality or the experiential dimension of faith. Kelsey's review of survey data shows that a significant percentage of Americans have had mystical experiences (39 percent) or are engaged in a search for a kind of experience that mainline religious institutions do not seem to provide (10 percent). In addition, post-test inquiries of survey respondents reporting mystical experiences showed that more than half of these persons had never told anyone of the experiences before the survey. And, more significant, the last person they would be inclined to tell about their experiences was a member of the clergy. Respondents felt that the clergy simply don't believe in such things anymore (1979:125–26).

Kelsey further acknowledges that if there are legitimate experiences relating to a mystical dimension of reality, would-be spiritual guides or spiritual directors should have firsthand experience of this realm. Otherwise, it would amount to a case of the blind leading the blind. The field, he concludes, is wide open and there is great need. Guiding people on the spiritual quest would appear to be an important thrust in pastoral counseling in the decades to come.

Beyond Self-fulfillment: Recovery of the Soul

The cultural hero of our time, according to Jacob Needleman, is the seeker. The seeker is one who courageously responds to the crisis in our cultural situation. The cultural crisis, in large measure, stems from our inability to feel the values we have with sufficient intensity. Energy or moral and spiritual force, then, is the real theme of "the great search" underlying the variegated life experiments of the past two decades.[1]

But what, more precisely, are we seeking? We are seeking to recover a dimension of our humanity that neither modern psychology nor established religion acknowledges. This lost dimension is the soul. It is the dimension of experience that is eclipsed by the desacralized conditions of the modern world. "Loss of soul" is a phenomenon that anthropologists have described in relation to so-called primitive cultures.

> In this condition a man is out of himself, unable to find either the outer connection between humans or the inner connection to himself. He is unable to take part in this society, its rituals, and traditions. They are dead to him, he to them. His connection to family, totem, nature, is gone. Until he regains his soul he is not a true human. (Hillman, 1967: 43)

This condition, James Hillman maintains, aptly describes our own cultural situation. Each of us is, in Jung's terms, "modern man in search of a soul."

This diagnosis has special implications for ministers and pastoral counselors. The proliferation of mental health centers, according to Hillman, will not help us find the soul. Indeed, no matter how healthy we get mentally, we still need soul. He goes so far as to ask, "Can anyone have mental health at all unless it be founded upon a sense of soul?" The contemporary loss of soul affects everyone, including clergy. The problem of many clergy today is to find the inner connection with the calling as well as to keep this calling alive. The natural tendency is for the minister to look elsewhere, borrowing and imitating methods that seem to work for secular therapists. But the task of the pastoral counselor, Hillman argues, is different from that of the analyst or clinical psychologist.

> His tradition goes back to Jesus, who cared and cured souls in many ways: preaching, wandering, visiting, telling tales, conversing, arguing, touching, praying, weeping, suffering, dying— in short, by living to the full his own destiny, true to his life. Let the clergy follow the *imitatio christi* rather than imitate psychotherapy. (46)

The minister's task is not to cure in the modern medical sense. As a shepherd who leads souls to God, surely the central task is devotion to the soul, which begins with care for the pastor's own soul. Thus the problem of pastoral counseling today begins with the minister and the relationship with his or her own soul.

The most valid encounter between psychology and religion, in Hillman's opinion, is taking place within the soul of the individual minister struggling with his or her calling. Through this struggle a new way of caring for the soul is emerging. It is a form of pastoral care that is based on the experience *within the counselor.*

The problem of finding the soul, then, must be taken seriously by the liberal mainline churches in our desacralized society. If these churches won't attend to this "sacred need," the implications are clear.

> He who has lost his soul will be finding God anywhere, up above and down below, in here and out there; he will cling to every straw of love blown past his doorway as he stands waiting for a sign. Without some sense of soul, there will, of course, be vast confusions of morality, uncertainties of action, decisions logically sound but not psychologically valid. (49)

Meanwhile, new religious movements and quasi-religious therapies flourish. The clinics fill while the liberal churches empty. In this context these churches may be well advised to look in another direction for which there is a long, although forgotten, religious tradition.

Jacob Needleman charts a course in this direction in his recent book, *Lost Christianity.* It is the search for "the Christianity that works, that actually produces changes in human nature, real transformations" (1982:4). Like Hillman, Needleman maintains that this search is the property of part of the mind that neither modern psychology nor established religion acknowledges: it is the search for soul.

The soul is not a fixed entity. It is a movement that begins whenever a person experiences the psychological pain of contradiction. It is spontaneously activated in a human being in the state of profound self-questioning, a state that is almost always inaccurately recognized and wrongly valued in everyday experience.

> "Lost Christianity" is the lost or forgotten power of man to extract the pure energy of the soul from the experiences that make up his life. This possibility is distinct only in the most vivid or painful moments of our ordinary lives, but it can be discovered in all experiences if one knows how to seek it. (171)

(138)

Part of the problem stems from our failure to distinguish between self-fulfillment as a mere quest for happiness and the deeper impulse toward self-transformation. The quest for happiness is little more than the vain effort by the mind to alter the emotions, or vice versa. Needleman explains:

> The power to alter the structure of human life, inwardly as well as outwardly, does not reside in a partial function of the psyche. Only that function which can be in actual relationship, actual contact, with all the parts of the self has the possibility of altering the self, or of serving as the channel for the force that can alter the whole of the self. (171–72)

That function is described as the power of gathered attention. An authentic practice of Christianity as a transformative religion will require practical techniques, such as contemplative prayer. Yet "the lost element in Christianity is the specific methods and ideas which can . . . lead us towards the level at which the teachings of Christ can be followed *in fact* rather than *in imagination*" (150).

The lost dimension of Christianity parallels what Louis Dupre describes as a general erosion of genuine transcendence in the modern world. We are witnessing, he suggests, the unprecedented phenomenon of a religion that is rapidly becoming desacralized. Thus genuine religion in the present—and, presumably, in the future—differs from that of the past in that it integrates from *within* rather than from without. Indeed, there is nowhere to turn but inwardly (1983:5–7). He summarizes the implications in his book on transcendent selfhood.

> The center of human piety has moved inward where the self encounters its own transcendence. The modern believer sacralizes from within a world that no longer possesses a sacred voice of its own. His initial contact with transcendence occurs in an inner self that is neither sacred nor profane. While in the past nature, verbal revelation, and ecclesiastical institutions determined the inner experience, today it is mostly the inner experience which determines whether and to what extent outer symbols will be accepted. (1976:29)

This deliberate confrontation with inner silence is the basis of the current urge toward spiritual life. "For only after having confronted his atheism can the believer hope to restore the vitality of his religion" (1983:7).

The import of Dupre's perspective is what it tells us about religion in the desacralized context of the modern world. Thus the search for a deeper spiritual life is more than a passing phenomenon on today's religious scene. It is nothing less than a movement for religious survival.

Needleman recognizes that the rediscovery of the inner world cannot itself be the answer to the problems of living. It can do little to solve the massive problem of social injustice. Yet our situation is hardly understood when it is debated in terms of antinomies such as spirituality vs. moral conduct, inner vs. outer, and so on. Mysticism and spirituality by themselves are not enough. The same is true of social action and therapeutic caring. "The lost element in our lives is the force within us that can attend to both movements of human nature" (217).

What, then, is needed? The self-fulfillment ethos is inadequate for meeting our most important personal and cultural needs. It must give rise to what Yankelovich refers to as a "social ethic of commitment." Nevertheless, Clecak has persuasively argued that the quest for fulfillment during the past two decades has been the central energizing thrust in American culture. And that personal fulfillment consists of salvation as well as social justice. It has been culturally salutary and still holds promise for our future.

Critics of the quest for fulfillment argue that this impulse reflects a culture of narcissists or survivalists. Lasch puts it this way:

> Narcissism signifies a loss of selfhood, not self-assertion. It refers to a sense of inner emptiness. To avoid confusion, what I have called the culture of narcissism might better be characterized . . . as a culture of survivalism. . . . Confronted with an apparently implacable and unmanageable environment, people have turned to self-management. With the help of an elaborate network of therapeutic professions . . . men and women today are trying to

piece together a technology of the self, the only apparent alternative to personal collapse. (1984:57–58)

Yet, even Lasch concedes that we are not likely to get any closer to an understanding of contemporary culture as long as we define the poles of debate as selfishness and self-absorption, on the one hand, and self-fulfillment and introspection on the other.

I have tried to suggest that the variegated life experiments of the past two decades may be better understood as a search for the rediscovery of soul. The search for self-fulfillment surely has its place. It is a contemporary way of describing the pursuit of life, liberty, and the pursuit of happiness. But this quest holds promise for genuine religious and cultural renewal only insofar as it points beyond itself. It too easily reduces to consumptive patterns that remain within the orbit of the having mode of existence.[2] The search described by Needleman, Hillman, and Dupre, by contrast, is the search for a qualitatively different mode of being that is symbolized by the term soul. It is particularly evident in the revival of interest in spirituality and contemplation. Yet it is also the only place where modern persons, in general, can experience integration and transcendence. Finally, this search is the quest for moral and spiritual energy that deepens and strengthens our possibilities for self-affirmation and communal solidarity.

The future vitality of liberal churches, as well as that of the culture at large, depends on their capacity to play a leading role in the search for the rediscovery of soul. They must continue their search for a distinctive identity and come to discover how the Christian vision of salvation can enhance and correct the cultural ideal of self-realization. Church leaders may need to confront their own atheism as they rediscover, once again, the courage to be.

PART

III

THEOLOGICAL REFLECTIONS

9

The Loss of Optimism as a Problem for Liberal Christian Faith

Joseph C. Hough Jr.

Liberal Christian faith in America is an ambiguous notion. In much of the contemporary discussions it is taken to mean the sort of religious belief and practice that is perceived to be common or even dominant in those denominational groups whose national leadership is ecumenical. If that is what is meant by liberal faith, predicting its future would be simply a matter of examining trends of the several indices of institutional vitality, such as memberships and contributions, evaluating those trends, and projecting the possibility for liberal faith in America (Jacquet, 1984:229ff., esp. 246 and 273ff.).

But it is clear that the ecumenical churches vary widely in their understanding of Christian practice and mission (Roozen, McKinney, Carroll, 1984:34ff.). For example, the difference between United Methodist churches in distinguishable social and geographic locations can be sharper than the differences between United Methodist churches and Southern Baptist churches in the same social and geographic locations. The same is true of the other "ecumenical" groups.[1] Moreover, anyone seriously involved in the life of any one of the ecumenical denominations has surely observed the emergence of powerful movements within those denominations that are contesting the control of the present ecumenically oriented leadership. This is creating the paradox of "liberal" churches whose faith and practice may be anything but liberal by any recognizable definition.

For these reasons, projections about the future of the ecumenical churches in America will probably fail to address the question about the future of liberal faith in America.

In light of this, I propose to focus on a particular expression of Christianity that is present in a significant number of congregations and what I perceive to be the theological foundations of that faith expression. I shall argue that liberal Christian faith, as I describe it, was, at its inception, characterized by a highly optimistic assessment of the possibilities of God's redemption in history. This optimism cohered nicely with the optimism of American democratic faith. As the optimism of liberal Christianity faded and the theological heirs of liberalism became increasingly critical of America, they were alienated from secular democratic faith. As a result, the appeal of liberal Christianity diminished and its influence waned. At the present time, liberal Christianity is a minority religious movement in America, and it is likely to remain in that position for the foreseeable future.

In a recent book, *Varieties of Religious Presence*, McKinney, Roozen, and Carroll (1984) have argued that among the churches and synagogues in America, there are four main types of concrete "religious presence" defined in terms of their mission orientation. Two of the types are otherworldly in their emphasis, placing little importance on the possibility of redemption of this world. Their focus is, rather, on the redemptive possibilities for the individual in spite of the world. In one case, the *sanctuary* view, mission is viewed as a search for sanctity within the world's chaos and disorder. The church is a retreat of peace in the midst of conflict and a place of respite from the cultural pressures of the world. The mission of the church, in this case, is to put people "in touch with the spirit" so that they, as spiritual beings, can experience the joy of the presence of God here and now. A second type, the *evangelistic* presence, views the mission of the church primarily as a call to save souls of persons sorely tempted by this world and prepare

(146)

those souls for their future life in a better world beyond the present one.

Two other types of religious presence understand their mission as this-worldly; that is, they are concerned with the possibility of God's redemptive activity in history here and now. The *civic* type understands mission to be support for the institutions of society, which are themselves examples of God's redemptive work in history. People of this type are, therefore, anxious to undergird those institutions, which for them seem to be morally appropriate and which foster those virtues and values that they perceive to be their own religious values as well. A fourth type, the *activist*, is equally concerned with salvation in history but activists are restless about the impact of secular institutions because they see that impact in conflict with religious values. They tend to be active in social reform because they see their religious values in conflict with the status quo; mission for them is always understood in part as social criticism. Yet that social criticism is seldom revolutionary. It is reformist and usually carried on within the context of a general appreciation of the possibility for progress in history by virtue of God's work and the resulting inspired human choices.

In this essay, religious liberalism refers to the sort of religious presence represented chiefly by the activist view of mission. Furthermore, it is assumed that this sort of religious presence is grounded theologically in a perspective most clearly represented by the Social Gospel in America, particularly in the expression of the Social Gospel articulated by Walter Rauschenbusch. Although this might be seen as unnecessarily restrictive by some, it will at least give some specific focus to this essay.[2]

Foundations of American Optimism

A major characteristic of liberal Christian faith in America has been its optimism about the future of human history. As in Europe, part of the optimism of liberal Christian faith derived from the growing hope for human progress generated by the founders and heirs of the Enlightenment. Profoundly impressed by the discoveries of the natural sciences and their potential to open the secrets of nature, philosophers of the time quickly determined to apply the powers of the human mind to the persisting problems of human health and industrial development. They soon expanded their horizons to human behavior and the problems of social organization as well. The world, natural and social, was seen to be malleable. Everything in the world was open to human investigation, and the exploration of the nineteenth-century philosophers unveiled to them a panorama of immense possibilities. Things could be better, and they were. Of that, few of the participants in the enthusiasm of the Enlightenment had any doubt. Human ingenuity could intervene to change history and nature. No longer were human beings simply responders to the mysterious forces and spirits of the universe. They were now the lords of nature and the subjects of history. As their reason was liberated from the fetters of superstition and fear, they could lead human beings toward a future of progress for their good and the good of future generations.

In America the optimism about the future emerging from the Enlightenment was supported by an optimism rooted in the life experience of white persons who came to the New World. This was true in America in a way that it never was in Europe. Here the future was opened not just by the preaching of visions inspired by scientific discovery, but also by the telling of hundreds of life stories about the opportunities for beginning a new life that had been actualized among simple folk who had seized on the vast resources that were available in the new world and relentlessly pursued the freedom of the open frontier. By the end of the nineteenth century the stories of their lives had been shared many times over. Nearly every white person had heard or told a success story about new beginnings and had shared dreams about new possibilities. "Nothing in all history has ever succeeded like America, and every American knew it. Nowhere else on the globe had nature been at once so rich and so generous, and her riches were available to all who had the enterprise to take them and the good fortune to be white" (Commager, 1950:5). To the average white Americans, "progress was not . . . a philosophical idea but a commonplace of experience" (5).

Material progress was not the only commonplace characteristic of American experience. The Americans had struggled to inaugurate a widely participatory society in which each white American could experience a growing sense of participation in the decisions about rules and laws governing their social life. From the congregations of the religious and the hundreds of other voluntary associations to the rules prescribing the processes of government decision-making, the white Americans were subjects of their lives and history in a manner heretofore unknown.

Thus was born secular "democratic faith," what Crane Brinton has called the only form of this-worldly utopian thinking in Western history to gain widespread acceptance of the many (1965:354–55).

> Central to this democratic faith is the view that a suitable physical and social environment can be devised and put into practice so that what in the West has been considered evil can be vastly diminished, perhaps eliminated. . . . Furthermore, the necessary changes in the bad environment, though they must be planned and preached by an enlightened minority, will—must in a democracy—be ratified by the majority of the people and even will, after the necessary universal education be initiated by the people. (359)

This secular optimism in America was different from another perspective too. The Enlightenment optimism of Europe had been, for the most part, anti-church. In America, from the beginning, it was not. Even in Europe the symphony of optimism generated by the Enlightenment was not altogether strange music to Christians, particularly those of the Reformation tradition. They had a strong belief in the God of Israel, who had promised a messianic age of unparalleled peace and prosperity. This is not to suggest any easy compatibility between traditional Protestant beliefs and the Enlightenment. The relationship was always uneasy and much of the time it was downright hostile. Yet the Reformers knew that authentic biblical faith had always been filled with hope. That hope, grounded in a firm belief in God's sovereignty, God's creative action to bring

(149)

forth the world, and God's active intervention in human history in the incarnation, had always engendered images and visions of a redeemed future for nature and history. Thus, although the Protestant Reformers were profoundly pessimistic about human nature, and therefore about the immediate future possibilities for nature and history, they never lost sight of God's promise for a new age, a new future, and a new kingdom.

For the most part, that new kingdom was not of this world. It would take shape in another world beyond this one or at the end of it. Yet, as Troeltsch has observed in his massive study of the social teachings of the churches, the gospel ideal itself contained within it assumptions about persons and God that would cause it to venture often "on the most searching interference with the social order" (1960:1:86). It is not surprising, then, that even during the early days of the Reformation on the continent of Europe there were rumblings among the chiliastic sects about creating a new kingdom even in the midst of the present corrupt earthly kingdoms.

Furthermore, at Geneva, a theocratic experiment was attempted, and the Marian exiles from Britain, who resided there for a time, were stamped with the experience. As a result, there developed among the English Puritan Reformation groups what A.S.P. Woodhouse has called "the method of analogy," by which faithful Puritans extrapolated political judgment from ideal visions about the order of life in the Christian community (1938:60ff.; Walzer, 1968).

Those intrepid Puritans who left England to come to America in the New World came, then, not simply for religious freedom. They came anticipating a new political experiment, one that would be a light to the nations and one based on their own perceptions of the proper rules of God for human communities, both church and society. They came hopeful and optimistic that in this New World something genuinely new could occur. Their vision was, as it were, of the coming kingdom of God in America.

At some point during the nineteenth century these religiously based hopes for a new future and a new world merged in America with the new images of the future of humanity emanating from the optimistic projects of the new sciences and the vision of the boundless natural material prosperity promised by the resource-rich American continent. Thus American democratic faith, although by and large a secular phenomenon, was not antireligious. Most Americans, religious or not, affirmed the importance of religion for the new social order. In fact, most Americans thought that the general acceptance of Christianity was one of the major reasons for their success. They were special objects of divine favor (Commager, 1950:163–64).

To be sure, the evangelicals who were dominant in American life did not become sanguine about the depravity of human beings. The sinner stood in need of conversion. But the converted sinner who saw the light easily became a recruit for the building of the kingdom. The most serious sort of judgment about human sins, therefore, was no barrier to the coming of the kingdom. Having been properly confronted by sin and having been shaken firmly over the fiery pit, the converted sinner understood that the practice of piety required involvement in the kind of social reform that would bring in the kingdom (Smith, 1957; McLoughlin, 1968:Introduction). But equally important, God was raising up persons who had "Christian instincts," even if they did not participate in organized religion (Rauschenbusch, 1916:122). Thus Walter Rauschenbusch would write:

All history becomes the unfolding of the purpose of the immanent God who is working in the race toward a commonwealth of spiritual liberty and righteousness. History is the sacred workshop of God. There is a pre-sentiment abroad in modern thought that humanity is on the verge of profound change, and that feeling heralds the fact. We feel that all this wonderful liberation of redemptive energy is working out a true and divine order in which our race will rise to a new level of existence. (121)

Rauschenbusch was not unaware of the ambiguity of history, but that ambiguity for him was a temporary phenomenon.

It is unjust to Christianity to call our civilization Christian, it is unjust to our civilization to call it un-Christian. It is semi-Christian. Its regeneration is in process, but it has run in streaks and strata, with baffling inconsistencies and hypocrisies . . . but insofar as the process has gone, it will warrant us in taking the completion of the job in hand with serene confidence. . . . The largest and hardest part of the work of Christianizing the social order has been done.[3] (123–24)

This overarching optimism that was characteristic of liberal American Christianity at the turn of the century cohered nicely with democratic faith. Although Rauschenbusch himself never quite said that the kingdom would come on earth, at least in *Christianizing the Social Order*, the possibilities were certainly promising. Some of his followers were not even that careful about their claims. In fact, for a time, to be a Christian in America was to believe in America as God's historical experiment in human redemption (Niebuhr, 1937:192ff.).

The theological perspective of Rauschenbusch was based on three central convictions. First, the God of biblical faith was the God who acted in history, in and out of the church, and the action of God in history was for the sake of human good. Second, God was absolutely sovereign over history, and that was the basis for profound optimism about human progress in history. Third, Christian piety was not only a matter of personal, moral, and religious behavior; it was also identified with participation in and support of progressive movements in history, particularly those movements that had the force of democratizing the major institutions of society. God was acting in history, in American history, progressively to bring in the kingdom on earth.

Collapse of the Vision

Such optimism about America remained characteristic of liberal Christianity in the main until after World War II.[4]

That event sobered liberal Christians and prompted a more careful appraisal of the human prospect. More than any other person, Reinhold Niebuhr signified the move from an unqualified optimistic liberalism to a chastened liberal activism. Profoundly shaken by World War I, and even more by World War II, Niebuhr wrestled with the ambiguities of history and the persistence and magnitude of human sin. In *Moral Man and Immoral Society* (1932) he had argued that we can hardly expect perfection from individual persons and that it was even less realistic to expect that institutions could be made to conform to the ideal of the kingdom of God. Thus Niebuhr became severely critical of any attempt to equate historical movements or institutions with the kingdom of God. Rather, the kingdom of God was seen to be an ideal that was a judgment on all history. Yet the ideal, after all, did remain an ideal. The force of American optimism was not lost. Democracy *was* the highest possibility in history. It was made necessary by sin, to be sure, but it was possible because of the capacity for justice that was God-given. The future of history was indeed fraught with danger, but it was also pregnant with possibilities. Thus, although the kingdom of God was no longer to be identified with actual progress in history, the ideal did exist as an influence on the future of history by inspiring the ongoing struggle for justice. Although liberal Christian faith had lost its innocence about limitless possibilities for redemption in history, it had not lost its optimism about significant struggles for redemption of history within history. This chastened optimism of American liberal Christianity dominated the religious thought of mid-century American liberal Christianity.[5]

The high point of its development came with the civil rights movement under the leadership of Martin Luther King Jr. In that movement there was certainly no uncritical adulation of America as the land of progress. Democratic faith had never reflected the black experience in America, and the American dream had been nothing less than a continuing nightmare for the overwhelming majority of black Americans. Yet it was with increasing uneasiness that the nation continued to hide the anomaly of discrimination under the wraps of equal opportunity. That growing uneasiness emerged after World War II into what Gunner Myrdal called an "opinion explosion" of democratic feeling. The force of war propaganda about the racism of Nazi Germany and the characterization of the war as a great holy crusade to preserve democracy had their effect. The American public after the war was ripe for change. The growing economic prosperity of the nation opened up new possibilities for the expansion of material well-being as well.

In this context Martin Luther King Jr.'s call to America to be truly what it was called to be and what it understood itself to be struck a responsive chord in much of the nation. King's criticism of America's failure to become a racially inclusive society was sharp but never strident. He called on the promise of America and appealed to the documents of democratic faith itself. He spoke to the moral possibilities of the American dream and tied those possibilities to the power of love to motivate persons to bring about change without violence. King's criticism of America, then, was not based on a pessimistic assessment of the American dream. It was, in fact, a criticism grounded in the optimistic assessment that the pervasive power of Christian love, manifested as nonviolent resistance, could move America toward a growing fulfillment of the ideals of democratic faith for all Americans, black and white. Although the persistence of bad faith was real, the hopes of democratic faith were realizable. Thus, although King never did expect perfection in American history, he was confident that progress was achievable, and even irresistible, if the movement perdured in its challenge and its hope.

To be sure, there was fierce opposition to this call to respond to the ideals of democratic faith for all Americans, particularly in the South, where the rules and procedures of democracy had been blatantly distorted into racist structures of exclusion from the procedures and processes themselves. Yet King's hope and optimism were not misplaced. So long as the focus was on the public rules and public laws of participation in democracy, the appeal of King to the Constitution as the authoritative challenge to the distortion of democratic life inspired a growing moral consensus. This led to far-reaching judicial and legislative attempts to shape the political process more in accordance with the American dream.

However, as King's crusade led him closer and closer to the more informal bases for discrimination and segregation in American life, his optimism faded and the moral consensus that had undergirded his movement began to fall apart. Soon more strident criticism of America emerged. Even King himself began to grow more pessimistic about the possibilities for change. His forays into the North to attack the persisting institutionalized discrimination of the huge urban centers convinced him of the intractability of racism. The faltering poor people's campaign focused on the abiding inequities of the economic system. Finally, his agonizing struggle over the Vietnam war ended in his opposition to the war and in his denouncement of American foreign policy as inimical to the poor and suffering people of the world. King's vision was becoming global, and that global vision led him toward a more and more radical pessimism about the prospects of American leadership in the quest for more liberty and equality in the world.

King's growing disenchantment with America as a nation was, in many ways, paradigmatic for the heirs of the Social Gospel in America. The optimism about America that was characteristic of King's early years was, in many respects, a move beyond, and even behind, the sober realism of Reinhold Niebuhr. His subsequent pessimism about America signaled the growing disenchantment of liberal Christianity with the nation. By the end of the 1960s most liberal Christian spokespersons in America had become increasingly critical of American policy in Vietnam. That criticism was joined with a growing pessimism about possibilities for justice in domestic policy as well. With the election of Ronald Reagan in 1980, the die was cast. American democratic faith had become, for liberal Christianity, a serious problem. The God who acts in history increasingly was seen to be the judge of American perfidy at home and abroad. Liberal Christians had cast themselves in the role of internal critics of America, and some proponents of the democratic faith began to see them as disloyal. National ecumenical church leadership and the generation of clergy educated in the liberal theological schools of America found themselves increasingly on the defensive.

Perhaps being on the defensive is not a strong enough characterization of this position of liberal American Christianity. With the revival of uncritically optimistic American democratic faith in the 1980s, liberal Christians are increasingly out of touch with the temper of the times. They are thus not only pessimistic about the future of America as a champion of democracy and economic justice in the world, but they are also becoming more and more alienated from the secular democratic faith with which their creative partnership was forged. It is, therefore, hardly surprising to discover that the new converts in the revival of the American democratic faith cast about for more congenial religious partners, those who understood and affirmed this historic linkage between the work of God in history and the progress and prosperity of America.

At this point a historical irony can be observed. Conservative religion, whose understanding of the mission of the church has traditionally been otherworldly and which has generally been wary of any expectations of the arrival of the kingdom of God in history, has suddenly attached itself to American democratic faith. America is seen as the guardian of faith against the looming threat of atheistic and materialistic communism, while the material success of the American economic system is seen as evidence of God's favor for the nation. In other words, the mission of America is to protect the freedom of faith to carry on its work. It is to be the dike against the dark satanic forces that would extinguish the light of faith, which is the only hope for the salvation of individuals. Because America has chosen to do this, it is the light of all nations.

Thus, while no self-respecting conservative theologian would identify progress in America with the coming of the kingdom of God in history—their kingdom is not of this world—most conservatives easily adopt the optimism of secular American democratic faith. What is good for America is good for the gospel and vice versa. A new alliance between evangelical religion and democratic faith has been born. The terms of the alliance are very different from those of the old one, but the sociological outcomes are about the same. Belief in God and belief in America cohere nicely. The kingdom of America is a worldly kingdom. It has little to do directly with salvation. But it is the worldly kingdom that most clearly provides the conditions under which the call to be saved for the next world can be preached and heard.

Thus, far from being critical of America, conservative Christian faith is grateful to America. Secular democratic faith is appreciative of this show of gratitude. This, more than any other single fact, constitutes the reason for the revival of conservative religion in America.

The alienation of liberal Christian faith from American democratic faith constitutes the sociological problem of liberal Christianity. But that alienation is symptomatic of a growing theological problem as well. As indicated earlier, liberal Christianity was rooted in a theological perspective based on the belief that God acts in history in a redemptive way. American liberal Christianity saw evidence of God's action in history in the emergence of the new scientific knowlege, the possibilities for generalized material prosperity, and the growing democratization of American institutions that widened the options for human liberty, equality, and dignity. The collapse of liberal optimism, however, did not eliminate completely the expectation for redemption in history. Although this optimism about history was chastened, so that any easy identification of the kingdom of God with actual movements in history was problematical, the belief that God was acting for human redemption in history remained much alive. That redemptive work would not appear as evolutionary growth or as uninterrupted progress. It would be manifest much more in a serious struggle for justice involving sacrifice and suffering. The kingdom of God would never come into history as such, but as an ideal it was both a judgment on human pretensions and a reminder of the enormous new possibilities in the future.

In the 1970s the theology of hope emphasized mainly those possibilities so that a new revolutionary optimism appeared. Here the disenchantment with American Western institutions was very real, but there was high hope for the future as a future of God's revolution to make all things new in history. This theological triumphalism, in part a product of a flirtation with Marxist utopianism, was short-lived. No triumphalist view of God's action in history could survive the growing realization that by ecological deterioration or by atomic war, the real end of human history was now plainly in view. Thus the deepest theological problem for contemporary liberal Christianity is not any pessimism about the particular history of any nation or group. The deepest problem for contemporary liberal faith is the concrete possibility of the end of all history. How does one understand the redemptive work of a God who acts in history when the politics of history threaten the end of world history and natural science foresees not only the end of world history, but also the end of galactic existence in the darkness of a "black hole" in space?

Three Theological Proposals

In this context, three sorts of proposals have been advanced that are pessimistic about the future of the world. In each case the disenchantment with the liberal prospect is clear. In that sense all of them are at least postliberal. Yet they also preserve, in one way or another, the call for something like an activist religious presence for the communities of believers. In that sense they are also heirs of liberal Christian faith. One proposal comes from those who see in human history primarily the evidence of the growing magnitude of human sin. The social order has become so corrupt that any talk of God's action to redeem historical movements and institutions is mistaken, if not perverse. There clearly is no evidence of the divine sovereignty in the secular history of the world. If one still believes in the divine sovereignty over history, then the evidence of the divine power in history has to be sought elsewhere. The place where God is acting in history, then, is the church. To be sure, the church has its problems too, but the action of God in history has always been and continues to be the creation of a faithful people who perdure in history, even in the darkest moments of historical chaos and cruelty (Fackenheim, 1970).[6]

Most Christians who hold this view have been influenced, to some degree, by the theology of Karl Barth. For Barth, all human history, even the best of it, is a manifestation of human sin. The presence of God in history is manifest as the gathered people of God living in obedience to the command of God mediated by the word of God as proclaimed in the church. In

Barth himself, pessimism about human history as such was mitigated by powerful optimism about God's power in history. Thus, while the Christian community never identifies any history with the work of God, it does see its own mission to live redemptively in history as God's obedient community. What is at stake, then, is not the identification of historical progress or movements in history with the kingdom of God. What is at stake is the integrity of the Christian community. That community is to live the life of the redeemed in the world, even though they have no illusions about the power and perversity of evil and sin. They live *as if* the world is being redeemed, and in so doing, they become a redemptive presence.

For some Americans, this Barthian perspective has been mediated by the writings of Jacques Ellul. Ellul's pessimism about history is far darker than that of Barth. He thinks that sin is so pervasive and extensive that it has assumed an autonomous structure of its own. It is manifest in the invincible movement of a technologically based society that has wedded knowledge and organization in such a way as to inaugurate the destruction of history. The God who acts in history has, in Ellul's view, abandoned history at least for the time being. The faithfulness of the obedient community, then, lies in its contention with God and its call on God to intervene miraculously in history. Until God responds, there is no hope for history. Meanwhile, the redemptive power of God is manifest as the persistent cry of the Christian community for God to return to history to redeem it.

A cry is not all that is to be done. The community also lives by its memory of God's acts in the past. It rehearses those acts and lives as if God will indeed act again. Thus, even in the pessimism of Ellul, the rehearsal of the acts of God and hope against hope for the future acts of God function as a continuing motivation for social criticism and social activism. However, this sort of social piety is heroic. It is not confident about the consequences of its action, nor is it certain about the possibilities of divine action. Its concern is for the integrity of faith as a witness to a hope for the integrity of God. What this sort of faith is uncertain about is not the divine power, but the extent of the divine disgust with the world, a concern that leads it close to despair—but not quite (Ellul, 1972).

This sort of Calvinistic pessimism has not made a significant impact on American Christianity.[7] Like the disaffection of intellectuals since the 1920s, it remains contained by the general optimism of American culture. Thus, as a theological option, it appears in America primarily as a growing focus on the reality of the church as the evidence of God's action in the world; a growing preoccupation with liturgical renewal of the church as the rehearsal of God's action; and the understanding of social criticism and social activism as Christian piety. It does not see that piety primarily as a service to the world or the advancement of progress. It is a matter of faithful obedience to the divine call to be the people of God in a highly ambiguous human situation. It is a matter of bearing witness to the truth rather than bringing in the kingdom.[8]

The obedient community may be called by God to struggle for justice and to sacrifice for the sake of liberty, or even to identify especially with the poor. In any case, however, social activism is a matter of the integrity of the believing community in a perverse world. It is not a manifestation of any optimism about the possibility of progress in history. The absolutely sovereign God will redeem the world in God's own time and on God's own terms. Meanwhile, what is important is not to identify the realm of God with wordly kingdoms. It is to live as if God will redeem history, even when there seems to be little basis for hope for the future.

A second theological proposal is advanced by James Gustafson in his newly published *Ethics from a Theocentric Perspective* (1981; 1984). Gustafson's reading of the problem with the liberal theology we have described is very different from that of the Barthian perspective. He shares with Barth the perception that the easy identification of liberal humanistic movements in history with the realm of God was and is a mistake. He is critical of Barth, however, because finally Barth remains preoccupied with human history and destiny as the telos of divine activity (1981:94–95). Like the liberal theology he criticizes, Barth retains the anthropocentric turn, the assumption that the works of God are primarily in the service of humanity. Even though, for Barth, God is God and the purposes of God are for God's own glory, those purposes are gracious toward humanity, and thus supportive of the preoccupation of human beings with *their* destiny and *their* history as primary concerns of the divine activity and intentionality.

Gustafson contends that even this anthropocentrism cannot be sustained. Nothing we have learned from the sciences in recent years supports the notion that the universe can be understood as being in the service of human history. Quite the contrary, what we know is that human beings are set in a pattern of interdependence, a "life pyramid," as Aldo Leopold described it (1966), on which we are radically dependent. It is our dependence on these interrelationships, rather than our sovereignty over them, that finally sets the terms of our place in the world. Put another way, for Gustafson, nature is more important than history as the focal point for our discernment of the purposes of God in the world.

Once nature assumes its dominance over history as the locus for divine disclosure, the perspective about the divine purposes must be radically altered. In fact, the whole question about God and humanity is changed. It is not so much the query "How is God working for human good in all things?" It is, rather, "Given what we know about the creative ordering of the world by God, how can we humans respond in such a way as to conform our lives to the ordering of the whole?"

There is here no theological warrant, as in Ellul, for "calling God into account" or hoping for a divine miracle that will finally redeem human history and assure eternal human good. "God will be God," says Gustafson repeatedly (1984:319ff.), and by that he means that the fundamental posture of human beings toward the world is acceptance of our human finitude, including the relativity of our value for God who values the whole as well as the parts and who values all the parts as well. The radicality of Gustafson's position is not clearly in view until it is understood that the relativizing of value extends not merely to the world of human history, but also to the world of nature. In the context of the divine valuing the earth, as we know it, is related to the whole of the universe. Like history, the destiny of nature is to serve the glory of God, and the meaning of God's glory is shrouded in the mystery of an interrelated and interdependent cosmos. Thus, although the world is the creation of God, and hence valued by God, its relative value to the whole of God's creative intentionality cannot be assumed to occupy any place of primacy.

Gustafson's theocentric perspective is grounded in the belief in the goodness of God. Like Augustine, he receives the world as it is, as the work of a good God, whatever happens in history. Moreover, human beings are not left without significant guidance for their moral activity. Wise discernment of the nature of God's creative work in the world leads Gustafson to urge an ethic of responsible participation in the interdependent relatedness of God's creation. Such responsible participation is characterized by concern for the common good of nature and society as the primary ethical disposition, and this entails a readiness to sacrifice the individual interests of the self for the sake of both present and future generations. Human choices can and do make a difference. The importance and value of the human is not underplayed. Things can and ought to be made better by responsible human participation. That is the hope and call of Gustafson's perspective. It is also the motivation for an activist posture in relation to the major social issues before us. In this sense, Gustafson remains in the tradition of those who understand Christian religious presence as active intervention in the sociopolitical struggles of our time (280ff.).

Yet, when this is said, it must be added that the deep reluctance to speculate about the divine intentionality in relation to history and the resulting distrust of attempts to identify any concrete understanding of the good for humanity with the divine good undercut any real optimism about the future of history. Such reluctance and distrust lead, on the contrary, to a profound acceptance of the ambiguity of all speculation about God's relation to our concrete hopes for redemption in history and the redemption of history.

The vigorous liberal optimism about history is gone. In its

place is a deeply religious acceptance of the possibility of the end of history and of nature as a whole as the political and natural forces of disintegration finally move them toward their final destruction.

Thus, in contrast to the first theological option mentioned, in this perspective one does not live *as if* God is redeeming history or will redeem this world in any identifiable sense. One accepts the ambiguity of history and the end of world history as concrete realities. They are accepted on the basis that the good for God is God's own mystery. But one does not live in resignation or in despair. Christians live in trust that the good is finally God's good, and that God's good is related to the good of the whole of creation. The chief end of humans is to glorify God— an old and traditional Christian affirmation—and glorifying God consists in living in humble acceptance of what is and acting responsibly in relation to our best historical and scientific understanding of the good of everything that is (283ff.).

Process thought is a third theological proposal that exhibits a chastened optimism about history and maintains a strong call for an activist religious presence. In this proposal, however, it is not any ambiguity about the presence of God in history or the divine intention for history that undercuts liberal optimism. It is, rather, a different understanding of God's power in history. For process theologians, the sovereignty of God is relative. By that it is meant that God is understood to be interdependently related to the world and deeply affected by what happens in the world. This, in turn, means that the divine intentionality, while being a major force in nature and history, is, to some degree, limited and shaped by the dynamic interaction between God and all creation. Thus, while the divine power is certainly effective in history, it is not totally effective. In addition, the nature of divine intentionality is dynamic; that is, because God is really affected by the interactions between history and God-self, the divine intention in relation to history can change. It is, therefore, not only permissible, but also necessary to speak of the divine action of God in history always in relation to an assessment of the realities of the concrete world-historical situation.

To be sure, not everything can be known about the divine intention, but the basic trajectory is clear. God is working for good, and our human experience of what constitutes good for us, at its deepest and wisest level, is analogically correct. Our good must be understood, as in Gustafson's perspective, as a good for us seen in all the complexity of our interrelations with the natural world and with one another. The "common good" of the whole is important for process theology, and the perspective is no more subject to the "anthropocentric fallacy" than is Gustafson's perspective. Yet, because of its conviction that human action and human interaction can make a difference not only in the shape of the world, but in the concrete development of the divine intentionality as well, it is much less likely that despair, or even resignation, could be compatible with this perspective.

Furthermore, process theologians are convinced that beyond the ambiguity of human history and the end of our natural world, there is an ongoing process of God's redemptive activity. Whatever happens in history, the final outcome of the divine relationship to the cosmos is redemptive. One could also say something like that from Gustafson's perspective, but the difference lies in the confidence with which the process theologians can speak of the coherence of God's intentions for good and our experience of what is good for us. God is "for life," and if God is for life, then a responsible human relation to the divine intention is the ongoing struggle for life-affirming and life-supporting social and political structures and the development of human behavior that is in accord with God's life-affirming intentions in the whole of the natural order (Cobb and Birch, 1981:176ff.). This call for living in relation to God's intention for history and nature certainly implies persistent and serious attention to our interdependence and our dependence on the world and on one another. Life affirmation is not merely the affirmation of my own life. It is the affirmation of the life of the whole, a profound respect for and care for the common good of nature and human society.

In summary, for process thought one does not live simply *as if* God is redeeming the world and history; nor does one live in the absence of knowledge about the divine intention for history. One lives knowing that God is deeply involved in a redemptive relation to history. That alone generates more optimism about the future than is possible for either of the other two perspectives. But even here the old liberal optimism is deeply qualified by the relativity of divine power over history and nature. The ambiguity for human life and the human prospect remains. We cannot be sure that the kingdom will come. But we can rest assured that in our struggle for the realm of God in history, God, too, is working with us and for us. We do know that God is working for our good in all things. What sobers us in the human struggle is the belief that the good God, who is for us, is limited by dependence on us and our world. Thus, although we can be confident about the divine intention, we cannot be confident about any concrete case of divine effectiveness. We can hope for the ultimate effectiveness of God, but that hope, like the "future" or "heaven," functions as a promise rather than as the ground of any easy optimism.

One can still view these proposals in continuity with the activist religious presence of liberal Christianity. In all three, Christians are called on to be deeply concerned for and responsibly participant in the choices that shape human history and destiny. But over them all hangs a critical uncertainty. There is finally no assurance that anything more than episodic "betters" or "worses" can be expected as a consequence of human choices in history. To be sure, in all cases we are still deeply affected by the divine power in history and moved by the divine self-disclosure in history. But there is finally no assurance that the future holds anything more or less than destruction and death. Thus, even though life presents us with possibilities for good, the meaning and ultimate outcome of it all is dreadfully uncertain. All these theological proposals call into serious question any sustained optimism about the human prospect. Because of that none of them will find acceptance by the converts of democratic faith. In that sense they hold no promise for the genesis of a neoliberal consensus on Christian faith in America. What they do represent is the possibility of a resurgent theistic perspective that will, in one way or another, challenge both the easy optimism of secular humanistic faith and the self-righteous moralism of individualistic and parochial Christian faith. As such, they will form the basis for a continuing active Christian presence, one that expands its conception of moral responsibility to the common good of the whole creation. But the confidence about history is so thoroughly qualified in all of them that they represent the end of the liberal theological program as we have known it.

10

Complementism: Liberal Protestant Potential Within a Fully Realized Pluralistic Cultural Environment

John K. Simmons

Looking back from the vantage point of the 1980s, Martin Marty observed that "to tell the story of mainline Protestantism in the 60s and 70s would almost be to tell the story of the culture itself in travail" (Baily, 1982:5). The saga of religiosocial turmoil hardly needs to be rehearsed. Such events as the civil rights movement, the Vietnam war, and Watergate, seemed to portend the irreparable fracturing of moral consensus. Eastern religions were "suddenly" discovered as new religious movements emerged from within and without the United States. Quasi-religious therapeutic programs and secular humanist world views arose to confront what was left of mainline Protestant hegemony. Even a glance at the titles of lead articles in church journals during the period reveals loss of authority, breakdown, confusion, searching: "Protestant Man on the Brink of Extinction," *United Church Herald*, 1967; "Protestantism: Dead or Alive?" *World Call*, 1968; "What Will 1971 Bring?"*American Baptist*, 1971; "Christians in Search of a Future," *The Episcopalian*, 1973; "Serving in 1974: Between Despair and Hope," *A.D.*, 1974; "A New Start in the Journey of Faith," *The Disciple*, 1974. Although there are numerous reasons for the apparent demise of mainline, or liberal, Protestantism, a close look at many similar articles suggests that the primary challenge has been pluralism.[1]

Pluralism has slowly but inexorably altered the contours of the American religious scene. Where once liberal Protestantism and American culture were practically indistinguishable, we now find ourselves asking the question Does liberal Protestantism have an American future? But how can this situation have developed in the United States, where, as Alexis de Tocqueville noted 150 years ago, the very possibility of pluralism rested on the underlying assumption that, despite denominational variety, the nation was, at heart, a Protestant Christian enterprise? If the Protestant Christian world view provided the "sacred canopy" under which the construction of a religiously pluralistic American polity took place, are we now to assume that, because of massive overcrowding, the roof is about to collapse?

Perhaps it will. Barring some totalitarian takeover, pluralism will always be descriptive of the American sociocultural scene. It can never be "removed." But there is reason to hope that friction caused by pluralism can give way to *fully realized* pluralism in American society. Whether or not liberal Protestantism "survives" as a healthy identifiable religious option depends on its resonance with the paradigmatic change that is occurring in the American cultural environment.

The power of paradigms in cultural formation and transformation should not be underestimated. If culture is the glaze over chaos, paradigms constitute "the stuff," the compounds that reinforce the tensile strength of the glaze. It is not surprising that when the paradigms that inform a culture are weakened, all hell (chaos) breaks loose because paradigms provide a consistent, mutually agreed on vision of reality. By offering organizational models that make reality interpretable, they determine how a people in a particular society see themselves in relation to all else.

Paradigms function on two levels that are vital to the formation of human identity. On the personal level, paradigms delineate individual identity by providing the cognitive aperture through which human beings view and interpret experience.

The ability to create, grasp, and use paradigms is indispensable to our orientation in the natural and cultural environment. On the collective level, paradigms determine our behavior toward one another by fostering a distinct sense of community and inspiring commitment to group endeavors within that community. The identity-forming, behavior-modifying power of paradigms is never more obvious than in the wisdom codified in the ten commandments, the four noble truths, or the Beatitudes.

Ironically, paradigms furnish cultures with the stability that allows them to outgrow their paradigmatic structures. Historically, the causes of paradigmatic breakdown have been numerous: the invasion of a sated society by barbarian hordes, the emergence of a charismatic spiritual or political leader, scientific discoveries, economic disasters, war, disease, famine, etc. The tensile test for paradigmatic strength is experience. If the paradigms embraced by a given society no longer adequately describe in-world experience, then the people in that society are faced with a crisis of interpretation. A new, stronger "glaze" is needed to prevent an eruption of chaos.

Today our society finds itself in just such a crisis of interpretation. In a globally interconnected world, new paradigms are needed to help us formulate individual and collective identities that are operational in a fully pluralistic culture. Although the conceptual and institutional framework of the developing paradigm is as yet unclear, the outline of such a framework may be found in Systems Philosopy (developed by Ludwig von Bertalanffy and Ervin Laszlo and recently adapted to the discussion of paradigm change by Fritjof Capra).[2]

Systems Philosophy studies the dynamics of self-organizing systems—liberal Protestantism being just such a cultural system. It stresses the essential interconnection and interdependence of all phenomena and monitors change, noting the coevolutionary tendency toward complexity, coordination, and creative adaption with and within the surrounding environment. For example, given the methodology of the old paradigm—to isolate and analyze—the question Will liberal Protestantism have an American future? might be interpreted

Will liberal Protestantism survive? From the new perspective, which recognizes that everything around us contains a large number of things and is exposed to a large number of things, the question becomes "How will liberal Protestantism creatively adapt?" Fritjof Capra writes: "From the systems point of view the unit of survival is not an entity at all, but rather a pattern of organization adopted by an organism in its interactions with its environment" (1982:289).

In a fully pluralistic cultural environment the presence of four characteristics will suggest a successful "pattern of organization": complementarity, communication, communion/community, consensus. Complementarity is a key function of self-organizing systems. In order for a fully pluralistic society to develop, human beings have to learn to deal with difference more harmoniously than they have in the past. Complementarity eclipses the glare of polarization by offering a unitary model, which, at the same time, respects difference and the integrity of the individual at all levels of society. Complementarity, the model for social interaction in a fully pluralistic world, generates a social environment characterized by communication, communion/community, and consensus.

The question is then: to what extent is liberal Protestantism adaptable to a social environment based not on competing privacies or polarities, but on reciprocating complements? In order to answer this question we need to turn to the past and look to the future. Peter Berger's work *The Heretical Imperative* (1979) provides a historical perspective on Protestant cultural interaction. Systems Philosophy offers a translation of this interaction into the evaluative terminology of new paradigmatic thinking. On this base we can begin to develop an informed prediction of the future of liberal Protestantism.

Complementarity

Pluralism is part of the American experience, yet it has increasingly become a negative experience. Why? *The Heretical Imperative* provides a comprehensive answer. If human beings must choose their world view from a plurality of competing belief systems, how is that choice to be made with a sense of authority? Where once in the premodern world people simply stood under the spell of religious tradition, submitting to it as one would to floods, earthquakes, or fires, now in the modern world a new situation is created. People are forced to choose their world view.

However, the multiplicity of possible choices in a pluralistic society undermines the process of world view selection. People need social support *authorizing* their choices. In a society that is increasingly pluralistic, human beings simply have to learn to live with Berger's "root insight":

> subjective certainty [in religion as in other matters] depends upon cohesive social support for whatever it is that the individual wants to be certain about. Conversely, the absence or weakness of social support undermines subjective certainty—and that is precisely what happens when the individual is confronted with a plurality of competing worldviews, norms or definitions of reality. (1980:43)

This leads to the inescapable fact that people must choose. Hence, from the Greek verb *hairein,* to choose, Berger dubs modernity the age of the "heretical imperative."

Yet we should never forget that although modernity has compelled us to choose from a multitude of institutional and cognitive possibilities, it is never an easy project. It is not simply a matter of pushing the shopping cart down the aisles of Weltanschauung's Supermart snatching a sack of Mystical Munchies, grabbing a bag of Yin-Yang Flakes, a package of Buddha-Biscuits, a can of Desert Father's Soup Mix. Always there remains an unsatisfied hunger for authority. It is not enough to choose. A person needs to feel that the choice is right. The paradigms present in the chosen world view need to describe accurately in-world experience.

Again, Berger is helpful by supplying us with three options (or modes) for dealing with choice and authority in a pluralistic world: the deductive option, the reductive option, and the inductive option. In the modern age, Protestantism has chosen one or the other of these options. But in analyzing each option it becomes clear that the inductive option—rooted in Protestant liberal theology—provides a workable model for *complementism* (fully realized pluralism) in the postmodern cultural environment.

The deductive option reaffirms the authority of religious tradition in the face of modern pluralism. Here we have the orthodox stance harking back to premodern times, when a person recognized only one way of looking at the world and one institution that represented that world view. Religious affirmations are deduced from something given a priori, which, in the case of Protestantism, is the Bible or Word of God.

This stance is actually counterpluralistic. The underlying mood is to go on as though nothing has changed. The deductive approach requires that people either remove themselves from society or try to organize such a vociferous social-support group that society is induced to conform to their authoritarian world view (Douglas and Tipton, 1983:21–22; Berger discusses the political stance of counterpluralism and countersecularity). For example, vacillation between these two retreat-or-attack strategies describes the history of fundamentalism in America. Ideally, as I have said, a religion—a set of paradigms—should conform to a person's in-world experience. An organization such as Jerry Falwell's Moral Majority can be seen as using the more aggressive deductive strategy when it comes to choice. A grab for political power with hopes of returning America to a lost Eden of biblical authority is an endeavor forcefully to change reality to mirror a priori religious truth.

The reductive option is secular, modernistic, and a source of the Protestant crisis. It strives for a reinterpretation of tradition in which "the authority of modern thought or consciousness is substituted for tradition" (Berger, 1979:71). The process is one of cognitive bargaining. A believer might give up one "Virgin Birth" but insist on retaining a "Resurrection from the Dead," depending on his or her willingness to allow modern biological theses to regulate acceptance or rejection of biblical miracles. And, as Berger points out, Protestant theological liberalism has engaged in the most intense bargaining with modernity. The danger, here, is that if you bargain everything away, you have total secularization and, consequently, no internal integrity, no place to turn for objective authority.

Looking back we can say that the vitality of American Protestantism, even in the mid-1800s, was maintained by a balancing of these two tendencies. As Martin Marty observes, "those who advocated revivalism, soul-saving, and rescue out of the world were the same people who wanted to devote virtually equal energies to the reform of the society" (1970:180). But shortly thereafter, the increasingly powerful presence of pluralism—fueled by such forces as Social Darwinism, industrialism, urban blight, immigration, and the New Theology—split Protestantism into two parties. On one hand, the conservative/evangelical/private/otherworldly strand embraced the deductive option. On the other, the modernist/public/Social Gospel strand dealt reductively with the pressures of a pluralistic cultural environment. Antagonisms between these two parties not only weakened the Protestant program in America, but also, in general, stultified progress toward a functioning pluralistic religious culture. Fundamentalism's belligerent attack on modernism only crippled the conservative position. Modernist efforts to create its own Garden of Eden and toss God out resulted in a religionless Christianity that was and is ineffective in assisting people with personal, spiritual problems.

The deductive and reductive options are both powerful tendencies in Protestantism today. They embody paradigms through which adherents understand their chosen religious tradition in its relationship with in-world experience. Yet the combativeness of the two paradigmatic perspectives diminishes the efficacy of Protestantism in general. What is needed is not a discarding of these forces, but a balance, reciprocity, complementarity between the two opposing tendencies. This can be realized in the inductive option.

The inductive option is paradigmatically resonant with a complementistic cultural environment. Moreover, liberal Protestantism can serve as an inductive model. Berger recognizes induction as the "middle ground" between the deductive and reductive options. In this sense it is nonauthoritarian in its approach to questions of truth. Authority does not lie in inerrant scripture or in the halls of modern secular multiversities. It rests in personal human experience that can be turned to as "the ground of religious affirmation. . . . Induction means . . . that religious traditions are understood as bodies of evidence concerning religious experience and the insights deriving from the experience" (1972:62, 63).

Protestant liberalism, since Friedrich Schleiermacher, has followed the inductive method, seeking a more perfect fit between personal religious experience and in-world reality. Admittedly, in this history of American Protestantism, the more balanced inductive stance, experientially rooted in Christian tradition yet open to social expression of religious insight, tended to slide into a modernist, reductive immanentism with an accompanying loss of Christian distinctiveness. Yet, as Berger attests, "the theological method . . . of classical Protestant liberalism, with its stress on experience and reasonable choice, is the most viable one today" (1979; see chapter on induction). The viability of the inductive stance rests on an inward authority that is not threatened by a one-of-many status in society. In fact, the nurturing of divergent viewpoints in a complementistic cultural environment is not only enriching, but also essential, since encounter and interaction with that which is "other" than oneself facilitates growth at the individual as well as the institutional levels of society.

If Protestantism is to "survive" in a complementistic world environment, new paradigms are called for that will regenerate a balance between deduction and reduction. Can there be a productive relationship between constrictive and expansive tendencies?

The systems view of life perceives the deductive/reductive dialectic as a positive struggle for complementarity best exhibited in the inductive mode. Avenues toward complementarity are opened by viewing liberal Protestantism as a "supraorganic [cultural] natural system" (Laszlo, 1972:30). A natural system is self-organizing, which means that "its order in structure is not imposed by the environment but is established by the system itself" (Capra, 1982:269). A clock, a Corvette, or a personal computer cannot be a self-organizing system simply because some "outer force" gives these objects their structure and function. An ant hill, a picket line, a rabbit, the San Francisco '49ers, the U.S. Senate, the United Methodist Church are all self-organizing systems. They can modify (reorganize) both structure (through evolution or edict) and function (behavior) to meet environmental demands.

The inductive option is, paradigmatically, just such a self-organizing system and reflects the dynamic principles of self-organization: "self-renewal—the ability of living systems continuously to renew and recycle their components while maintaining the integrity of their overall structure; and self-transcendence—the ability to reach out creatively beyond physical and mental boundaries in the process of learning, development and evolution" (Capra, 1982:269). Each system exists in a state of complementarity between self-assertive (self-renewal) and integrative (self-transcendent) tendencies. It is the totality of the environment in which one lives, moves, and enjoys being.

In Protestantism the deduction option can be equated with the self-renewal, self-assertive tendency. The fundamentalist predilection for a singular source of authority is not inherently misguided; it is a system's drive toward distinctiveness, an understandably important aspect of self-survival. The reductive option can be equated with the self-transcendent, integrative tendency. Again, the immanentism manifested as desire for cultural adaption is the natural yearning of a system to integrate with the environment. But the environment cannot be allowed to swallow "a part" of its own self. It is the distinctiveness of the part that makes the whole a particularly effective system.

In the inductive option, complementarity is found between the deductive and reductive options. Berger reaches for this when he writes:

> Against the right [the deductive option], this position [induction] means a reassertion of the human as the only possible starting point for theological reflection and a rejection of any external authority [be it scriptural, ecclesiastical, or traditional] that would impose itself on such reflection. Against the left [the

reductive option], the position means a reassertion of the supernatural and the sacred character of religious experience, and a rejection of the particularly oppressive authority of modern secular consciousness. (1979:154)

Here is the theological position that liberal Protestantism struggles toward today as it engages paradigmatic change. The reductive element becomes inductive as the traditional symbols and strong sense of sacred authority present in the deductive approach are reencountered in community.

For example, writing in *The Disciple,* Ronald E. Osborn observes that "the mood of our times swings violently from one extreme to another. Every six months finds us marching in a different parade" (1974:19). Against this reductive parroting of cultural change, he senses the need for balance. "In contrast to such nervous voguishness we need to strive to comprehend the breadth and balance of Christian truth—individual and social, priestly and prophetic, human and divine, devotional and theological, active and contemplative. We need to submit ourselves to the whole counsel of God" (1974:19). Osborn's call for balance is just one of many similar examples of the inductive sensitivity in a liberal Protestant's assessment of the changing cultural environment.

If liberal Protestantism has engaged in the most intense bargaining with modernity, it seems quite understandable that during "modernity's identity crisis," liberal Protestantism would exhibit more internal upheaval, more identity problems. However, this may simply be the normal activity of a natural system in its attempts to maintain itself in a time of furious change in the cultural environment. Furthermore, the sensitivity to "move inductively" will promote successful patterns of organization within the postmodern complementistic world. Since this is the domain of liberal Protestantism, it could be that liberal Protestantism is, in fact, a healthier natural system than generally perceived, working its way through a trying period of paradigm change.

Again, church journals support the inductive perspective. Philip E. Hughes recognizes that "the need for adaptability in the ministry of the church in the face of changing circumstances and patterns of society is not open to dispute. The evangelical, pastoral, and compassionate heart of the ministry, however, does not change" (1975:11). Integrative tendencies are balanced by the maintenance of that which is distinctively, traditionally Christian.

Another Martin Marty article is particularly germane: "Congregations Come Alive! Mainline Churches May Be in Trouble but Many Are Alive and Kicking." A study of Marty's lists four factors that account for the against-the-trend health of a local congregation:

(a) Members had a fairly clear idea of what they were about—and were united around a basic but not confining set of beliefs.
(b) The congregation had taken deliberate steps to provide exciting worship and growth in personal life.
(c) Leadership in the congregation was sure of itself—the pastor was secure enough to project goals and models, and the lay leadership was able to relate to his sense of direction with a quality of freedom and independence.
(d) The congregation had a mission to the community, providing members with a sense of both the frustration and thrill that comes with making a difference in the world. (1979a: 28)

Clearly, the inductive characteristics of complementism—communication, community/communion, consensus—are present in this situation on both a personal and an institutional/social level. This pattern of organization works because Christian-spiritual-inner life is balanced by community-secular-outer activity. A basic but not confining set of beliefs provides a firm foundation for interaction among members of the group but does not restrict personal spiritual growth or limit change within the community.

Communities such as this congregation should be encouraging for liberal Protestantism, since the pattern of organization adopted by a religious group will determine if it "survives." In a complementistic culture environment the most effective pattern of organization will be one that draws on and incorporates differing viewpoints. Induction is just such a pattern of organization. Because liberal Protestantism has historically embraced the inductive pattern of organization, one may logically assume that liberal Protestantism does, indeed, have an American future.

Communication

What will the future be like in a complementistic cultural environment? Certainly communication among divergent groups with a variety of world views will be a key characteristic. Richard J. Neuhaus declares that "Christian truth, if it is true, is public truth. It is accessible to public reason. It impinges upon public space" (1984:19). Although individuals may privately hold any sort of view, from the sublime to the ridiculous, it is only in the public realm that these views can actually "acquire" truth. Thus, as David Tracy warns, "without a serious commitment to the public realm, the shared, the communal, the realm where all must finally meet, there is a grave danger. For without that commitment pluralism itself could become another trap, another private consumer good, another excuse to retreat into one's own private reservation of the spirit" (1983:276). In a complementistic world such commitment is generated naturally by the complementarity that will exist between private and public realms. Organizations that creatively adapt to this paradigm change will have "a foot" in each realm and will be open to genuine conversation with other groups, conversation that will be held in the "public square." Whether the source of one's authority is the Bible or Aristotle, secular humanistic ideology or therapeutic programs, all are invited and all may speak in the public square. This conversation is protected from nakedness and overdressing by the following criteria: "intelligibility (coherence), truth (warrants evidence), right (moral integrity) and equality (mutual reciprocity)" (Tracy, 1983:280). Reciprocity is an important term, an inductive term, as it implies inclusion and dialogue. Each group understands its place and purpose within the cultural conversation as an indispensable particular in the universal public realm. Distinctiveness augments the conversation, yet no monopoly can or will be permitted. Church journals indicate that liberal Protestants are prepared for new possibilities of communication. For example, "in the 80s mainline churches will need to recover legitimacy by speaking with fresh authority, being morally credible and gifted in determining the real needs of people. As we head into a new decade we must remain open to the new possibilities that no one can foresee" (Marty, 1979b:22).

Community/Communion

One new possibility that should be realized in the complementistic society is a revitalized sense of community. As liberal Protestants become more adept at articulating distinctive Christian convictions to variegated groups within the public realm, their own experience of community will be strengthened. As a people-among-peoples, one-among-many, liberal Protestants will know a new freedom once they accept their role as a creative minority. They will be free to be distinctively Christian and to be in communion with other Christians without triumphalistic, covenantal concerns about controlling the sociopolitical arena. Like the pompous Englishman who is still haunted by some specter of past imperialistic splendor, doomsayers who predict the imminent demise of the United States if it ceases to be a "Christian nation" should wake up! The sun has set on the British Empire *and* Christian America. The situation is no longer a game of pluralism/counterpluralism with Protestant Christianity in the referee's chair. Nor is it a case of "us-against-secular-humanism." Secular humanists and liberal Protestants are people-among-peoples and both groups need to accept that one cannot expect preferential treatment in a complementistic cultural environment. What they can expect is to cultivate distinctiveness within their respective communities, bring that unique perspective to the public square, and communicate it! All for the common good.

Consensus

In America, even with the institutionalization of secular humanism, there has been a "broadly common morality." Peter Berger warns that moral pluralism may be eroding this taken-for-granted moral consensus. "Moral pluralism is becoming increasingly prevalent, and it is much harder to institutionalize than religious pluralism." Imagine statements such as "My moral preference is for arson in labor disputes," or "I happen to be a rapist," or "I'm into spying for the Soviet Union" (see Douglas and Tipton, 1983:18). Would this imagined rejection of the underlying ideals that have informed Americans' sense of the common good really take such extreme forms? Berger's assessment of the dangers of moral pluralism reveals a common neoconservative prejudice that is more consciously expressed by Richard Neuhaus: "Very basic notions of religious freedom depend upon an understanding of religion as the bearer of transcendent truth to which the nation is accountable" (1984:142). What Neuhaus' comment suggests is that there is no freedom without religious freedom and the religion that bears the transcendent truth that provides the moral basis for all other freedoms is the Judeo-Christian world view. The nation is morally accountable to this particular transcendent truth. Again we witness Protestant Christian refusal to relinquish its claim to a position it has already lost: center stage in the American sociopolitical arena.

In response, I would make two points. First, secular ideologies have transcendent truths that inform the common good. These truths make human beings accountable for the same high standard of moral behavior as do Judeo-Christian truths; they provide the basis for a moral language through which the nature of the common good can be communicated in public forums. Second, transcendent truth embodied in religious tradition is sufficient but *not* necessary ground for moral consensus. In a complementistic cultural environment, religious tradition and secular ideology have the same access to the public square where moral privacies complement but are not swallowed by public hunger for moral consensus.

One example of a secular ideology that possesses truth that transcends individual desire and informs the common good is that of the ecology movement in America. Roderick Nash offers a fascinating explanation for environmental ethics attracting such a broad group of adherents. "What is intriguing as an explanation is the possibility that an ethical attitude toward nature is the latest in a succession of American concerns for the rights of exploited or oppressed human beings. The new environmentalism simply transcended the limitation of species" (Tobias, 1984:176). Ever cognizant of the moral basis for life, liberty, and the pursuit of happiness, the American concept of rights has been expanding from the Declaration of Independence, to the Emancipation Proclamation, and the Nineteenth Amendment, through the Indian Reorganization Act and the National Labor Relations Act, and on to *Brown* v. *Board of Education of Topeka*, and the Endangered Species Act (180). American society will have its rapists and its Soviet spies, but these forms of behavior are moral aberrations. A basic respect for the rights of all living beings is clearly very much alive in America and provides a secular foundation for moral consensus.

Although the liberal Protestant perspective is not necessary for the formulation of American moral consensus, it is sufficient with all the vitality that sufficiency implies. Although it is not the purpose of this essay to dabble in theological speculation or outline an agenda for liberal Protestants, a strong case could be made to support the fact that the paradigm change leading to a complementistic society occurred 2,000 years ago with the birth of Jesus Christ. The three revolutions described by Paul in his letter to the Galatians (3:23–28) point to the incarnation as a major change in the way reality is to be interpreted.

> Now before faith came, we were confined under the law, kept under restraint until faith should be revealed. So that the law was our custodian until Christ came, that we might be justified by faith. But now that faith has come, we are no longer under a custodian; for in Christ Jesus you are all sons of God, through faith. For as many of you as were baptized into Christ have put on Christ. There is neither Jew nor Greek, there is neither slave nor free, there is neither male nor female; for you are all one in Christ Jesus.

No longer are we "restrained" under a way of perceiving being that locks us into competing privacies and polarities but are welcomed into a new complementistic world. The sense of evolving freedom that demands its own agenda resonates with the secular environmental viewpoint. A moral agenda for today virtually springs from these three ancient revolutions in human freedom: *"Jew nor Greek"*; the defusing of combative nationalisms; end to cold war polarization; disarming of the nuclear threat: *"slave nor free"*; sanctuary; solidarity; closing of the gap between rich and poor; freedom from excessive consumerism, which make people slaves to lack as well as abundance: *"male nor female"*; not just the feminist movement, but also the overall understanding that opposites are necessary complements, not causes for conflict. Biblical exegesis aside, the point is that while American moral consensus is not exclusively dependent on religious truth or secular knowledge, it *is* informed by both, creating a broadly accepted understanding and respect for human freedom that transcends individual preference in the cultivation of the common good.

It is appropriate to end as I began, with a reflection from *A.D.* William Nelson declares that "we should not fear changes that are to come but accept them, recognizing that Christ is a contemporary companion, prophet, and judge, urging us on to make his gospel real in this world" (1974:17). Liberal Protestantism has little to fear from the changes that will result in a complementistic cultural environment. Because of the liberal Protestant predilection for the inductive mode of religiocultural interaction, the characteristics of communication, community/communion, and consensus are already descriptive of their pattern of organization. Although liberal Protestantism will never regain its dominant position in society, as a creative minority, there is every reason to believe that this heritage will be an indispensable contributor to American culture in the emerging, fully pluralistic era.

11

Liberal Protestantism and the Language of Faith

Barbara Brown Zikmund

It is difficult to define what we mean by "liberal Protestant," and there is a lack of agreement about what is happening to the tradition. Generally speaking, liberal Protestantism involves a particular type of Protestant thinking that flourished in America in the early twentieth century (1910 to 1930). It places itself in relationship to sixteenth-century left-wing Reformation history, but its unique character was forged out of a nineteenth-century American evangelical consensus. By the early twentieth century many liberal Protestant denominations functioned as Establishment groups of Anglo-Saxon white Christians (Congregationalists, Presbyterians, Methodists, Episcopalians, Lutherans, Disciples, and northern Baptists). Smaller liberal bodies, such as the Friends and the Unitarians, were theologically liberal, but because of their smaller size their influence has remained marginal (Cauthen, 1962; Averill, 1967; Hutchison, 1968, 1976).

Robert Handy argues that the "Protestant era" in American history ended in 1940. By that time immigration and internal population growth created a pluralistic mix of "Protestant, Catholic, and Jew." Still later Americans became self-conscious about "civil religion," upholding "liberal" values unrelated to any specific confessional camp (1984; also see Herberg, 1955; Bellah, 1974).

Operationally, however, the leadership of white mainline Protestantism continues to operate out of a "liberal" value system. Two things keep this liberal bias alive in many Protestant denominations. First, the ecumenical commitments begun with the Federal Council of Churches have been stretched and expanded. In the past seventy-five years church merger conversations (including the Consultation on Church Union [COCU]) and participation in national and international ecumenical organizations (National Council of Churches [NCC] and World Council of Churches [WCC]) have forced many church people to deal with diversity. Even those denominations that have become more "conservative" or "narrow" at the local level ignore local attitudes and continue to court one another in the spirit of ecumenical "liberalism" nationally and internationally. Second, the racial and social crises of the civil rights movement, the women's movement, and the Vietnam war (which became the peace movement) have allowed many denominations to avoid theological controversy. In its zeal to meet the challenges of injustice in the world, mainline Protestantism has been protected from the truth about itself. This explains why many liberal Protestants find "liberation theologies" so appealing, for they seem to combine ecumenical vision with a call to social justice.

In the late 1980s, however, discontinuity between the grassroots mind and national denominational leadership is no longer masked by social action or the natural membership growth created by post-World War II population growth. Mainline Protestantism is being forced to come to grips with what it is and where it is going at the end of the twentieth century.

What Has Happened to Mainline Protestantism?

There are five developments in mainline Protestantism that disturb and explain the contemporary situation. First, the context for defining liberal Protestantism has changed. In earlier situations when liberal Protestantism became self-conscious, it argued for rationality or common sense over against blind faith or dualistic assumptions about religion and science. Today the "enemy" has changed. An apologetic for liberal Protestantism must be made in the opposite direction. Instead of arguing for more openness in the face of fundamentalism, liberal Protestantism today offers opportunities for commitment in a predominantly secular world. Liberal Protestantism has its greatest appeal to secular persons who have rejected religion, not to those seeking a way out of stifling religiosity.

When contemporary people are asked why they go to church, the reasons they give are rarely theological. The church is a keeper of values, a helpful service organization, a place to feel at home, a spiritual insurance policy (just in case some of that hell and damnation stuff is true) (Rauff, 1979). Liberal Protestantism, therefore, is most effective when it makes its case for a meaningful Christian life in the midst of secularity. It may be said that the Christian church is the one organization to which we ought to belong precisely in order to be "disturbed." Christianity challenges our selfish habits. Whereas in earlier times liberalism helped people to escape from the disturbing and unreasonable aspects of Christian orthodoxy, today authentic liberalism has its greatest power when it calls the unchurched or once churched to face disturbing realities and responsibilities in contemporary life (McElvaney, 1980).

Second, liberal Protestantism needs to realize that it is no longer part of the political and social establishment. We live in a century where the status of the Christian church is steadily diminishing. Political ideologies and other living religions actively compete with Christianity for power. Non-Western peoples have rejected the imperialistic assumptions of historic "Christendom."

The time has come when Christians in general, and mainline Protestants in particular, need to relinquish their majority mind-set. Although the Christian church remains the single largest religious group in the world, it lacks the prestige and power it once commanded. On the American scene mainline Protestant churches have lost membership and influence. Liberal Protestantism increasingly exists on the edges of power.

This may be a blessing. Roger Williams, colonial rebel, noted the way in which power has been the downfall of Christianity.

The unknowing zeal of Constantine and other emperors did more hurt to Christ Jesus His crown and kingdom than the raging fury of the most bloody Neros. In the persecutions of the latter, Christians were sweet and fragrant, like spice pounded and beaten in mortars; but by those good emperors . . . I say, by this means Christianity was eclipsed and the professors of it fell asleep. Babel or confusion was ushered in, and by degrees the garden of the churches of saints were turned into the wilderness of whole nations, until the whole world became Christian or Christendom. . . . When Christianity began to be choked, it was not when Christians lodged in cold prisons, but on down-beds of ease. (in Miller, 1963:136–37)

We may despair over the formal loss of ecclesiastical influence in society, in relationship to other religions, or over against other Christian groups, but our new marginality could be a blessing. People on the edges of responsibility and power often have special opportunities to bring important insights to leadership. Liberal Protestantism needs to stop thinking and acting with a majority mind-set and discover the strength and freedom of marginality.

Third, related to the reality of marginality, basic understandings of legitimate leadership have changed in contemporary society. American democracy, at its inception, assumed the validity of benevolent elites. The Constitution vested authority in propertied, educated male citizens. Ordinary people were not expected to understand the intricacies of political power. They simply followed good leaders. Today elitism is suspect and leadership is more and more difficult. Mass democracy assumes that majorities must have real power and that pluralistic voices must be heard. It may be less efficient, but liberal ideology says that it is more just.

Ironically, although liberal Protestantism embraces many of the values of mass democracy, its basic character depends on some important elitist assumptions. Logic and rationality are at the heart of liberal Protestantism. It assumes that people will believe when they understand, that people will act correctly when they know the consequences. It depends on educated laity with personal concern about their faith and their churches. Mass society, however, is not always logical and rational. Mass society regularly fails to appreciate the radical individual freedom of liberal Protestantism.

In the past decade the women's movement has been quite successful in liberal Protestantism. More and more women have moved into positions of power in denominational life. The numbers of ordained women have increased dramatically and long-standing male elites are learning to share power.

This change has come about so quickly (in 1985 more than 50 percent of seminary enrollments in liberal Protestant seminaries were female) that some observers believe that ordained ministry will become a "female profession," like nursing or primary school teaching. Because Protestant clergymen have historically been associated with the private sphere and linked to feminine cultural characteristics (being loving and kind), it is not difficult to accept women as clergy. When this happens, however, clergymen could perceive what they consider a "declining" ministerial profession. The understanding of woman's second place in the created order, which has been dominant in Christian history, may return to haunt liberal Protestantism long before it affects other branches of Christianity. And even if these changes are interpreted as positive, celebrating the increased numbers of women clergy as reducing long-standing barriers between laity and ordained leadership, the question of elitism remains (Russell, 1979: 125–26).

How can liberal Protestantism, with its codes of individual responsibility, thrive in a world where educated elites are vulnerable? As an educated white woman, it is difficult for me to maintain my solidarity with oppressed peoples of color. I value education and rest my theological assumptions on "Enlightenment values." Many ethnic and racial groups do not accept these liberal Protestant assumptions about the world. As they call liberal Protestantism to accountability they jeopardize its future in two ways, by refusing to follow elitist leadership and by rejecting some of the assumptions on which liberal Protestantism is grounded.

Fourth, the image of liberal Protestantism has been closely connected with particular policies developed through rational/scientific thinking. There is a saying that politics is the "art of the possible." Politicians spend time and money to arrive at workable solutions for the good of the body politic. Liberal Protestants have cared about and influenced the formation of public policy.

Over the years, however, liberal Protestantism has both triumphed and suffered because of this involvement. When specific policies have not produced promised results, people have rejected liberal Protestantism itself. Social Gospel thinking pushed liberal Protestantism into social engineering, but social engineering was limited. Social Security, welfare, school busing, farm subsidies are all examples of liberal Protestant concerns finding concrete political expression. For example, in the name of "equality," busing was legislated. When busing failed to do all that it promised, people rejected busing and even began to question the principle of equality behind the policy. In becoming so closely associated with particular political policies, liberal Protestantism risks its effectiveness. It loses political credibility with each policy failure, and sometimes its basic presuppositions are undermined.

Finally, liberal Protestantism not only needs to deal with a new understanding of its appeal, its marginal place in the social landscape, its rationalistic elitism in the context of mass democracy and its close alignment with faltering policies, but it must also wrestle with significant internal changes. Growth in white liberal Protestant denominations has slowed to a standstill, especially when we look at the increase of white middle-class members. New church growth in every mainline denomination, where it exists, flows from new populations. It rests on churches of predominantly ethnic origins (blacks, Hispanics, and Asians) that are organized to serve new urban populations and burgeoning immigrant groups from Latin America, Asia, and the Pacific islands.

Liberal Protestantism literally does not know itself anymore. Its theological commitment to integration and pluralism remains strong, but its life is torn asunder by diversity. The

(188)

problem is even more complex than it first appears because the immigrant Christians joining and expanding liberal Protestant denominations often do not understand or value the history and stance of American liberalism.

The missionary movement of nineteenth-century Protestantism went out into all the world to share the faith. It was incredibly successful. Many peoples of diverse cultures and values accepted "Jesus Christ as Lord and Savior." But for many converts this meant giving up indigenous beliefs and becoming Westernized. In retrospect, many liberal Protestants are embarrassed by this imperialistic history.

In time, however, Christians in the "younger churches" realize that they do not have to reject their roots in order to be Christian. New contextual theologies are possible. As new national self-consciousness changes the maps of the world, Christianity outside the United States takes new forms.

Ironically, it is not these "new third world Christians" who choose to emigrate to America. Rather, the most Westernized and conservative segments of these populations who have connections and relatives in America are the ones who emigrate. Since the 1960s thousands of new immigrants, most of whom are Christian and steeped in an old-style missionary faith, have come to America. These new immigrants have a "colonial mind-set" that is quite unlike the emerging Christianity in the nation they leave, and they are out of step with the current situation of liberal American Protestantism. Yet, when they arrive, they naturally seek out those mainline Protestant denominations with a mission history in their homelands.

The stage is set for misunderstanding and conflict. These new members are different. They speak different languages and have different cultural values, but they also differ theologically. They have beliefs and assumptions that undermine the apologetic, rationalistic, and activist legacy of liberal Protestantism. Indeed, the accident of mission history and the tendency for the most thoroughly "converted" to emigrate mean that more and more members of mainline liberal Protestant denominations literally do not understand the liberal traditions of their church.

(189)

These five trends may be slightly overstated, but the point remains: mainline liberal Protestantism wrestles daily with external forces and internal pluralisms that threaten to destroy its identity and its future.

The United Church of Christ: A Case Study

In the early history of my denomination, pluralism was viewed as temporary. Integration, assimilation, and cooperation were expected eventually to produce common understandings and common histories. This asssumption has recently been rejected. In the United Church of Christ (a 1957 union of the Congregational Christian Churches and the Evangelical and Reformed Church) we now speak of the value of diversity. We like to talk about "unity in diversity." We expect to benefit from pluralism. Varieties of racial and ethnic perspectives, we say, will redeem our church and our faith from patriarchal and European cultural biases. The problem is that we do not know how to value and benefit from pluralism and to keep the integrity and rootedness of our faith and our church. We have a problem typical of liberal Protestantism in the late twentieth century.

In my own life the dilemma is clear. I grew up in a large urban Congregational church. It was white and affluent. When the civil rights struggle emerged in the late 1950s, I, and many members of that church, embraced the integrationist cause. Eventually we welcomed a black family into our church. My church believed that integration was good. I believed that the rich traditions of black religious life should enrich my faith.

Next came the women's movement. I became aware of the patriarchal bias of my church and the fact that women were not treated equally. I pressed for change and worked to release women's gifts within my church.

In both cases I am grateful to those who pushed my church to make room for everyone. I felt a moral responsibility to speak out against oppression and to seek a more inclusive church. I still believe that we cannot let the sins of racism and sexism hold our churches hostage, even when change is painful and the price is dear.

Nevertheless, as I consider my own denomination I have come to believe that a simple representative or inclusive ideal in the midst of our increasing pluralism does not solve our problem. Making sure that every constituency group or caucus is adequately represented at every level of the church may express our vision of "church," but it leaves us tired and divided. I express myself very personally here.

As my church sought to respond to its pluralism, the system became so ponderous in its efforts to be inclusive that it ceased to function effectively. We began to make jokes about how many members it took to change a light bulb. Excellence deteriorated into mediocrity. Speed and risk became impossible. In addition, I did not like what happened to me personally as a result of this response to pluralism. Instead of being energized in situations where representatives from all corners of the church came together to "truly share" the needs of the people of God, I felt isolated and uprooted. I was still a token. Only this time all of us were tokens. It was a new kind of tokenism. In earlier times one or two blacks or several women were added to a situation controlled by the dominant group. We were there to assuage guilt and press for accountability. We were marginal and yet sometimes we were powerful.

In these new situations, however, no one group is dominant and all of us are powerless. We are a conglomerate. Each of us comes with our home loyalties. Most of us believe that we do not need to put down our sisters and brothers in order to have our concerns heard. But each of us functions as an isolated representative far from "home." It is hard to remember who we are.

Over the past few years I served on several national consultations to deal with theological and ecumenical concerns in my denomination. I went to many meetings and I met many good people. I learned a great deal. But I also learned that theological reflection done in those carefully selected representative liberal Protestant groups was inadequate. Even when each of us gave the project our best selves, we could never "be" at our best. This is because each of us functioned in token isolation from the natural communities of faith from which we came. We worked as an artificial conglomerate. The longer we worked together, the more untrustworthy our work became. I am now convinced that theological integrity cannot be achieved in three-day meetings at conference centers far from home. I do not trust my own capacity to stay in touch with my theological roots when I am uprooted and isolated repeatedly from my faith community. I do not believe that liberal Protestantism can keep its "soul" operating this way.

As I reflect on the situation I see three ways out: (1) We can accept our increasing diversity and deal with it by cultivating new homogeneous churches and denominations that will naturally grow when "like" people come together. The "church growth" movement has formalized this solution. (2) We can view pluralism as a temporary stage and seek to reexamine and reclaim the earlier assimilation/integration ideal. (3) We can look for some new way to understand our identity as Christians and the theological task that preserves our liberal Protestant commitment to justice and equity and does not destroy the integrity of diverse Christian communities.

It is easiest to give up on diversity and pluralism, especially within denominations, and simply argue that churches should seek to attract "like" persons. Individuals and families need to find the right match, and in that homogeneous community all persons will be enabled to nurture their faith and share their witness in the world. By trying to go back to foundational principles and remain rigorously inclusive, churches actually limit their potential for growth and frustrate members. It is poor stewardship, goes this argument, to spend so much energy dealing with diversity.

If that approach seems irresponsible, and I believe that it is, we can retrieve the assimilation model—maybe not a melting pot, but some mosaic, hybrid, or unifying theme. This is more in keeping with the ethos of liberal Protestantism. We should try to name our oneness in Jesus Christ in terms that transcend cultural particularities by drawing on some of the historical foundations of Christianity. The work of the ecumenical movement that invites Christians to retrieve common creeds, confessions, and catechisms is one example of this approach. In the craving for security in our complex world many liberal Protestants believe that this is possible.

Theologically, I have problems with both of these approaches to religious pluralism. The first solution presumes that oneness in Christ can be upheld by glorifying differences, not by working them through. The second presumes that Christian theology for these times can be done deductively. If we can just find the key era, or the basic document from which all Christians can derive a common theology in the midst of our diversity, then we will be one in Christ. Both of these alternatives, however, do not really deal with pluralism adequately. What are we to do?

Liberal Protestant Theology in a Postliberal Age

In earlier times it was possible to bring together certain elites with common liberal Protestant traditions. Theology flowed from foundational principles with ease. Today our pluralism makes this impossible. Either the theology is insensitive to the reality of pluralism, or it is shallow and fails to provide an intelligible world view.

As I have reflected about the future of liberal Protestantism in this environment, I have found the writing of George Lindbeck in his recent book, *The Nature of Doctrine: Religion and Theology in a Postliberal Age* (1984), most intriguing. I do not agree with the full scope of Lindbeck's case for a postliberal theology, nor do I accept his narrow definition of theology, but I find his descriptive analysis of the differences between liberal and postliberal thinking helpful. It fits with my personal experience within the United Church of Christ. It reinforces my intuition that liberal Protestantism needs to use its intellectual and rational assumptions radically to change its approach to questions of religious faithfulness. Perhaps we are not called to make an apologetic based on foundational ideas or experiences from which religious life derives meaning. Perhaps we are asked to recognize that religious life is embedded in particular communities that make existence meaningful in different ways. Theology in a postliberal era may not be "post-liberal." It may be the natural extension of the liberal perspective come of age.

Lindbeck suggests that the ecclesiastical and theological

camps that govern our thinking do not *need* to be defined by existing categories. The choice is not between accommodating to modern rationalism or returning to premodern orthodoxy. There is a third, postliberal (new liberal?) way of conceiving religion and religious doctrine (7).

If the task of theology is to give religious people linguistic ways to articulate a meaningful view of life, historically there have been two ways of doing this: premodern and modern. Premodern theology finds meaning *within* the world view of the faithful. It may be irrational or illogical, but within a particular community it is meaningful. Modern theology tends to look for meaning *outside* its basic texts or symbol systems.

Orthodoxy and conservatism find meaning in transcendent reality; liberalism grounds its interpretation in foundational human experience. Both groups, however, use these cognitive or experiential-expressive methods (as Lindbeck calls them) to define and defend religious credibility and faithfulness.

A cultural-linguistic model, or a postliberal stance (as defined by Lindbeck), changes the modern definition of context. Instead of focusing on inner logic, or outer experience, we are invited to discover religious meaning in the world of religious language and metaphor. This position refuses to return to a premodern naivete. It recognizes, however, the "degree to which human experience is shaped, molded and in a sense constituted by cultural and linguistic forms" (34). When we approach religious meaning in this way we acknowledge the fact that we cannot think, feel, interpret, or even "be" human unless we learn to use appropriate symbol systems. Religious meaning is always grounded in the language and communal life of a people; it is not found in some universally common experience diversely articulated by different religions. Any religion can be judged faithful when it authentically interprets the textual materials at the core of its life, even when they differ dramatically from other perspectives, texts, or interpretations.

Lindbeck's analysis and critique of liberalism is helpful. He notes that the religious journey for liberals usually starts with experience, with an account of the present, and moves toward the future. It is highly individualistic. Each individual, out of innate religious yearning, embarks on an individual quest for personally meaningful symbols of transcendence. Religion, however, is communal. Churches are more than private consultants to individual searchers. Churches are religious communities "that socialize their members into coherent and comprehensive religious outlooks and forms of life."

In the immediate future Lindbeck argues that classic liberal Protestant rationalism, with its emphasis on the commonality of human experience, may be useful. It provides a common rational framework for diversified religious quests. In the long haul, however, the fragmentation that rational individualism produces is absurd. It ultimately destroys community. Lindbeck writes: "The viability of a unified world of the future may well depend upon counteracting the acids of modernity." It will "depend upon communal enclaves that socialize their members into highly particular outlooks supportive of concern for others rather than for individual rights and entitlements, and of a sense of responsibility for the wider society rather than for personal fulfillment" (127).

In the past the great strength of theological liberalism has been in making religion experientially intelligible, uncovering universals, accommodating to cultures, seeking commonalities, and translating particularities into foundational insights. When we think about this from the standpoint of cultural-linguistic experience, this really cannot be done. Religions are like languages or cultures; they make sense only from within. They cannot be taught by seeking objective, united concepts about nouns or verbs. Grammar will never convey meaning. And no one really learns to speak or read a foreign language by studying its grammar or by reading something in translation.

Religion is like a language. Different religions will never be understood or explained by describing concepts or common experiences in another language. This is what liberals have tried to do in using the languages of science, philosophy, and psychology to affirm their faith. We will only learn to speak the language of faith through practice in communities which speak that language. And communities of faith, therefore, can only be understood on their own terms, never by transposing them into alien speech, however universal that language might appear to be.

At first this approach seems to force me into some premodern anti-intellectual stance. It leaves behind Enlightenment rationalism and is preoccupied with canonized texts. On closer examination, however, faith described in this way allows me to retain my liberal Protestant conviction that religion should be intelligible or credible, and it preserves the importance of social witness in the world. We can make ethical judgments about various religions. Its reasonableness "is largely a function of its assimilative powers, of its ability to provide an intelligible interpretation in its own terms of the varied situations and realities adherents encounter" (131).

It this is true, then the future of liberal Protestantism lies not in its ability to redescribe the faith in new concepts or its skill in expressing foundational concepts that unify diversity. Liberal Protestantism will survive only when it effectively teaches the language and practices of Christianity to potential adherents. The emphasis will be on nurture, development, teaching, and socialization. Religion understood in this way does not worry about translating particular experience into common philosophical categories.

At the present time, because everyone in American culture knows something about Christianity, this focus on the unique "language" of the Christian community is difficult to claim. We are literally inoculated against the biblical world view. We continue to look for new translations of the gospel into existential, depth psychological, or liberationist language. The future of liberal Protestantism, however, with its desire to value diversity and preserve interpretive freedoms, may be served best by celebrating the capacity of human beings to live authentic happy lives in communities of faith caught up in biblical language and world views.

Does liberal Protestantism have an American future? "No," if we look at the standard definition of liberal Protestantism and if we continue to reinforce the individual spiritual quest. Liberal Protestantism needs to claim its communal language. It may have a future if it can deal honestly with the postliberal age and the limits of rationalism. Vital communities of faith will be found among liberal Protestant denominations when they successfully provide a framework whereby people can live creatively with biblical meaning and respect the integrity of others who live with it differently.

PART

IV

POSSIBILITIES
FOR THE
FUTURE

12

Constituencies for Liberal Protestantism: A Market Analysis

Donald E. Miller

The proposition is accurate that, *in general*, liberal, mainline denominational churches are declining while conservative and sectarian churches are growing (Kelley, 1977; Roof, 1978; Hoge and Roozen, 1979). It is also true that a few liberal churches are growing while some conservative churches are declining in membership. The goal of this essay is to assess the potential future clientele of liberal Protestantism in light of recent assessments of ongoing changes in American values.

First, I address the generalization that liberal Protestant churches are declining and identify some of the most common explanations for this trend. Second, a brief case study is offered of a large liberal church that is growing. I ask why it is growing and what implications the characteristics of this church have for the growth of other liberal churches. Third, some assumptions are addressed concerning why people are religious and what functions religious commitment, particularly of a liberal style, fulfills. Fourth, the normative and theological question is asked, What is the role of the liberal church in America? I conclude the essay with some suggestions regarding the revitalization of liberal Protestantism.

At no point in this essay is the equation made between growth as either morally positive or negative. Indeed, some factors contributing to numerical decline may be morally exemplary and some sources of growth may be morally questionable. My own bias should be explicit from the beginning, which is that the liberal church potentially has an important role to play in shaping American society (Miller, 1981).

Explanations for Decline

The decline of liberal Protestantism during the past two decades has been explained in a number of ways. Dean Kelley's now classic explanation is that liberal churches do not demand enough from their members. He offers a formula in which ultimate *meaning* is equal to *concept* plus *demand* (1977:51). His model for this equation is growth-oriented conservative churches, which place high demands on their members in terms of both moral and life-style prescriptions. Implied in his argument is the assumption that if liberal churches only demanded more of their members, they, too, would grow. Kelley's thesis provoked a great deal of controversy. One rebuttal was that liberal clergy were not too lax, but too strict and demanding, especially in the progressive stances they took on civil rights issues, Vietnam, farm workers' right, nuclear arms, women's rights, issues of economic equality, and so on. According to this rebuttal, people quit going to liberal churches because the clergy were too demanding, not because they were too lax.

Other socially active clergy argue that the reason they lost members during the heyday of political involvement in the sixties and seventies is not because of their moral stances, but because they neglected their members' spiritual needs (Regas, 1972). If spiritual nurture had occurred, and if individual needs had been met, then almost any amount of prophetic action would have been tolerated by members. Hence the decline in membership figures for liberal churches is a function of a one-sided ministry. The antidote for church growth is a balanced ministry of moral challenge and spiritual nurture.

There are two other explanations for liberal church decline rooted in clergy negligence: one faults the religious education programs of the sixties and seventies and the other points the finger at a theological crisis among liberal clergy. During this era the programs for young people were dominated by the therapeutic philosophy of the period (Rieff, 1966). More emphasis was placed on expressing feelings than cultivating commitment or understanding of the Christian tradition. Sensitivity group encounters led by clergy substituted for Bible study and did little to encourage commitment, and in fact, in the name of "honesty," probably contributed considerably to an ethic of individualism.

Another explanation related to "honesty" is the intellectual openness of liberal clergy concerning their own theological doubts and questions. Clergy failed to provide a solid reference point against which liberal church members could define their own beliefs. Surely members of liberal churches seek moral order and theological certitude as much as do conservative church members, albeit of a more tolerant sort. What has been lacking in liberal churches is a well-articulated liberal theology (Gilkey, 1981). The consequence of liberal clergy uncertainty is that church members have either sought out more conservative forms of religious participation where the answers are less open-ended and tentative, or, more likely, they have left the church altogether in a spirit of disillusionment.

Other explanations for the decline of liberal Protestantism are based in modernization theory and cultural change. Advocates of these positions argue that affluent Americans, the client population of liberal Protestantism, have in the past two decades become increasingly individualistic. Authority external to the individual, such as resides in institutions or traditions, has lost its compelling force, and instead, the individual has become the measure of all things. Those embracing the spirit of the age attend church if it is fulfilling, not out of a sense of the authority of the institution. Life is not lived in conformity to externally imposed codes or rules. The primary locus of the sacred is the self; and worship, if practiced, is a means for getting in touch with one's own inner voice (Luckmann, 1967).

Related in many ways to the cultural explanation is the view that we have become a therapeutically based culture in which psychologists and psychiatrists have taken over the role of the clergy (Rieff, 1966; especially chapter 8). People are no longer interested in being "saved"; they want to be free. Repression, control, and authority are associated with an era of communally based "book religions" (e.g., Judaism, Islam, and Christianity). What people want now is release, catharsis, and internal control. Externally imposed guilt is perceived to be the height of inauthenticity: "Woe unto those who remain fixated at that primitive stage where the voice of parents, priests, and civic leaders dictate feelings of moral obligation." For the therapeutically oriented, guilt is an ugly word to be dropped from their vocabulary.

Another culturally based explanation places the blame for liberal church decline on the fact of intellectual and ideological pluralism (Berger, 1967; chapters 5—7). The shrinkage of the world into a global village as a result of a vastly expanded media technology has taught people the lesson of cultural relativism much more effectively than was ever done in cultural anthropology courses. Amid the clamor of competing truth claims, there are two alternative responses. Either people become jaded and cynical, dismissing even the modest theological claims of the liberal clergy, or they recoil into the secure posture of an authoritarian religious community (e.g., conservative Protestantism), where the answers are clear and unambiguous. It is momentarily liberating to believe that the social order is a fiction, a social construction based solely on self-interest, power, and social consensus, but it is not personally comforting to think that all is arbitrary, that there is nothing worthy of ultimate commitment. But many people do not think that deeply and find sufficient distraction from these "nauseous questions" in a nightly diet of T.V. entertainment and weekend shopping.

Another theory explaining decline states that America is finally catching up with the plight of institutional religion that exists in much of the rest of the modern world, especially Western Europe, where church attendance is one quarter less than it is in America (Wilson, 1976; 1977:176–78). According to these theorists, during earlier periods of America's history, churches fulfilled a number of nonreligious functions: they were an important source of community in a highly mobile society, and perhaps even more important, they served as discriminating indicators of social status. Now, however, affluence has spawned a sufficient number of other "communities"—interest group gatherings, country clubs, fraternities of various sorts—to compensate for the role previously served by religion. Even the family is assuming a new role. Particularly for the upwardly mobile, the family is a communal enclave, offering respite from the nearly all-consuming pressures of the work world. Thus, when working parents have spent minimal time with children during the week, they find it divisive to go off to church on Sunday morning where they are again separated from one another in age-segregated programs.

In making my own assessment of the decline of liberal Protestantism, I am tempted by aspects of almost all these theories. It is undeniable that there have been enormous cultural shifts in the past two decades. It is also true that liberal clergy have often been out ahead of the moral sensitivities of their congregations and have alienated many of their members as a result. In the final section of the essay I circle back to these important issues and pose some alternative strategies for coping with these causes of liberal church decline. But first, I want to look at a church that is defying the generalization that the liberal Protestant church is declining.

All Souls: A Case Study of a Growing Liberal Church

An example of a liberal church that is vital, healthy, and growing is a well-established Episcopal church that has just celebrated its one hundredth birthday. All Souls (not its real name) is located across from city hall in an ethnically diverse city of about 125,000 persons. The sanctuary is filled every Sunday morning with nearly 1,000 persons. It has an annual budget of $1.5 million that has grown substantially in the past five years. The church supports numerous outreach programs: a drop-in center for the hungry and lonely, a shelter for the homeless; it has spawned an extremely active interfaith center addressing the issue of nuclear war; it is actively involved in issues related to Central America and political refugees from

(205)

that region. During the Vietnam war the church established a Peace Operations Center. The rector of the church visited Hanoi in the sixties, and more recently, several parishioners, members of the staff, as well as the rector, have visited Central America on peace missions. There is an active group of people addressing issues of international and national hunger, and so the list continues of issues and programs that emanate from this church.

By some predictions, All Souls Church should be in the doldrums, having alienated almost every member on one issue or another in the past several decades. Indeed, on some issues there has been a small exodus from the church. But every few months a new group of thirty to forty adults, mostly young and middle-age professionals, is accepted into membership in the church; babies are being baptized, and there is a surprisingly strong program for children and young adults in the church.

Although this description may suggest to some that the "kingdom of God" has already been established here on earth, the success of All Souls can also be viewed through sociological eyes. What is the client market for All Souls? What is it doing to attract new members? How is it meeting the needs of its members, and what are the mechanisms of commitment?

Five generalizations, many of them overlapping, can be given regarding the attraction and client population of All Souls. First, the church is a catch basin for disenchanted members of other churches. An amazingly large percentage of the congregation are not born and bred Episcopalians. They come from all sorts of religious backgrounds. Not a few are "burned out" or alienated Evangelicals who were either rejected by their former churches or, in disgust, went looking for a more tolerant and open religious option. The church also has a healthy sprinkling of Catholics who left the Roman Church because of the Catholic position on birth control or divorce. There are even a few Jews in the congregation, often spouses of members, who seem to have comfortably found a place to worship. The invitation issued by the rector before every offering of communion—"Wherever you are on the journey of faith, you are welcome at the Lord's table"—seems to encompass and make welcome a wide variety of people.

Second, the church tends to attract a large number of "Yuppie" types (Young Upwardly Mobile Professional), for whom the church represents, among other things, social status and upward mobility (or alternatively, the desire to associate with upwardly mobile people). One suspects that the beautiful Gothic architecture of the church and the professional quality of the music on Sunday morning fit well with the polished Turbo-diesel Mercedes sitting in the church parking lot. In some ways, All Souls is a Yuppie version of Robert Schuller's Crystal Cathedral, only polyester leisure suits have been exchanged for wool herringbone coats and Hart Schaffner and Marx labels, and lawyers, investment counselors, and educators populate the church, rather than engineers, sales representatives, and middle-level management personnel.

Third, there are more than a few old-fashioned political liberals for whom All Souls represents a bulwark against the rising tide of political conservatism. The church serves as a platform for promulgating many liberal ideals, as well as for responding in direct ways to the casualties of the current administration's policies at home and abroad. At a time when it is difficult to feel much excitement about the state of the Democratic party, All Souls is a bastion of liberal political vision.

Fourth, All Souls is a counter to the utilitarian individualism of our age. The church provides an opportunity in its Sunday morning worship service for an experience of mystical self-transcendence. On a regular basis the liturgy and sermon invite the participant in worship to look beyond oneself to acknowledge a source of life, creativity, and beauty that is larger than any purely humanly created reality. In our era of utilitarian individualism (Bellah, 1985a) this is a rare opportunity, one that many people are hungry to experience. On a typical Sunday morning it is most common to see people wiping tears from the corners of their eyes. Whatever else is going on theologically, worship for many people at All Souls is more powerful than most psychotherapy sessions.

All Souls is also a community, of sorts, for its members. I say "of sorts" because outside of worship, the majority of social interaction occurs in committee meetings: planning programs, doing reviews of programs and staff, deciding budget allocations, figuring out how to increase the number of pledging units within the church, and so on. Altogether too rare are moments of unstructured communication. Fellowship follows a model of collegial interaction well learned by church members in the business world.

Fifth, for many persons All Souls provides considerable therapeutic intervention in their lives. Not only does the church deal with problems of guilt and brokenness, but also sage advice about childrearing, divorce, sexuality, job failure, alcoholism, and the like is offered from the pulpit, as well as being liberally present during a regular Sunday morning forum that follows the worship service.

In summary, if my somewhat intuitive analysis is correct, people are at All Souls for a variety of reasons, some purer and more honorable than others, but for all members the church obviously fills an important void in their lives. Although one might be tempted to reduce All Souls to its social status, aesthetic, cathartic, therapeutic, or communal functions—and it does offer all those—there is something more at the core of the religious experience of its members and that would appear to be its moral and self-transcending qualities.

Some Assumptions Regarding Religion's Appeal

In attempting to understand why liberal Protestantism is declining and what its future might be, it is important to understand what the appeal and attraction of religion is; then we can address the specific question of the viability of liberal Protestantism in particular. There are two broad categories of reasons for people going to church: (1) specifically religious motivations and (2) reasons that are rooted more in social and psychological functions associated with church identification.

While I do not want to generalize that *all* people are religious, it is nevertheless noteworthy that religion fulfills for many human beings the same needs. Whether the church is All Souls or the New Revelation Tabernacle, certain elements are common to the experience of religious people. What differs from one religious community to another is the stylization of these needs and the way in which they are fulfilled. Also differing is the behavior inspired by the symbolization associated with particular rituals and beliefs.

At the heart of every religion is the attempt to place the events of everyday life within some overarching ultimate perspective. Generally, these perspectives are cosmological, explaining the present with reference to both the beginning and the end (telos) of human history. Central to these cosmic perspectives is the assumption that what occurs is not random or capricious: there is order to the universe, and therefore meaning to one's own experience. This ultimate perspective explains death, suffering, as well as defines one's vocation in life. In short, what differentiates religious from nonreligious people is that the latter believe that they make up the rules of the game of life themselves, whereas the former are convinced that life should be lived in terms of an order that exists independent of one's own individual fantasy of it. Hence one motive for those attending church, whether conservative or liberal, is that the church serves as a mediator of a divine moral order.

There are also social and psychological factors related to churchly commitment. For example, one major attraction of the church, again liberal or conservative, is the quest for community. Although a modicum of sociability may be experienced at work, the office or factory is an incomplete community, at best. Many people seek a much more integrative community, one that spans age-groups and unites rather than divides one's centers of loyalty. To some extent the country club or neighborhood may provide a context for an age-inclusive community, but what is lacking in such settings are the very things that a religious community provides: regularized mechanisms that deal with the rhythms of failure and forgiveness, despair and hope, death and rebirth. Hence the church remains a major alternative as the locus of community.

The church may also be attractive to parents with younger children who are concerned about socializing them into appropriate moral and civic values. Hence it is not surprising that in America there has been a correlation between church attendance and the birth rate. Also, one might predict that those churches catering to client populations with a higher birth rate would be growing faster than those with a low birth rate.

Finally, but certainly not exhaustively, the church deals with social status desires. On a personal level, the church as a voluntary association offers numerous opportunities for office holding and leadership. To some individuals blocked in career advancement, or lacking social prestige from the vantage point of the larger society, the church is a place where they can receive recognition and commendation for their service. As already indicated, membership in a particular church may symbolize to oneself and others a particular social rank.

The point of identifying some of the factors undergirding churchly commitment is to argue that church growth and decline, whether liberal or conservative, is predicated on how adequately these various religious functions are met.

Decline in the liberal church can be traced to one of several factors: (1) fewer people desiring a transcendent reference point for their lives, (2) the sacred cosmos of the liberal church not being compelling (or believable), and/or (3) liberal churches not providing the social psychological functions that people associate with religion. Let's look at some of the differences separating the liberal and the conservative church with a motive of asking what is the distinctive contribution of liberal Protestantism.

The Role of the Liberal Church in America

Despite the similarities between conservative and liberal Protestantism, there are enormous differences in both epistemology and moral outlook that result in their appealing to very different audiences and having very different roles in society.

On the issue of epistemology, Robert Bellah very adequately captured the difference between conservatives and liberals in his well-known distinction between historical realism and symbolic realism (Bellah, 1970). Historical realists equate religious truth with sacred history as it occurred, thus making salvation dependent on a literal belief in the Virgin birth, resurrection of Jesus, and so on. Symbolic realists are interested in what these events point to or stand for. Historical realists tend to be biblical literalists, proof-texting scripture in support of their moral and religious convictions. Symbolic realists are much more sensitive to sociological and hermeneutical issues in the interpretation of scripture.

As set over against conservative Christianity, liberal Protestantism has three fundamental roles. *The first role is to provide a religious community for those with a postmodern mentality.* The conservative theological platform is not believable to a major segment of the American population. These are people who are not intentionally hostile to traditional doctines of Christian theology, but such doctrines simply are not comprehensible to them. On a purely cognitive level, then, liberal Christianity provides for such people an intellectually defensible alternative to both conservative doctrine and its polar opposite, agnosticism. The truth of Christianity for liberal Protestants is not a matter of whether certain supernatural events occurred, but the vision for humanity of the man Jesus of Nazareth. The liberal church has been open to all forms of biblical and historical criticism, rooting the reality of faith in practice and worship, not in rigidified dogma.

A second and related role for the liberal church is to serve as the religious community of the culturally sophisticated and affluent. While liberals would be the first to dispute the moral integrity of a homogeneous church, in fact the liberal church is made up principally of well-educated, middle- and upper-middle-class people, most of whom are Caucasian. The church-growth theorists are descriptively accurate when they say "birds of a feather flock together." Such a dictum is understandable inasmuch as people of different cultural and socioeconomic groups have different needs and stylize their religious expressions differently. Hence the needs of the cultural elite need to be addressed, and my suggestion is that serving such a client population should be one of the tasks of the liberal church.

A third role for liberal Protestantism is to serve as a prophetic witness to traditional liberal values: pluralism, tolerance, free inquiry, and freedom of expression and choice. It is not that these values are exclusively the property of the liberal tradition, but they do stand in sharp contrast to those on the religious right who would restrict free choice in issues related to, for example, sexual preference and childbearing and who furthermore would make Christianity the normative religion of the United States. The differences between liberal and conservative Protestants are manifold.

The tradition of liberal Protestantism stands in defiant protest against a colonial political philosophy that poses the United States as the guardian of the free world against godless Marxist states. Liberal Protestantism in America, dating back to the Social Gospel movement, has stood on the side of the poor, sympathizing with labor movements, resisting monopolistic business practice and exploitation of workers, and supporting guarantees of basic medical care, an adequate diet, and shelter. Liberal Protestantism has also been an advocate of public education as a form of social intervention. Stated normatively, in a highly individualistic culture, liberal Protestantism has a valuable moral function to remind us that we are one human family, linked in interpenetrating webs of collective responsibility. Conversely, conservative Protestantism has tended toward a much more individualist interpretation of social and economic issues.

Using my earlier example of All Souls Church, it is clear that a liberal Protestant church can be a powerful presence in a city. Two short examples illustrate its potential impact. As part of its one hundredth anniversary celebration, the church decided to give a "gift to the city." A church member of considerable intellectual stature and social skills was commissioned to interview a hundred citizens in the city, from all backgrounds and classes, asking them about the quality of their own lives and those with whom they work in the city. The result was a professionally published booklet outlining the needs of the city and several moral imperatives regarding problems in the city. In the year since the report has been published, it has become an important reference point for defining the moral state of the city. Some 3,000 copies of the report have been read by school administrators, members of the city council, directors of agencies, law enforcement personnel, and so forth.

The second example can be cited briefly. The church decided to build a new facility for its work among the poor and homeless of the city. The residents and businesses in the area of the proposed new site protested having "criminals" in their neighborhood. At the zoning hearings where the issue was to be decided, the church was able to turn out more than 600 persons to be an effective presence in support of a zoning variance. My point in this and the preceding example is simply to say that there is a role for the liberal church as an advocate and agent for the welfare of all citizens, especially the disenfranchised of our society and the world.

Revitalizing Liberal Protestantism

In thinking about the revitalization of liberal Protestantism, one of the beginning steps is to identify the target audience for the liberal church. In this regard we may be served well by examining the client population of All Souls.

First, I noted that one constituency of All Souls is renegade Evangelicals and Catholics. Particularly in the case of the ex-Evangelicals, these are people who have been touched by the spirit of modernity or else they would have stayed in the conservative fold. One has to ask, therefore, whether the liberal church is a stepping stone to a secular mentality or whether it is possible for them to find in the liberal Protestant church something other than a reactionary counterforce to Evangelicalism. A community like All Souls gets fair mileage out of distinguishing itself from the conservative camp, but it is equally important that the liberal church be able to define what it stands for, rather than simply to state what it is against. All Souls does offer an affirmative spiritual and moral agenda to which people can commit themselves, and this, in part, explains the church's growth.

Thus, in assessing the future of liberal Protestantism, I believe that one recruitment market is disillusioned Evangelicals and Catholics. Burned-out Evangelicals will come because a supernatural world view no longer fits their experience, and further-more, the defensive moral legalism of conservative Protestants does not fit their openness to the arts and culture. Liberal Catholics are a target audience if they have been alienated on one of the marriage- or sex-related stands of the Catholic Church: abortion, contraception, divorce, or an exclusive male priesthood. Hence I anticipate that both Evangelical and Catholic churches will create a significant fallout for liberal Protestantism.

Second, All Souls seems to attract an inordinate number of young, upwardly mobile professionals. These people are proud of their church. All Souls is a symbol that they flaunt as loudly as they do the names of their children's private schools and family club affiliations. Far from being ashamed of their religious affiliation, it is one element of the larger mosaic that symbolizes their social standing and life-style. It would be wrong, however, to caricature these peoples' religious commitment as being entirely frivolous. The rich and upwardly mobile also have religious needs. And it would be too cynical to offer the Marxian interpretation that their need for religion is simply to justify their wealth. Rather, many Yuppie types received strong socialization into the countercultural values of the 1960s and have genuine moral and spiritual concerns even though they may have exchanged, for now, their hippie beads for vested suits.

Hence young, upwardly mobile professionals are a second important target population for the liberal church. Although part of the attraction of religion, for them, is certainly aesthetic, that is not necessarily bad—despite Kierkegaard's polemic against aesthetic religion. Worship should be creative, beautiful, and emotionally moving. Furthermore, there are worse forms of fiscal irresponsibility than building and maintaining cathedral-like structures; let the city landscape have a few spires to go with its towering office buildings! But another reason not to discourage those who come to church primarily for aesthetic reasons is that the Yuppies possess tremendous potential for doing good in this world. They tend to be well-connected professionally, they are people of power and influence, and they have a tremendous amount of drive and initiative. Hence anyone with a shred of pragmatism in his or her bones would want to open the door widely to such individuals in hopes of channeling them into the service of "Christ's kingdom."

Third, the church needs to hold on to the old-time political liberals who have been its heart and soul. These are the people who are the bedrock of the liberal church. Usually they are older, their spirits and bodies bear many a wound from past political battles, but they have been purified by fire and their commitment is unwavering. Unfortunately, the numbers of political liberals are waning rather than waxing. Few new recruits are coming from our colleges and universities. Hence, undoubtedly, the ranks of political liberalism outside the church are not a fertile field for recruitment, at least at the present.

Fourth, for those most caught up in the cultural ethos of utilitarian individualism, the liberal church can be a significant counterpoint of community and nonutilitarian values. A significant market, then, for the liberal church is precisely those who are most alien to it: those caught up in routines of consumerism, psychotherapy, and bootstrap, self-congratulatory economics. This may seem like a strange target market, but if utilitarian individualism breeds people who are empty, lonely, and bitter, and the liberal church offers a warm, open, and accepting context for self-transcendence, then it is not unreasonable to assume some growth in the ranks of liberal Protestantism from this quarter.

If the liberal church is going to appeal to these four types of client population, then it must make certain that it is a strong community itself. The liberal church needs to get beyond committee meetings as the prime expression of community. Likewise, in its commitment to the poor and disenfranchised of the human family, it must offer more than empty symbols of concern. Integrity must be the touchstone of all that the church does.

Fifth, the liberal church performs a number of therapeutic functions for people, but it does so within a transcendent and nonindividualistic context. The psychotherapeutic industry in

America is responding to real needs, but it is also, in many cases, morally bankrupt (McLemore, 1982). Indeed, many of its cures are worse than the disease. The liberal church potentially deals with many of the same issues as are confessed within the therapist's office, but its solutions (forgiveness, reconciliation, community) are offered within a theological framework that links people to one another and unites the human family with the ground of creation. The temptation of the liberal church is simply to provide, at perhaps less cost, psychological counseling services that parallel those available on the open market. This is sure death in my view because in so doing, the unique role of the church is lost. The church should counsel, but its clergy should always stay true to their priestly vocation in offering absolution, freedom, and spiritual renewal.

In identifying the five target audiences for liberal Protestant recruitment I do not mean to imply that the route to revitalization will be easy. Indeed, the explanations for decline cited at the beginning of the essay are serious impediments to the future well-being of the liberal church. Without bold leadership and some important changes in the mode of operation of the church, I expect liberal Protestantism to continue its current patterns of attrition. But I am convinced of the mission and role of the liberal church in American society, and in conclusion I wish to comment briefly on three previously discussed factors—intellectual, cultural, and clerical—as sources of the current demise of liberal Protestantism.

Conclusion

I suspect that despite the apparent vitality of All Souls, all is not well internally in the hearts and minds of many of its members. Although many of them probably could offer profoundly moving descriptions of their religious experience, they would be hard pressed to explain this experience theologically. Unlike their fundamentalist friends, they lack the born-again vocabulary that describes life-changing events. Furthermore, they have been so schooled in psychological interpretations that they can't easily impose the vocabulary of "the Spirit" on

(216)

their self-transcending experiences. Indeed, most of them would have difficulty talking about God, although they most certainly believe in whatever that word symbolizes. We are in a profound cosmological shift, and liberal Christians are among the hardest hit. They accept the relativity of all claims to authority, yet they nevertheless experience claims on their person that seem ultimate and absolute.

In the "good" liberal churches, I strongly suspect that there is no less religious experience occurring than in the conservative churches—indeed, in some there may be more! The problem is one of interpreting this experience. The liberal churches that are declining, I would submit, are those whose liturgy engenders little, if any, self-transcendence. Thus the key to the growth and survival of the liberal church is tapping, through the worship experience, the wellsprings from which all religion grows. The church can never compete as a social club. It has to maintain its unique character as an institution that mediates between the human and the divine.

A primary task of the liberal church in the future will be to create a vocabulary that explains the experiences of members. Undoubtedly this vocabulary will be less exclusivistic than the explanations of their conservative brethren. But these explanations need carry no less authority. What will be deadly for the liberal church is if it limits opportunities whereby its people can create a revitalized theology. What the liberal church needs is the North American equivalent of "base communities"—the vital communal basis for Latin-American liberation theology. Liberation theology cannot be imported to North American liberal Protestants. Liberal Christians of this hemisphere need to create their own experientially based religious communities and their own distinctive theology.

As mentioned earlier, another factor contributing to the decline of the liberal church is the cultural shift toward utilitarian individualism. For individuals influenced by this world view, the church is seen as authoritarian. The liberal church, in particular, is unattractive because of its emphasis on corporate responsibility and systemic explanations of war, poverty, unemployment, etc. Fundamentalism is much more sympathetic to an individualistic approach to social problems than is liberalism. Hence it is not surprising to see the alliance between the religious right and the policies of the current administration.

To bank too much, however, on the long-term dominance of political conservatism is myopic. True, the liberal political agenda is in shambles, but the bankruptcy, both figuratively and fiscally, of the Reagan Administration creates the possibility of a turnaround in the fortunes of the liberal perspective. When, and if, there is a reversal the liberal church should be the benefactor of a new political alliance. I am also of the opinion that the shallowness of utilitarian individualism will, for many people, run its course, and when it comes up wanting there will be a ready market of those who are hungry for a more communitarian, metaphysically rooted alternative. In the meantime it is incumbent on the liberal church to maintain its integrity and then creatively figure out ways to present itself as an option to this satiated and disillusioned constituency.

In the opening section of this essay the clergy were cited as contributing to the decline of liberal Protestantism. The argument was threefold: (1) that clergy were too progressive, thus alienating many in their constituency; (2) that well-trained clergy have themselves become caught up in the philosophical and theological perplexities of our age, often contributing more fog than light to their congregations' desire to have something to which they can commit themselves; and (3) the therapeutic mentality of many of those involved in the religious education program has done little to counter the individualistic and relativistic spirit of the age.

Finally, perhaps what the liberal church needs are a few more of Dostoevsky's Grand Inquisitors who will keep their doubts to themselves and provide moral and spiritual leadership instead. More fundamental, however, is that liberal clergy need to recover a genuine spirituality of their own. Their contribution to the political realm is unique only if it emerges from a sacramental context of hope, love, and worship. Spirituality is not the exclusive province of conservative Christians; there is an equally vital, although perhaps less expressive, tradition of spirituality among liberal Christians, and it is this that must stand at the center of all political action. If a new theology is to emerge that will give both identity and direction to the liberal church, it will emerge out of the balanced contexts of worship, moral commitment, and theological reflection.

13

Winning Lost Sheep: A Recovery Course for Liberal Protestantism

Benton Johnson

Liberal Protestantism has reached the low point of its long and influential American career. In the decade before World War I it was a growing and vibrant presence in American culture. Although badly wounded by the skirmishes and the secular drift of culture during the 1920s, it soon recovered its nerve and its voice, thanks to brilliant innovators like Reinhold and H. Richard Niebuhr and Paul Tillich. Its current slump is far deeper and more long lasting than its little depression of the 1920s. If current trends continue, within a generation or two the liberal denominations may have gone the way of the old state churches of northern Europe.

There is a good probability that they will go that way. Unless new themes and new programs restore their energy, they will almost certainly go that way. Their revitalization, however, is both desirable and possible. In this essay I propose a strategy for renewing the strength and influence of the liberal Protestant community in the United States.

Assessing Weaknesses

The first step in any strategy for renewal is to achieve a realistic understanding of what has gone wrong and why it has gone wrong. The second step is to take inventory of whatever strengths, or assets, the liberal Protestant tradition still possesses. Only then will it be possible to chart a recovery course that has a realistic chance of succeeding.

Demographic weakness. The first, and most obvious, weakness of the liberal denominations is their loss of membership, a loss that by now runs into the millions. There are, to be sure, some signs that the rate of loss has recently slowed. A few denominations are now reporting modest gains, but there is no real evidence that a turnaround has begun. Thanks to the excellent research by Robert Wuthnow (1976), Dean Hoge and David Roozen (1979), Clark Roof (1982), and others, we now know a great deal about the demographic dimensions of the membership loss. It is now firmly established that the prime source of the loss is the failure of many young adult children of the members of the liberal denominations to affiliate with a liberal religious body. There has been no mass exodus of older adults. Even the conservative members who grumbled about the social action projects and the political preaching of the 1960s have tended to stay put. Although the evangelical branch of Protestantism has attracted a sizable handful of the liberal youth, and another handful has joined such new religious movements as Rajneeshism or the Unification Church, the great majority of these young people are today without religious affiliation. Liberal Protestantism's "lost sheep" have joined the ranks of America's religious "nones."

The decline of the liberal churches has been exacerbated by their relatively low birth rates over the past twenty years and by an apparent falloff in what was probably an important source of their growth during the 1950s, namely, a pattern of membership transfer first documented by Rodney Stark and Charles Y. Glock with data collected in the early 1960s. The pattern involved an intragenerational shift of membership from the conservative to the liberal denominations. Recent data suggest that this pattern of membership switching is less common now than it was a generation ago. As a result of all these trends, the liberal churches have acquired a lopsided age composition. Compared with the population at large, they are disproportionately made up of people over the age of fifty. As a consequence, their death rates are relatively high and will become higher still unless they are able to replenish their ranks with younger people, especially younger people with young children. The evangelicals, by way of contrast, are faring quite well. Not only are fewer of them switching to liberal denominations, but also their birth rates are higher than those of liberals and they do a better job of holding onto their young people. Although they are probably not growing at a rate faster than the increase of the American population as a whole, they are a steadily increasing proportion of the *Protestant* population. In terms of size and growth potential alone, the evangelicals are closer to becoming the dominant power in American Protestantism than anyone outside their ranks would have thought possible a scant fifteen years ago.

Theological weakness. The second weakness of the liberal denominations is the depletion of their theological resources. Although this depletion is difficult to document with the precision possible in survey research, few would dispute that it has occurred.

Theology is the general theory that, in its popular form, mobilizes the collective energies of a religious community. When a community's theological resources drain away, its energy level declines. Orthodox Christianity taught a doctrine of divine rewards and punishments, both temporal and eternal, that for centuries enabled religious leaders to mobilize and direct individual and collective energies for moral ends. When modern criticism deprived this doctrine of its power, classic liberalism, especially in its American versions, was able to replace this depleted resource with another that was readily at hand, namely, the hope for the perfection of human society and personality, a hope originally inspired by millennial theology but made newly compelling by the secular spirit of the age and by the apparent improvement of the world. Despite protests from conservatives, the transition to liberalism was made fairly smoothly. There was no widespread demoralization, apathy, or sense of crisis. Then, several decades later, Reinhold Niebuhr's scathing critique deprived this resource of its power by destroying its credibility. World War I, the depression, and the persistence of collective evil convinced him that the sentimental optimism that had become the real faith of the liberal bourgeoisie was neither biblically sound nor in accord with the basic processes of history. Niebuhr's message came at a time of trouble for the Protestant community and acted as a tonic on it. One of its effects was to stimulate an exploration for new theological resources.

As recently as a quarter of a century ago, many Protestant leaders had good reason to be optimistic about the prospects of these new explorations. Sydney E. Ahlstrom, for one, was delighted with the renewal of theological activity, a renewal he declared to be a "renaissance unparalleled since the age of the Reformation" (1960:30). Only ten years later, Ahlstrom, along with many other liberal Protestant intellectuals, had reached a different conclusion. The cultural revolution of the 1960s had profoundly reshaped the religious landscape. The theological renaissance was over. Theology itself had turned critical and destructive and was undermining the very foundations of Christian belief. It soon became apparent that both the earlier secularized millennialism and the new explorations of the Niebuhr era had succeeded only in postponing the day of confrontation with the "old claims of scientific and historical investigations" (1970:7).

More than fifteen years have now passed since Ahlstrom wrote these words. Although little is heard today about secular theology or the death of God, neither is a theological revival under way. Instead, there is demoralization, apathy, and decline. "Where," Edwin Scott Gaustad asks, "are the Beechers, Abbotts, Coffins, and Fosdicks of yesteryear, or the Niebuhrs and Tillichs of yesterday?" (1983:75). Liberal Protestantism seems to have run out of ideas. It is suffering from a bad case of resource depletion.

Loss of self-esteem. The third weakness of liberal Protestantism is a mood, or general framework of thinking, that has been in existence for so long, especially among its intellectuals and other opinion leaders, that it is seldom discussed and almost never challenged. Some will not consider it a weakness, but rather the expression of a fully justified evaluation of current reality. They will prefer to have the liberal churches decline further rather than change their own thinking about them and the culture they represent. But this mood is an impediment to the churches' recovery, and it must therefore be counted a weakness by those who want them to recover. I refer to this mood as a loss of self-esteem, by which I mean a loss of respect for the values and preoccupations of the liberal Protestant community and the class in which it is embedded, particularly the values and preoccupations of its ordinary members.

The proximate source of this mood is the severe criticism of bourgeois culture, including bourgeois religious culture, made by Reinhold Niebuhr throughout most of his career. His target was the optimistic, self-serving ethos of the middle class, an ethos that has replaced a biblically grounded view of humanity and its real condition and has obscured the underlying dynamic of class interest as well. Bourgeois ideology, he wrote, "thinks the Kingdom of God is around the corner," whereas in reality it merely reflects the "sentimentalities and illusions of the comfortable" (1932:80, 82). In Niebuhr's view, Christians needed to rediscover the biblical theme of sin, to abandon the conceit that the liberal churches and their culture are the exemplars of human progress, and to align themselves with oppressed peoples in their struggles for liberation and justice.

Niebuhr's relentless critique of bourgeois religion and culture was justified considering the circumstances under which he wrote. At the very least, it was a healthy corrective to the naive and toothless utopianism then common in the liberal Protestant community. In addition to creating a new interest in theological work, it infused the old Social Gospel with a pragmatic, tough-minded spirit. Moreover, it convinced successive cohorts of young liberals, especially among the clergy, that a life of political struggle against oppression is the highest form of Christian practice. But Niebuhr's critique and challenge did not persuade many lay people to shed their bourgeois prejudices. Perhaps more would have been empowered to do so if the theological explorations of his time had succeeded. In any event, Niebuhr's call to duty was a hard one. It amounted to a penance for the bourgeoisie, a penance that carried no hope of salvation.

In the 1950s, when it had become clear that most lay people chose not to heed the call, a new generation of religious leaders who shared Niebuhr's general perspective on bourgeois religion launched an attack on lay piety that was harsher and more broad-ranging than any attack of Niebuhr's. What troubled this new generation was that the postwar upsurge of interest in religion did not seem to reflect any serious theological or spiritual quest or any concern for social justice. The most popular religious voices of the decade were not those of neoorthodox intellectuals or social activists, but writers and preachers like Norman Vincent Peale, who treated religious faith as a tool for achieving personal happiness and success, and Billy Graham, a product of a revitalized fundamentalism with its traditional emphasis on individual salvation. Much of this revival seemed motivated by a search for security and a desire to enrich private life. Moreover, if the revival had any political content, it was an affirmation of American values and institutions, although without the heady optimism and self-assurance of the old celebratory liberalism. All in all, the hallmarks of the revival were conformity, security, and confident living. The response of religious intellectuals was to attack middle-class religiosity and middle-class biases with all the resources they could muster. Owing to the theological situation, however, they could not threaten the laity with personal damnation or the nation with divine punishment, nor could they inspire them with a hope of salvation or of a millennial kingdom just around the corner. The best they could do was to scold, debunk, ridicule, debase, belittle, play heavily on guilt, and encourage people to feel bad about themselves.

By the early 1970s the prejudices and idols of the laity had been systematically smashed. Among the major targets were the laity's self-centeredness and preoccupation with the comforting aspects of religion, its lack of social concern, and its racism, militarism, sexism, and homophobia. Not even the parish church or God was spared. The attacks were broadly paralleled and reinforced by a rising tide of secular criticism of trends in middle-class life. After 1965 a new generation of secular militants launched their own attack on the white bourgeoisie. By the end of the decade many white liberals, both religious and secular, were convinced that they were a sorry lot. As Gaustad has recently put it, "all that guilt eroded self-confidence and left leadership flaccid" (1983:176).

Survey research has pretty well established that a shift of value commitments, centered among white college-age youth, seems to be the major reason for the membership losses sustained by the liberal churches. The shift was spearheaded by the large baby boom cohort that began reaching maturity in the mid-1960s and was expressed in its most visible and extreme form in the great countercultural revolution that swept across elite college campuses and adjacent communities at the end of that decade. The prevailing view is that whatever the causes of the shift might have been, they were secular in character and that, to use Hoge and Roozen's words, the shift "hit the churches from the outside" (1979:328). Although I cannot prove the point, it seems likely that among the numerous sources of the alienation of young people from the liberal churches was the antibourgeois climate of opinion that many religious intellectuals helped to create. Moreover, it was they, not the secular critics, who declared the parish church irrelevant and killed the Christian God. In the 1960s the major work of trashing bourgeois religion was done by church people themselves.

Assessing Strengths

There are a few religious intellectuals whose commitment to radical social transformation has led them to abandon any interest in reforming the liberal churches. Harvey Cox, for example, has recently asserted that the "main stimulus for the renewal of Christianity will come from the bottom and from the edge, from the sectors of the world that are on the margins of the modern/liberal consensus." He believes that "the modern era itself is ending" and that liberation theology and the base communities of Latin America "are the germ cells for the next era of our culture" (1984:206, 268, 267). Although history may prove Cox right, his prognostication, in my opinion, is both naive and romantic. Moreover, its assumption that the bourgeois enterprise is doomed has the unintended effect of handing over the spiritual and political initiative of the American middle class to fundamentalists, new agers, and right wingers. Although history may prove me wrong, I believe that the United States and its middle class will be an influential force in the world for a long time to come and that a revitalization of the liberal churches is a spiritually and politically responsible task. It makes sense, therefore, to take inventory of the strengths on which a revitalization movement might be built.

The strengths of the liberal denominations may be conveniently divided into two categories, material assets and cultural assets. The material assets continue to be impressive. Despite the decline in membership, the liberal churches still claim the allegiance of many millions of Americans. Thanks to generations of offerings, endowments, and bequests, they own or control impressive physical facilities, including colleges and seminaries. Moreover, a large portion of their constituency are well educated and affluent and occupy strategic positions in society. Through a wide variety of means, including funding and promoting, they are in a position to make a difference in national life.

Although the cultural assets of the liberal churches are many and varied, I call particular attention to two of them because they should be sources of a legitimate pride that can facilitate the recovery of self-esteem and because they contain dispositions that may be useful in shaping a course for the recovery of the churches' strength and influence. The first cultural asset is a diffuse concern for the whole state of humanity, and the second is an openness to new ideas and programs and a willingness to ally with outside groups and perspectives that are not vicious or destructive. In short, the liberal religious tradition has a great breadth of concern and an ability to be flexible, to change directions now and then. Of course, these assets have not invariably worked to the benefit of humanity or of liberal religion itself. Emile Durkheim has rightly noted that many a vice is simply the exaggerated expression of a virtue. But on the whole, these basic dispositions should be counted as strengths.

The tradition of diffuse concern is the legacy of a churchly, as opposed to a sectarian, mode of orientation, especially a sectarian mode that is either apocalyptic or introverted. American liberalism has inherited the specifically Puritan interest in both the individual soul and its nurturing matrix, the church, and in the whole state of society, from the family to art, science, the economy, and government. In this regard, Niebuhr's critique was not a change of emphasis; it was a correction of the simplistic theories and overblown hopes that liberals had entertained, as well as a warning that the road to a better world would be long and hard. It never occurred to the Puritans, to the early liberals, or to Niebuhr to withdraw into religious ghettos or to seek death in a frenzy of righteousness. Those who shared this tradition of diffuse concern were sometimes meddlesome, arrogant, and willing to make sweeping moral judgments on matters about which they knew little, but they did not abandon any sphere of life as beyond redemption.

The tradition of openness and a willingness to change directions and seek allies in pursuit of larger objectives is also part of a churchly orientation. In its virtuous form it is an example of what Max Weber called an ethic of responsibility. In its less virtuous form it involves a compromise of principle or poor judgment in forming alliances. It is this disposition of openness to change, activated by a portion of the Puritan clergy of New England, that made possible the creation of the great interdenominational coalition of evangelicals that exercised such an influence on American culture and politics from the 1820s until well after the Civil War. It is this disposition that made possible the shift to liberalism and the Social Gospel by a leading portion of this coalition at the turn of the century. It is this disposition that made liberal Protestants receptive to the new directions laid down by Niebuhr and his associates in the 1930s. And it is this disposition that a few years later helped to gather the scattered forces of fundamentalism into today's evangelical movement. Each of these changes of tack was an innovative response to crisis. The time has come for liberal Protestantism to change course once again.

Charting a Recovery Course

Having taken inventory of some major weaknesses and strengths of liberal Protestantism, we are now in a position to ask what, if anything, can be done to chart a recovery course having some prospect of success. The only weakness for which a recovery course cannot now be charted is the churches' theological predicament. The problems standing in the way of theological renewal are formidable. Not only must such a renewal pass today's strict tests of intellectual credibility, but it must be able to energize large numbers of lay people as well. Although some theological resources can and should be used in other efforts to strengthen the churches, the depletion of theological resources is a problem with which the churches will simply have to live for the time being. The other two weaknesses can be overcome. The churches can recruit new members, by using their remaining assets for devising new programs, and they can do something to recover a sense of self-esteem.

Winning lost sheep. What sorts of people should the liberal churches attempt to recruit? Because the churches are becoming dangerously unbalanced demographically, it makes sense to recommend that they try hardest to attract young adults. From what segments of the population should these young adults be sought? It has long been the hope of liberal Protestant leaders to build churches that include people of all classes, races, and ethnic groups. Although this is a noble aim, it has never been achieved, especially in such a socially heterogeneous nation as ours. The most likely pool of new members is white Christians of middle-class background. To be more specific, the most likely pool is made up of liberal Protestantism's "lost sheep," the very young people whose failure to affiliate is the principal reason for the churches' decline. Others, of course, should be made welcome, but the chief recruitment target should be people brought up as liberal Protestants who now have no religious affiliation. Moreover, liberals would do well to learn from the experience of evangelicals concerning the factors that make for church growth. As a general rule, local congregations that are relatively homogeneous have higher growth rates than do other congregations. At least in the early stages of a new recruitment campaign, a special effort should be made to gather congregations or cells of young adults outside existing parish organizations or facilities, perhaps using homes, apartments, and rented conference rooms instead.

There is another reason for gathering recruits apart from existing ecclesiastical structures. Because most of the lost sheep no longer find the church interesting or relevant to their concerns, a recruitment campaign that merely invites them to return to the same old church will not succeed. Even if such a campaign were packaged with all the skill of a modern advertising agency, these well-educated, discriminating youth would soon see through the deception. They need to be assured that something important has changed, that something new has been added. On this matter, too, liberals can learn from evangelicals. Ever since their own recovery programs got under way more than forty years ago, evangelicals have established a highly successful series of special ministries to specifically targeted groups (e.g., high school students, athletes, collegians). These ministries do not compete with local churches, but are organized apart from them, and their particular emphases are geared directly to the concerns of the targeted groups. The wing of the recent Jesus movement that had evangelical sponsorship is an excellent case in point.

Some guidelines for program planning. What content should these new outreach programs have? That must be partly determined by trial and error, as the evangelicals have discovered, but I recommend that three considerations guide the decision of what programs to try. The first consideration, which should really go without saying, is that the programs be consistent with the broad cultural traditions and resources of liberal Protestantism, although, of course, they should be new in focus or content. The second consideration is that no effort be made to compete directly with secular programs or services readily available in most large communities. It simply makes no marketing sense, for example, to duplicate social action programs either of the left or the right, just as it makes no sense to duplicate the human potential movement's personal growth trainings or seminars, or indeed any other service currently popular in the "Yuppie" market. The third consideration is that the new programs should address concerns, worries, and aspirations that are common among young middle-class whites. This means that they should consider borrowing from and refashioning some of the programs or services that have appealed to such people. The Jesus movement, for example, did not duplicate the counterculture of the 1960s, but addressed many countercultural concerns and adopted some of its style. Years ago revivalists learned how to put barroom tunes to pious uses. Surely modern liberals have not lost the gift of creative borrowing.

A program suggestion: toward a new cure of souls. In planning specific programs for engaging the lost sheep, particular attention should be given to addressing the concerns that have made regimens for the cultivation of personal power and effectiveness so popular with middle-class whites throughout the twentieth century. Beginning with the New Thought movement and continuing down through the present time, there has been a great outpouring of inspirational literature, formulas, therapies, and trainings designed to enhance people's ability to take control of their lives. In recent decades there has been a veritable explosion of technology in this area. During the first half of the century many liberal Protestant leaders had no difficulty supporting and contributing to the quest for personal growth and power. Harry Emerson Fosdick's famous book, *On Being a Real Person* (1943), comes immediately to mind. It was not until the 1950s that liberal intellectuals decided that the laity's preoccupation with peace of mind and positive thinking encouraged self-absorption at the expense of an attention to theological and social issues. From that time to this, liberal intellectuals, both religious and secular, have been deeply suspicious of the new systems of popular therapy, and a great gulf of distrust has grown up between them.

And yet these new systems have been popular, and there is no sign that their popularity is waning. It is no exaggeration to assert that the new therapies, taken together, are the most popular new "religious" movement of the century among middle-class whites. There are excellent sociological reasons why this should be so. If the liberal churches are to resume their growth and influence, they will have to come to terms with these new therapies and the concerns they address. Liberals will not be able to drive them away by condemning them. Instead, they should consider borrowing from them in an effort to fill a serious void of their own, namely, the void created by the collapse of the cure of souls.

The cure of souls is that aspect of Christian theory and practice that addresses people's hopes, fears, and anxieties in a manner that provides moral guidance for their lives. It is a mechanism for shaping and regulating the human spirit within the framework of a shared morality. It was a central feature of the various systems of Christianity until the close of the first, or pre-Niebuhr, phase of liberal Protestantism. Now it is virtually a lost art. As a result, there is a serious disjuncture within the liberal churches between matters pertaining to private, or personal, life and matters pertaining to social and political issues. This is yet another reason why the churches have lost their ability to empower people for service. There are three basic sources of this disjuncture. The first and most obvious source is the inability to use the old promises of divine favor and disfavor as motivating influences or interpretational devices. The second is the more recent suspiciousness of a celebratory liberalism that promises personal triumph and abundance while screening out the evil and tragic side of life. The third is the shrinking of the moral sphere itself, which is a legacy of the concerted attack on bourgeois morality that got under way in the 1960s. In

(232)

some circles today the very word morality conjures up visions of constricted life-styles, compulsory heterosexuality, and virginity at marriage. Moral choices at the level of private life are widely held to be matters of individual discretion. What is left of the cure of souls in liberal Protestantism is a pastoral counseling informed by secular client-counselor psychotherapies, most of which also leave moral judgments in the hands of the client. What is left of morality is a concern for social and political issues that is often expressed in a form as authoritative and commanding as that of the Puritans but without the motivating influences the Puritans could employ. In liberal Protestantism the private and public spheres have become so uncoupled that pastors are reluctant to offer moral guidance in the jungle of private life and are unable to mobilize personal energies for public service.

The techniques and processes developed by the human potential movement not only enable people to express and work through private problems, but also create experiences that raise people's energy levels. Moreover, since most of these techniques and processes occur in group settings, many of the experiences are shared, with the result that a state of collective consciousness, which Durkheim referred to as effervescence, is often generated. During such periods, groups develop an intense sense of bondedness, which, after all, is the foundation of all morality. Moreover, it is a sense of bondedness based on spontaneous love and good will rather than on a sense of obligation or duty. In short, there is nothing grudging about it. This situation contains many promising possibilities for creating ways to thematize private concerns in a context that facilitates the formation, or rather the re-formation, of moral consciousness that can apply both to private and larger social issues. Not the least promising possibility is that the atmosphere of good will and harmony that group processes can produce provides an excellent setting in which to address some of the most vexing and polarizing issues within the churches today—issues of sexuality and gender, issues of peace, and issues of how to relate to the third world. At the very least, the setting would help to mitigate the anger, self-righteousness, cynicism, and hypocrisy with which these issues are often addressed.

Postscript on theology. Any effort to find liberal Protestantism's lost sheep must be recognizably Christian if it is to benefit the churches. Yet the theological situation makes it difficult to offer a fully robust and confident expression of Christian faith. It is important to be honest on this matter and not resort to pretension or evasiveness. The lost sheep may be capable of responding to certain expressions of Christian symbolism (e.g., the symbolism expressed in songs), and as time goes by they may become even more responsive. But they will probably resist many of the ways that Christian symbolism has been presented in the churches in their youth. They will certainly resist the vagueness, the meanderings, and the cheap rhetorical devices all too common in the pulpit. Fortunately, many middle-class young adults are not looking for closed belief systems, but for plausible frameworks for understanding the world and for guiding their own lives. Christianity remains as plausible a framework as any other spiritual system that has attracted the attention of liberalism's lost sheep during the past decade and a half. In view of Christianity's historic claims to have the whole truth, the claim to mere plausibility is a weak one. Even so, it is often possible for weak claims to prevail over claims that are even weaker. There is something to be said for Reinhold Niebuhr's view that much Christian teaching has the character of a "necessary symbolism" of humanity's condition (1929:120). Surely Christianity still has something worth saying on reincarnation, the divinity of humanity, and the imminence of the Aquarian age, doctrines in which many young adults place a certain faith.

Whether liberal Protestantism continues to decline or turns the corner toward recovery is a choice its own members have to make. The decision to recover should be an easy one. The hard task will be to chart a course that will bring it about. I hope my chapter provides a small start in that direction.

14

Can a Mainstream Change Its Course?

Leonard Sweet

While sociologists have been providing statistics in glorious abundance that demonstrate the ailing condition of liberal American Protestantism, historians have been debating whether the theological center of gravity has shifted from left to right. There are at least three ways of thinking about the future of the tradition. One is to argue that liberalism has had such a breathtaking amount of influence on American religious life that it has won nearly all its battles. Conservatives learned from liberals the lessons that religion and politics do mix and that issues of justice and human rights must be placed at the center of religious consciousness. Indeed, if anything, liberal clergy have retreated somewhat from the realm of social activism. The past ten years have witnessed a new phenomenon: liberal clergy busy signing themselves "Doctor" having spent their energy budgets on continuing education degrees rather than on social action. Large numbers of conservatives are now as sophisticated as liberals in their use of critical instruments in presenting theology to the satisfaction of the physical and social sciences. The difficulty, then, of using standard liberal battle cries as touchstones of liberal belief is that no one is against them. Liberal Protestantism is alive and well in left-wing evangelicalism, regardless of its condition in the "mainline" churches (Sweet, 1984a:44–45).

A second tack was hinted at back in the early twentieth century by University of Chicago theologian Gerald Birney Smith, who argued that fundamentalism was, at heart, nothing more than a variant version of modernism, with both sharing the same world of liberal Western Enlightenment values (1928). Tyron Inbody has most recently pressed home this case that liberals and conservatives inhabit the same intellectual universe. He shows how both can be defined culturally, ideologically, and socially on a common basis—located solidly within middle-class, individualistic, North American bourgeois culture (1985:85–90; also see Krauthammer, 1983:12–15). Both are preoccupied with eschatology. Hal Lindsey's *Late Great Planet Earth* (1970) is matched on the liberal side by such apocalpytic tomes as Jonathan Schell's, *The Fate of the Earth* (1982), Christopher Lasch's *Culture of Narcissism* (1979), and Robert Heilbroner's *An Inquiry into the Human Prospect* (1974). If a roll call of doom is to be heard, it will be played in both conservative and liberal camps.

A third way of approaching the question, and the one I reflect on in this essay, is through the perspective of "mainline" (or what historians increasingly refer to as "oldline") religious denominations. Does liberal Protestantism have an American future? Some say no. Like the Smithsonian dinosaur, the structural skeleton remains. But the heart that beats in it has stopped. Others say yes. Mark Twain style, the rumors of liberalism's demise have been greatly exaggerated. The future could still belong to the "sleeping giant" of liberal Protestantism if only it would awaken to its strength and vitality. Liberal Protestantism *may* have an American future, but only in altered form and as a more marginal force. The real question becomes, Can a mainstream change its course?

The course of what has been "mainstream" American religion needs to change in the direction of, first, a reconstructed theology; second, a revitalized ecclesiology; third, a rehabilitated patriotism; and fourth, a reconstituted supernaturalism. This amounts to a fourfold agenda for the revamping of oldline American Protestantism.

A Reconstructed Theology

Liberalism requires a reconstructed theology. We have known since Karl Barth that liberalism holds erroneous assumptions about humanity and history. Liberal inattentiveness to nature is a theological act of negligence, with an attendant loss of mythopoeic nourishment and sacramental vision. The mobility of liberalism's approach to personal ethics has led to an absence of moral depth and only slight moral intelligence. Ethics has become little more than egoism; its main question is, What do I feel like? Liberal accommodationism has allowed medicine to replace religion as the guardian of morality in American society. Fundamentals of liberal theology—freedom, equality, and justice—have been stripped of most meaning, as support for "civil rights" has degenerated into indiscriminate support of special interest groups where "rights" equals "desires" and "self-fulfillment." The individualism resident in liberalism's pedigree has combined with pluralism to make a rather unseemly doctrine—everyone has a right to do whatever one wants to do.

Theologically speaking, you never step twice into the same mainstream church, and a theologian like Harvey Cox is a *tabula* of the traumas and temptations of contemporary liberalism (Sweet, 1984b; 1982). A labyrinth is best that has no center, but not so a life. The attempt to mix liberalism with something spiky like liberation theology, which many hoped would liven up the "mainline" religious scene, has not always been an effective cocktail. The unceasing effort of liberal theology to provide culture a voice for God has meant that the main character has too often gotten lost. Nobody talks about God, or at times is even allowed to. The youth group of an "oldline" church in Rochester, New York, had two rules that its high school-age members had to agree to before they could join: first, everything said would be held in strictest confidence, and second, they would not discuss religion. Indifferent and untutored at deciphering God's guises, liberal Protestantism has not given its members eyes in the night. The recent interest in "spiritual formation" has meant that liberals still retain a few rags of respectability to clothe the spiritual nakedness exposed by the forces of modernization. But so far the spiritual formation movement reflects more the privatization of religion than the communal dimension of faith. In short, if liberal theology has an American future, it will not be gained through a trivial revival of old liberal values.

Part of what is needed for a fundamental reconstruction of the basic premises of liberalism is a renewed spirit and piety. Liberalism has been so busy transforming the Christian tradition that it has forgotten to transmit it. The rediscovery of the lectionary has returned the Bible to many sanctuaries, but it is an ecclesiastically edited Bible, a "reader's digest" scripture that omits difficult passages and seriously mangles the Old Testament. Instead of constantly playing simple-simonism with culture, liberalism must come to see itself as heir of the Christian tradition and on that basis engage itself in constructive, critical conversation with the tradition. Complaints about religious illiteracy collect a lot of detail from various studies that document the basic ignorance of the American people about some of the simplest questions of the faith.

Not only is liberalism not on speaking terms with its scriptures and tradition; liberals also don't know their conservative opponents. The failure of liberal intellect and imagination is nowhere more evident than in this absence of a liberal apologetic. In large part, religious language has been taken from the liberals. The jargon of liberal theological discourse, the portmanteau words, is drawn from the worlds of psychology and business. The dominant passwords of the church today—caring, sharing, inclusive, intentional—symbolize the lack of identity and the uncertainty of address that characterize the liberal theological mind. The liberal agenda for theological reflection must include a recovery of mental toughness, tradition, and scripture. It must also regain the characteristically liberal stress on experience.

The liberal soul is cavernously empty: vital piety is seldom present. It is easier to awaken an evangelical social conscience than to warm a liberal heart. Liberals need to get back under their own flag and liberalize liberalism. Oldline churches would be more faithful to their tradition if they were less concerned about making churches full of people and more concerned about making people full of God.

To say that there is a deficiency of religious experience in oldline churches does not smoke well in the pipes of many liberals. One of the most paralyzing delusions today is the notion that liberals lead lives rich and deep in experience. To be sure, Robert Bellah's study of popular American piety (*Habits of the Heart*, 1985a) demonstrates repeatedly that Americans make feeling the ultimate criterion for everything. On everything from morals to money, the basis for decision-making in American culture is to consult one's feelings. Bellah has even discovered that the dominant reason Americans go to church is to feel good about themselves.

This is the rub, and the nub of the problem. What liberals are used to feeling is themselves. Experience today refers to human experience—to the experience of the self and to tracing every tiny tendril of the self's emotions. Even religious experience is predominantly an experience of the self and not of God's initiating disclosures in one's life and in the life of the community of which one is a part. Actually, the situation is even more serious than this suggests. Much of personal religious experience is not only dominated by the self and unchecked by the community, but it is also defined by others. In other words, what experiences there are tend to be derivative and vicarious.

Perhaps the biggest reason why vital piety is often foreign to contemporary liberalism is that authentic religious experience only takes place within the context of individual personhood and community, and both are difficult to find in modern life. In the powerful book entitled *The Denial of Death* (1973), the philosopher Ernest Becker discusses what he calls the "paradox" of "twin ontological motives." Every person experiences two internal urges, or motives, that pull in seemingly opposite directions. First, there is the urge to be *a part* (*two words*) of something larger than oneself. One might call this the tug of community. Second, there is the urge to stand *apart* (one word) from everyone else, to be different and unique. One might call this the tug of individuality (152–55). These two words, community and individuality, function as a Siamese truth. The tug of truth is a dialectic between the individual and the group, the part and the whole, the person and the community, or between uniqueness and representativeness, the two words Victor Hugo used to sum up his life—*solitaire, solidaire.*

It is important to grasp this distinctive duality to life because it is precisely these two basic human urges—the urge to be a part of a living, forgiving community and the urge to stand apart as an original, a unique human being—that are being frustrated and foiled by modern culture. It is more than a matter of isolating the two tugs from each other, as if the two stand alone independently of each other. The attraction of Marxism is that it has a collective, corporate, social view of human life and destiny. But it does not know what to do with the individual, thinking that what is best for the social order is best for the individual. The attraction of capitalism is that it has an individual view of human life and destiny. But it does not know what to do with the community, thinking that what is best for the individual is best for the community.

The real problem is that liberals try to experience God today in a culture where the two very things that nourish religious experience—being the kind of person God calls one to be in community with others—are hard to come by. As the world gets smaller, the spans between people get bigger. As technology brings humans closer together in electronic ways, it pushes humans farther and farther away from one another in ways of intimacy and trust. As a result, the church is less an experience of relatedness, wholeness, and authenticity than of simulation, segmentation, and atomization.

Since the late nineteenth century, when entrepreneurial capitalism was transformed into corporate capitalism, the individual person has been absorbed into the corporate enterprise. The structural constraints of a competitive free market economy—the constraints to consume, the constraints to produce, the constraints to experience, the constraints to achieve—are just as severe as the controlling attempts of a socialist economy. Both pressure humans to feel and act and think in certain ways: in one system these ways are defined by the state; in the other they are defined by a corporate bureaucracy. Is it possible to visit Bloomingdale's without feeling a constraint to consume? Is it possible to attend school without feeling the constraint to achieve? The power of economics and technology to change individual, eccentric behavior into mass, centric behavior is more effective than the barrel of a gun. This sacrifice of individuality means that society is increasingly made up, not of interlocking individuals, but of interchangeable lives.

Science and technology, not religion, have become the opiate of the masses. This is one reason people have lost their edges, their rawness, and thus their freshness. Social ostracism greets eccentricities, and derision grinds idiosyncracies until our personalities lose their "character"—they are well rubbed and scrubbed by the modern forces of banality, brutality, and impersonality that attack sharp images and smooth everything into one homogeneous mass of conformity. Not surprisingly, oldline denominations are becoming increasingly authoritarian and repressive. Yes people prosper and "characters," "free spirits," and "independent thinkers" are more and more isolated and silenced.

One of the hardest tasks imaginable is for the church to build up character in a society that destroys characters. But a testimony of nonconformity is demanded of Christians today. All too often even the church strands its members during the week in a barren conformism from which they emerge only on Sunday to play at building community, by sitting, singing, and sipping coffee together as a coffee-table community. Even if it looks good on the outside, this community is seldom consulted or cultivated from the inside. This is why many people find the liberal church chilly, comfortless, and confining. This is also why the last place people expect to have a religious experience is at church.

The liberal religious legacy calls the church to deeper forms of religious experience than Peeping Tom religion or coffee-table community. Being an eyewitness is not enough. One must become a heart-witness. On the night Blaise Pascal experienced the burning reality of God's presence in his life, he wrote these

(241)

words on a scrap of paper, which from then on he always kept in a shirt or coat pocket close to his heart:

> From about half past ten in the evening to about
> half an hour after midnight.
>   Fire.
> God of Abraham, God of Isaac, God of Jacob,
> Not the God of philosophers and scholars.
> —Quoted in Duclaux, 1927:111

The fire of the Holy Spirit must burn on liberal hearts the feeling of God's forgiving love, which Graham Greene described in a reverberating phrase, "The . . . appalling . . . strangeness of the mercy of God."

Religious experience in the liberal tradition must not be confused with that of conservative summer camp religion with its guitar-strumming, hand-clapping, bonfire toasty warmness. Such feelings are more likely to spring fresh from the coals than from the soul, and they have a limited life. They need continual stoking to stay alive. It is this superficial, marshmallowish kind of religious experience that elicited Will Barrett's comment in Walker Percy's *The Second Coming:* "If the born-again are twice born, I'm holding out for the third go-around" (1980:272). Nor is religious experience in the liberal tradition that of camp meeting religion, with its spiritual eruptions and irrational swoonings, as illustrated in the emotional gurgling of an overcome brother at a nineteenth-century camp meeting revival: "Brethren, I feel—I feel—I feel—I feel—I feel—I can't tell you how I feel, but oh!, I feel! I feel!" (quoted in Pratt, 1920:184). Emotional conversions can become self-consuming—they burn out in the believer's mind. Still, religious experiences of the campfire or camp meeting religion variety are better than none, and even wild and untamed experiences can be gardened through discipline and community life.

A distinctly liberal religious experience is not naked, raw, or divorced from reason and restraint. Rather, experience is informed and enriched by theological insights about the traditions of the faith and by scientific insights about life, nature, and society. The dominant dualism of today is not between body and spirit, but between feeling and thought, emotions and reason. Liberalism points a way toward overcoming such dualism with its belief in the rationality of experience and its conviction that emotion could facilitate rather than obstruct reason. Faith's experience of God's love, forgiveness, and presence in the liberal tradition is not something irrational, disruptive, or beyond control. Thought and will need to be constitutive elements of any distinctly liberal piety.

A Revitalized Ecclesiology

There must be a redirecting of liberalism along the lines of a revitalized ecclesiology. The biggest problem of the church today is that it does not know what its role is. Despite all the goal-setting sessions and church self-study projects, the church still does not know who or what it is. In their confusion and uncertainty, liberals have looked around to those who seem to know who they are and what they are doing, and they want to be like those people. In a society where an M.B.A. is now a more prestigious degree than a Ph.D., the attraction of managerial techniques has proven almost irresistible.

Almost every single oldline church today might be called the church with the bureaucratic face. Ministers as managers have as their master metaphor for ministry not the pulpit, but the desk. With the triumph of the managerial revolution in the oldline church has come the ascendancy of technique over spirit (Hutcheson, 1979). Ministers are conceived of as professionals, and a church is known by the activities it keeps. A good church is a panting church, a church that is busy, getting a lot done, with lots of programming, lots of task forces, lots of cars in the parking lot, lots of things to do to keep its members active, and, especially, lots of committees.

Liberals have, in short, forgotten Pentecost. The purpose and mission of the church is to be the body of Christ. The church *is* not a structure. The church *has* a structure. The church is not managed. The church is led. The primary function of the church is not to be an aesthetic, cultural movement. The primary function of the church is not to be an intellectual or missionary movement. The primary function of the church is not to be a political or social justice movement. The primary purpose of the church is not to change the world, or to preach to the world, or to serve the world. The primary function of the church, from which stem all other functions, is to be the body of Christ—quite sacramentally, Christ enfleshed, incarnated, embodied in presence and in power.

Like birch trees, Christians grow in clusters. They search for the sky together. There is an irreducible communal component to living the Christian life. You cannot be a Christian any other way save as a member of a community. One Christian is no Christian. You cannot be a Christian without a church.

The fundamental act of oldline religious life today, however, is not its community dimension, but its privatization. Despite all the "fellowship groups," "fellowship dinners," and "fellowship nights," people are still pulling their own way. Community is hard to come by. The privatization process, of course, started long ago. Beginning with Martin Luther and proceeding apace to Descartes, the discovery of truth began to move toward the privacy of subjective illumination and away from community, tradition, and authority.

Emil Brunner has pointed out how the figure of Daniel Defoe's *Robinson Crusoe* (1719), an Enlightenment best-seller, symbolizes the eighteenth-century philosophy of life and its ideal of the self-sufficient individual. Add to this Adam Smith's law that says if you do well for yourself, you will do well for the community, and it is not hard to see how we have arrived at the place where it is every man for himself, every woman for herself, and no one wanted to owe anybody anything. Emile Durkheim, who pioneered the understanding of religion in its most "elementary form" as a way of getting people to relate to one another, calls this "the cult of the self" (1975:61).

"Today religion in America is as private and diverse," Robert Bellah observes, "as New England colonial religion was public and unified." When Americans first hear the word religion, Bellah asks, what do they think of? It is certainly not "church" (1985:220,226). The Hutterite belief that individuals can achieve salvation only if the entire group is saved appears as odd and alien as the Hutterites. The privatization of life's pilgrimages, rites of passage, and rituals makes religion predominantly a private affair. According to a Gallup poll, 76 percent of churched Americans (and 86 percent of the unchurched) believe that people should arrive at religious beliefs independent of any church or synagogue (Princeton Religion Research Center and the Gallup Organization, 1978). Americans want "freedom," which they define in solitary terms: "being left alone"; "not having other people's values or standards forced on me"; "the right to pursue my own life my way." Such a definition of freedom and the church do not mix. People are free only when they belong to an organized living community. Not when they are off on an island somewhere.

Because of its inadequate sociology of community (Ajzenstat, 1984), liberalism has become basically a nonorganic religion, offering bounteously to its members experiences of dismemberment. It stands in desperate need of a revitalized understanding of the church and of the function of community. "Community" has become one of those buzz words that can be so annoying that one reaches for the fly swatter. One must be clear about what is meant by "community." Not just any community will do. It must be a particular kind of community with a particular kind of spirit.

A community of "caring and sharing," "a community of togetherness," a "loving" community is not an adequate understanding of the kind of community the liberal church needs. One could say the same thing about the Rotary, the Eastern Star, or the Ku Klux Klan. "Caring and sharing" groups may be less in keeping with the gospel than what a pastor-friend calls in his church bulletin "grace and shit" groups. The community created by a revitalized ecclesiology is also not a collective. The modern state unleashes tremendous individualizing and collectivizing forces, depersonalizing people into both atomistic individuals and impersonal masses. Individualism and collectivism are both dangerous, for God's commonwealth is neither an assortment of spider webs in which each reigns supreme (anarchy) nor an ant hill in which all function mechanistically (totalitarianism). A biblical fellowship will protect the interests of the community at the same time it preserves the identity of the individual. It will make room for the rebel, the heretic, and the virtue of nonconformity at the same time it encourages discipleship, obedience, and the virtue of fidelity. It will realize that not all members of Christ's body are equal, but all are equal members. There must be a place for the individual person within the community and a place for the community within the individual person.

The new community will have a particular kind of Spirit. Spirit is indigenous to many kinds of community. One speaks of team spirit, community spirit, school spirit. But the church is a community that has as its spirit the Spirit of Jesus Christ. It is a Christbody community, a community organized around the spirit of self-sacrificing love. Its distinctive way of looking at things and distinctive style of doing things are shaped by Jesus Christ. To become a Christian, then, is to become part of a Christbody community. One cannot have the one without the other.

The church is not a voluntary society, a human gathering that one forms and joins out of a community of self-interest. It is a divine creation, which means that it is both a divine gift and a human task—one that lives the life of Christ and incarnates Christ's real presence in the world. The title parson has not had wide currency in the liberal tradition and properly so, for it more accurately should be used of the community itself than of its leadership. "Parson" came to refer to the way the pastor functions as the *persona Christi* in and to the congregation, whereas the pastor's function is to help the congregation become the *persona Christi* in the world. This is the true meaning of ordained ministry—the raising up of leaders by the church who can build koinonia communities.

Churches need pastors because they need persons possessing unique spiritual powers to order and start a movement, who have devoted their lives to the building of communities. Unfortunately, most seminaries are not geared for training this kind of leader. Lowell Fewster (1981), a specialist in evaluation instruments and techniques, undertook a study to determine what aspects of pastoral leadership graduates from one well-known seminary were least prepared for. He found that the major complaint of graduates from this seminary was that they felt ill-prepared to be spiritual leaders of a parish. The body of Christ does not need any more pastors who see ministry primarily as preaching, or counseling, or administration, or education, or any other single specialization of ministry. It needs leaders who are body builders, leaders who can build and strengthen koinonia congregations in which the variety of spiritual gifts is exercised—women and men who can form and facilitate the life of a community. The most pressing need of the church is for its members to stop thinking of church membership as "going to church" and instead think of it as "being the church."

People are hungry for community, and they will pick it up wherever they can find it. One way of writing the history of modern American religion, with its cults and rock concerts and fundamentalist subculture, would be to explore this search for surrogate communities. The Moral Majority and the New Religious Right have recognized this perhaps better than anyone. As much as we hate to admit it, not everything Jerry Falwell says is wrong. When he talks about the trinity of endangered values—family, flag, God—he is expressing the void that people feel in their lives because of a lost sense of belonging to a community, whether it be the home, the nation, or the church. The surprising persistence of nationalism and the astonishing spread of socialism can be attributed, at least in part, to the tenacity of this quest for community and as a reaction against a mechanized, impersonal, alienating world of extreme individualism.

The problem is not that oldline churches do not yearn for a revitalization of this understanding of the church as Christbody community. They do. Nor is the problem that oldline Protestants have been unwilling to invest more of the church's institutional life in small group programming, or in what Europeans call the "little flock movement." They have. Numerous local congregations who have tried unsuccessfully to resurrect small groups and intimacy, some even to the point of "koinonitas," can attest to this. So what is the problem?

First, and most obvious, liberals have put the cart before the horse, with attention to "methods" preceding understanding about the nature of the church. Howard Snyder, who is both an expert in church renewal and an urban pastor, contends that many churches have "added on small groups as another program when they should have been recreating the level of community" (1982:22). Christians first must unlearn an understanding of the church in which the word coffee is often only another expression for the word fellowship. Church is not an organization you join, but an organism of which you are a living member, attached to other members of the organism as surely as the five people in mountaineering are attached to the same rope. You may scrape against one another, get tangled up in troubles of someone else's making, get vexed at the dirt someone kicks your way, or even come not to like some of the other climbers. But beyond those feelings lies the awareness that together you constitute what the Germans call a *Schicksalsgemeinde,* a "fate community" that rises or falls together. You share a common destiny.

Second, with a revitalized ecclesiology there will come a greater restructuring of life around Christbody community and a willingness to sacrifice for it. I shall never forget being stunned in my first parish when I received a phone call asking if I would be willing to meet with a family that was thinking of moving into our town. Before this family would consider taking the position offered to them, they wanted to meet the pastor of the local United Methodist church and visit the church. What determines whether Christians uproot their families and move to a new city? It is usually a faceted decision involving considerations of salary, job, school, neighborhood, recreation—too often everything but the church.

Third, we must begin to think more in terms of building up community than of building up ourselves. Even many who travel through life in Christbody communities do so as lone wolves in migrating packs. We like to be individuals in crowds, which is far afield from communities vibrant with individuals. Individuals in crowds are people who like to do their own thing around people, with people watching. The body of Christ is the last place on earth where people do their own thing. Christbody communities are charismatic entities in which *mea culpa* (my sin, my guilt) is replaced with *nostra culpa* (our sin, we are all guilty), in which duty to others is ascendant over duty to self, and in which the gifts of the spirit are used for the upbuilding of the community and not for the self.

Fourth, many of us are too sophisticated for ecclesiology revitalized along these lines. A couple of years ago I attended a church in which each Sunday they spent an inordinate amount of time on "parish announcements." They made an especially big deal of anyone who had a birthday that past week. As they sang gleefully "Happy Birthday," I embarrassedly slunk down in my seat, recalling childhood memories of church in which the "birthday person" (and it always seemed to be someone over eighty) had to march down the aisle to the altar and insert a penny for each year into a lighthouse with a beacon that lit up each time a penny was inserted. Yet there was something going on here that was precious and significant: private milestones became public celebrations, and a family-patterned community was being formed.

Liberal oversophistication is also apparent in oldline churches' persistence in what various people have styled "R-rated worship"—adults only worship. Somehow liberals have imbibed the notion that God prefers to hear adult voices over children's sounds emanating from our sanctuaries. Children belong in church. It is just as much their church as it is their parents' church. Children should come to see everyone in church as part of their extended family. They should feel the freedom to treat members of the church as they would members of their own family—climbing up into their laps during service, asking them to take them to the bathroom, passing notes around. I heard recently of a church that changed its front door for another one. When asked why they were replacing a perfectly good door, the carpenters responded that the administration board decided that no church should have a door children couldn't open.

Finally, liberal churches have not demonstrated that they know how to care for and feed their members. Liberals are not physical enough. A Christbody community shares a common nervous system. When one member of the body suffers, all suffer. As Paul puts it in Romans 12:5, "We, though many, are one body in Christ, and individually members one of another." Nothing need ever be said, and it is felt by the others. The entire organism sends its healing resources to that part of the body in need and pain. In the words of an old Zulu proverb: "When a thorn gets into the toe, the whole body stoops to pick it out."

A Rehabilitated Patriotism

Oldline Protestantism needs a rehabilitated patriotism. Patriotism is a word that has behaved badly over the years and never so badly as when used by Sen. Joe McCarthy. More than any other person he is responsible for the liberal inability to celebrate I Am an American Day. He so abused patriotic emotions that it has been difficult, if not impossible, for liberals to claim American national sentiment. But it must be reclaimed (Neuhaus, 1984:55–77). By forfeiting questions concerning the meaning of nationhood and democratic faith to conservatives, liberals have ensured that the only definitions of patriotism available to people will be ethnocentric rather than international ones. They have also projected a self-image of themselves as being unpatriotic and un-American. Democracy needs patriotic citizens who think of responsibilities as well as rights, who allow for dissent, and whose civic consciousness embraces the future (Janowitz, 1983). One of the most revealing challenges facing America's oldline leadership is whether or not it can be open to a rehabilitated patriotism, an enlightened, critical love of country in which the flag is not burned or used as a blindfold, but is proudly brandished while having its blemishes and dirt continually brushed off.

Because of an unsatisfactory connection to political culture, oldline churches have made it seem as if prophetic witness necessitates disengagement from patriotic sentiment. For this reason, and for others, a rehabilitated patriotism must make different arrangements for the church's social and political witness from the ones that are already in place. Oldline Protestants need to reconsider the voluntary society.

Over the past sixty years oldline Protestantism has been a boxing ring in perpetual session. In one corner are conservatives, who insist that the church has no business getting involved in direct political action. In the other corner are liberals, who insist with equal vehemence on official churchly political commitments. No fighter can win this match. Both are right.

The notion that the church's robe of righteousness is so pure that it should never brush up against the dirt and mire of politics is an impertinent and unscriptural attitude. The church cannot reject politics. The question is how political responsibility is to be exercised. The fundamental political responsibility of the church is to be the church. Or as Stanley Hauerwas puts it, the church's "first political act is to be herself" (1983:100; 1977:140). If one accepts this premise, then that celebrated motto of William Temple about the church—"The church is the only institution which exists solely for the sake of those who do not belong to it"—must go overboard. Hauled on board instead must be a holistic definition of the church as a Christbody community when referring to its organic character and a particularistic definition of the church when referring to its constituent parts or vital organs.

On the first page of Chairman Mao's little red book one reads that if you want to have a revolution, the first necessity is to have a strong Communist party. It is no different with the church. If the church is to labor to make society more just and humane, and even to revolutionize it, the church must be strong as a Christbody community. At the same time, however, both local congregations and denominations as organs of the church should deliberately distance themselves from direct political action on behalf of specific causes and campaigns. Why?

First, history shows repeatedly that what the church in one era proclaimed as the latest word from heaven it could denounce in another era as the latest word from the pit, and vice versa. Whether or not the church has sipped from the same cup as culture has depended mostly on expediency. Or as one nineteenth-century etiquette manual stated, "Whether or not it is polite to drink out of the same bucket as your pony depends on the distance the water has to be drawn." The Constantinian era of the church may be coming to an end, but the church will always be subverted and compromised by political, social, economic, and cultural forces. Robin Gill argues forcefully in his *Prophecy and Praxis* that "churches, as churches, are already too involved with the world and, as a result, too constrained by it, genuinely to proclaim specific moral, social, and political implications of the Gospel" (1983:20). Christians lead a double life, for they live in two kingdoms, two cities (Augustine), two realms (Luther). In the realm of God, divine action is clear, decisive, and messianic. In the realm(s) of the world, God's action is hidden, ambiguous, and providential. The kingdom of God in the New Testament is not a political movement, social reform program, or apocalyptic regime. That would be to replace faith with ideology raised to idolatry. Rather, the divine kingdom is the revelation of God in consummate power and strength. To ideologize and build utopia is to live in one commonwealth that is both church and state. The church must always stand with one foot in heaven and the other foot on earth.

Second, the church must admit a pluriformity on issues of the day if it is to be true to its purpose of being the body of Christ for all people. Given the plethora of positions Christians take on the same issue, one may correctly conclude that there is no such thing as Christian action, but only Christian motivation.[1] Some Christians are led to pacifism out of their belief in God's love and justice. Other Christians are led to take up arms, either in military forces or guerrilla movements, for the same reason. Congregations must be able to contain both, for both are motivated by the same throbbing heartbeat of Christian love and service. Why is it we are more likely to admit a plurality of views on how Jesus came into the world than on how peace will come into the world? For the body of Christ to present to the world one political face would be to make it ethnically and economically inclusive and ideologically exclusive. The church can live under the banner of the hammer and sickle as well as under the stars and stripes.

Third, it is the responsibility of the church to cross culture but scarcely ever to legitimate it. By "crossing" culture is meant both spreading the healing message of God's suffering, redemptive love over a world in need and standing in perpetual judgment on that culture when it is guilty of oppression and injustice. The church as a Christbody community must proclaim Christian truths and condemn society for departing from them. It must demand social justice even more strongly than it has in the past. But it does not have to take a stand on every social or political issue of the day or endorse one particular platform or political modality over another on how justice is to be achieved.

Saul Bellow says that he left New York for Chicago because he was fed up with intellectuals who had to have an opinion on everything. Some have left the church for similar reasons. My grandmother used to say that if you stir a cowpile, it will stink to the sky. But if you leave a cowpile alone, it will turn to chips. There are some social and political cowpiles that the church can best eliminate by leaving them alone.

The church is not called to enter and inhabit political structures, but to denounce all social, economic, and political structures that inhibit justice and peace and to provide a framework within which issues of the day may be discussed and debated among the faithful, even if no consensus is reached. This does not mean that the church will criticize equally all political or economic systems. Sometimes moral distinctions will be made that open up one system to greater criticism than another. But the church will not legitimate any historic system or give it the "Christian" blessing.

Finally, a local church is exerting a political function and effecting political consequences merely by being a congregation. Every time someone says, "Why doesn't the church do something," guilt scampers to mount some crusade that is doomed from the start. What is not realized is that the church is already doing something by being the church. The church incarnates God's realm wherever congregations make compassion, mercy, and justice practical realities of life. It is doing on earth, in the words of the disciples' prayer, what is being done in heaven. As such it challenges the world with the witness of a new social order. What ultimately threatens the world is not the clenched-fist quality of political action groups, or the stick-the-tongue-out haughtiness of social resolutions, or even the twist-the-arm pressures of financial support. What causes shaking and quaking to take place is the presentation to the world of an alternative, counterfactual model of community. "We best criticize the world," William Willimon has written well, "by being the church."

> In its very existence, the church serves the world, not by running errands, but by providing a light, that is providing an imaginative alternative for society. The gospel call is an invitation to be part of a people who are struggling to create those structures which the world can never achieve through governmental power and balanced self-interest. (1982:8)

The reform of political and social structures may be one of the least important keys in the cause of God's commonwealth. This is because structures do not provide people with meaning; structures do not answer life's deepest questions; structures do not stretch the soul. Changing structures may not be as revolutionary or subversive as we imagine. Or even as difficult. After all, which is easier: to overthrow a government or change people's hearts and minds? Congregations fulfill their political responsibilities by bearing witness to a new world, criticizing the old world, and prophetically pointing the way to the world's redemption.

But if congregations are not to be seen as agents of political reform, how can the liberals be right in their insistence that the Christian church give corporate witness and work to liberation? How can one claim that political inactivity on the part of the oppressed is inexcusable at the same time one denies that political activism is a mission of a congregation? This is where the church as a Christbody community needs to rediscover and redeploy one of its own forgotten organs—collective action through voluntary societies, which rightfully serve as the prophetic arm of the church (Berger, 1977:130–41; Hutcheson, 1981a:62–79). The use of official denominational structures to implement social policy is a relatively new experiment in American religious life and, in the words of Hutcheson, "an experiment that has failed" (1981b:994–97, 996). One reason the denominational structure of American Protestantism is a shambles is that the church has conceived of its mission to be a voluntary society rather than to raise up voluntary societies.

Voluntary societies are the hyphens that allow the church to be in the world but not of it. Hyphens both link and separate. They link the church to the world in mission but separate the church from the world in thought and spirit. A voluntary society is a non-sectarian, non-profit social group voluntarily created and joined that occurs outside denominational or congregational structures and that is formally organized to secure a specified objective. The breaking up of movements into single-issue crusades has been described as the "Balkanization" of American life. But ever since the early nineteenth century there have been single-issue crusades through these voluntary societies that called Christians from all denominations to band together around a common crusade, raise their own money, and work through political, economic, and social involvement until that goal was achieved, whereupon the voluntary society would be dismantled. Voluntary societies were the most significant ecumenical expression and activity in the first half of the nineteenth century. These organizations, while often founded by clergy, were run and led by the laity. Denominations, which mainly addressed issues of faith and order, gave official encouragement to voluntary societies (even ones that contradicted one another) but no official approval. Voluntary associations were so strong and active by 1840 that their combined budget exceeded that of the federal government. In 1860 one third of the population of New York City were members of at least one church-related voluntary society (Foster and Singleton, 1975; Doyle, 1977).

The reasons for a rediscovery of the voluntary association are so obvious that one hesitates to set them down. First, the work of social justice is more than the work of the clergy. In the past laity have been hampered in their social witness because the church has rooted its understanding of social ministry in its denominational bureaucracies or in something weak and limpid like local church "social concerns committees." It is the responsibility of congregations to be strong enough communities so that their people can garner the theological resources, psychological confidence, and spiritual energy to get involved politically in social melioration and not have their efforts be doomed from the start.

Second, it is time Christians became realistic about the strength of the powers and principalities that work in our world. The notion that one is making a difference in the arms race when each local church forms its own little task force to deal with nuclear weapons, or even when each denomination forms its own denominational task force to mobilize support, is naive. Church members are rightfully reluctant to put their energy in something akin to launching toy sailboats on the ocean's tides and expecting them to reach China. If the church is interested in something more than simple gestures toward God of goodwill and sincerity, it must get serious about a united witness. People with similar convictions must draw together into one common, national, or even multinational group and cease dissipating all that energy in unchanneled and uncoordinated strategies for social change. Voluntary societies not only enlist broad support, but they also allow for fast and efficient action. They are places where even relatively small numbers can have large influence through the discipline and commitment of highly motivated members.

Third, the church must take sides. This is its prophetic role. But there are two sides to taking sides. It is the responsibility of the church to provide the world with a background of Christian principles attached to concrete, contemporary situations against which voluntary societies labor in the foreground to implement particular political programs and social policies. The prophetic role of congregations is in the realm of the general. The prophetic role of voluntary societies is in the realm of the particular.

Few have ever stated this better than William Temple:

> The method of the Church's impact upon society at large should be twofold. The church must announce Christian principles and point out where the existing social order at any time is in conflict with them. It must then pass on to Christian citizens, acting in

their civic capacity, the task of reshaping the existing order in closer conformity to the principles. (1943:36)

The adoption of such a position leaves the church open to criticism from both liberals and conservatives, as Temple realized:

> The Church is likely to be attacked from both sides if it does its duty. It will be told that it has become "political" when in fact it has been careful only to state principles and point out breaches of them; and it will be told by advocates of particular policies that it is futile because it does not support these. If it is faithful to its commission, it will ignore both sets of complaints, and continue so far as it can to influence all citizens and permeate all parties. (37)

Until a network of voluntary societies is established, congregations must continue to fulfill both a general and a particular prophetic role. A situation of great background but no foreground is the least satisfactory of prophetic options. It causes the quality and character of the church's prophetic task continually to be compromised and reduces the church's ability to speak the words most urgently needed.

A Reconstituted Supernaturalism

A reconstituted supernaturalism is the fourth agenda for the revitalization of oldline Protestantism. Liberals must be nudged off the sidewalks onto the grass, fields, and forests of life. To improvise on a phrase from the children's book author Shel Silverstein, "where the concrete ends" is where the full dimension of the faith begins. Liberals have gotten by living without the supernatural. But for those who are dissatisfied with unadventurous piety, for those with the ability to let rip in life, for those courageous, reckless, and honest enough to explore faith's frontiers, one must venture into a world dense with magic, mystery, and miracle. We have tended to downplay such high expectations for fear of being seen as part of the Peter Pan School of Religion—a fairy-tale faith that has never grown up, that believes in religious fairies, and that takes flights of fancy into never-never lands far removed from the ground of real experience. Liberals pride themselves instead on a down-to-earth, grown-up faith that is solidly anchored in reality, ruddered by reason, and propelled by God working through the scientific method.

At the very time the bloom is off the scientific rose, scientists themselves are often more humbly realistic about what science can do and what hopes we should have for it than are most Christians. The four most influential philosophers of science in recent times—Karl Popper, Paul Feyerabend, Thomas S. Kuhn, and Imre Lakatos—all show that science is a fallible and less reliable guide in leading us to knowledge than we have commonly supposed. Jacob Bronowski, in his influential study *Science and Human Values,* reminds us that "there is today almost no scientific theory which was held" in the eighteenth century. Most often "today's theories flatly contradict" those of the Enlightenment: "many contradict those of 1900. In cosmology, in quantum mechanics, in genetics, in the social sciences, who now holds beliefs that seemed firm fifty years ago?" (1958:87).

When it comes to reliability, religion is no less vulnerable than science. Disease leaves us in the dark about most of life's ultimate questions. In the words of Sir Brian Pippard, "a physicist who rejects the testimony of saints and mystics is no better than a tone-deaf man deriding the power of music." Yet liberal Christians subscribe to the monstrous falsehood that scientific thinking is the only route to truth. Leaving to science all wonder-working powers, liberals are open to the microchip miracles of technology at the same time they resign faith to the realms of the possible and appropriate. We have come to expect the spirit of high adventure and discovery to pervade the life of science, but not the life of the Spirit.

A resurrected supernaturalism will take oldline churches away from the familiar and into threshold experiences. A threshold experience is that step beyond which life begins to take on new colors, words mean different things, and emotions speak different messages. The first threshold experience is the experience of mystery.

God has a particular liking for the magical and mysterious.

The law of the waves and wind tips us off as to how God works: you can't see where they come from and where they go. As a rabbi has spoken, "if there is not more than one explanation to an event, then it is not of God." God works mysteriously, anonymously, unpredictably. In fact, Flannery O'Connor's definition of fiction is the best definition of a reconstituted supernaturalism: "mystery that is lived" (1970:125).

Christian mystery is sacramental and incarnational. Like one of those beautiful summer evenings that all have seen but so few have felt, it is not something that exists to be observed and analyzed, but something that exists to be lived and experienced. The awesomeness and availability of mystery are everywhere. "The whole of existence intimidates me," Søren Kierkegaard wrote. "From the tiniest fly to the mystery of the Incarnation, everything is unintelligible to me, most of all myself" (Rohde, ed., 1960:19). All creation is mangered in mystery. All around us can be found what Nathaniel Hawthorne termed "mysterious hieroglyphics," hieroglyphics of holiness that invite our involvement in the mystery of creation. The Puritans believed that God created the world and gave us the senses to perceive it in order that these mysterious, sensuous experiences might lead us to God. Strange things happened at nineteenth-century Methodist camp meetings, where the sensual and spiritual blended into one, because once a year these Methodist pioneers let their faith roam freely throughout the supernatural dimension.

If liberals are to stray from the concrete, take off their shoes and socks, and experience under their bare feet the mysteries and surprises of life, they must begin to develop a second threshold experience. The Renaissance philosopher and Neoplatonist Marsilio Ficino called it "angelic thinking" (Sears, 1963:105, 128), the ability to think spiritually as well as mentally—in images and likenesses, myths and metaphors, dreams and poetry.

The supernatural is where things that are unseen and spiritual encroach on things that are seen and physical. The supernatural can be quite forbidding, even spooky, and it is only beginning to be trusted. We sense that God has provided us with resources, reserves, and other sixth senses that no one has even imagined. And because psychologists have given scientific credibility to dreams, we do not send to the funny farm people like Graham Greene, who attach great importance to these thoughts of the soul and who trace the genesis of some of the creativity (e.g., Greene's books *It's a Battlefield* [1934] and *The Honorary Consul* [1973]) to dreaming. A debate on the merits of dreams is now about as controversial as a debate on the merits of the Beatitudes. But for the most part we keep in good repair our prejudices against God's other "forgotten languages": ESP, remote viewing, and other paranormal phenomena. Dreams are about as far as liberals are willing to go into the world of "angelic thinking" and "spiritual senses."

Archibald MacLeish once warned all would-be travelers into the unknown: "Once the maps have all been made, a man were better dead than find new continents." Understandably, liberals are like everyone else—more inclined to clutch the old maps than to step forward toward new continents. But there is a difference between being ignorant about something and being stupid about something—the latter is dangerous and disrupts life. And liberals are utterly stupid about threshold experiences that contradict Western ways of reasoning and call humans to new forms of angelic thinking.

There are two kinds of Christians. Those who know nothing of miracles and those who know of nothing else. Liberals are to be counted almost exclusively among the former. To live life on acceptable terms with the miraculous—to be neither among those who know nothing of miracles nor among those who know of nothing else—is the last threshold experience required of a faith lived in friendship with the supernatural.

The biggest blockage to coming to terms with miracles is the prevalence of a wrong understanding of what miracles are. When Dostoevsky wrote, "Children, do not seek miracles, for miracles kill faith," he was pointing to the miracles sought by people who believe that if you are close to God, you are far from trouble. Religion of this variety majors in pretty smiles, blue skies, with no hint of Gethsemane or Golgotha. Peter Hodgins, son of Pastor Kenneth and Barbara Hodgins of Jamestown, New

York, died at six after a long bout with bone cancer. Every day he lived with that cancer a miracle took place. No matter how painful or uncomfortable the day had been, Peter's evening prayers always included these words: "Lord, camp your angels around our house, and on our lawn, and on everything that is ours, in Jesus' name. Amen." The miracle Peter and others like him discovered in life was not that God cured the hurt, the "thorn-in-the-flesh," or the cancer, but that God camped angels on their home, prison, lawn, and everything that was theirs, angels that kept them going with joy, grace, and dignity in the face of tragedy. There is no pit so deep that God cannot pull you out of it. There is no loneliness so isolating that God cannot reach you. There is no rejection so brutal that God cannot bring you back. There is no valley so low that God cannot walk you through it. That is the true miracle.

The hocus-pocus healing of "faith-healers" has given miracles a bad press. Harold Wilke, who has spent a lifetime helping oldline churches to probe the question, "Is Our Theology Disabled?" tells the sick and handicapped that when someone informs them "If only your faith were strong enough, you would be healed," they should respond with "If only your faith were strong enough, you would heal me" (1984:130). The liberal religious tradition has no business abandoning healing to religious quacks and charlatans, or to the medical profession.

In the medieval period a visit to a moldering bone housed at some church shrine was often effective psychotherapy. Why are people who see 900-foot Jesuses the only ones who realize that physical problems often have spiritual roots? The church, which used to see its mission as the "cure" of souls, is now satisfied with the mere "care" of souls. The closest most of our churches come to holding healing services is when we let AA groups use our facilities for the healing sessions they call "meetings." Some healing is in our hands. Some healing is out of our hands. But healing belongs in the church.

Will renewalist currents be strong enough to change the mainstream's course? If so, will oldline denominations try hard to make a place for renewalist movements (and indeed foster as many as possible), allowing them to do their work and then become part of the establishment? Or will oldline denominations fight against them, preferring the pain of decline to the pain of reconstruction, revitalization, rehabilitation, and reexamination. History and sociology are on the side of the latter. If the former is to happen, it will take more than a silver bullet and a slug of whiskey to help denominations through the ordeal.

Notes

Introduction

1. For a succinct characterization of liberal Protestantism in historical context in America, see Hutchison, 1976:3–4.

2. Martin Marty (1970:170–79) has suggested that this division within Protestantism resulted in the "two party system." He labels one party "private" and the other "public" Protestantism.

3. By 1920, Hutchison points out (1976:3), "liberal ideas had become accepted and respectable in more than a third of the pulpits of American Protestantism and in at least half the educational, journalistic, social, and literary or theological expressions of Protestant church life." (The northern and southern Methodists were reunited in 1939 to form the largest of the "mainline" denominations.)

4. See the collection of essays in Dean R. Hoge and David A. Roozen, eds., *Understanding Church Growth and Decline, 1950–1978* (New York: The Pilgrim Press, 1979).

2. Liberal Protestantism: A Sociodemographic Perspective

1. A new "mapping" of American religion, its groups and trends is provided in Roof and McKinney, *The New Shape of American Religion* (1986).

2. The six remaining families are *Catholics, Jews, moderate Protestants* (Methodists, Lutherans, Disciples of Christ, white northern Baptists, and Reformed members), *black Protestants*, and *conservative Protestants* (white Southern Baptists, Adventists, Nazarenes, and members of the Churches of Christ and smaller evangelical, fundamentalist, pentecostal, and holiness (groups). See Roof and McKinney (1986), chapter 3.

3. These surveys provide a wealth of information on the American population. For a codebook on items and marginals, see Davis (1984).

4. The proportion of the population who identify themselves to the pollsters as members of a liberal Protestant group is considerably

higher than the proportion of the population accounted for by these groups in their membership reports to the *Yearbook of American and Canadian Churches.* The reported membership of the Episcopal Church, the Presbyterian Church (USA) and the United Church of Christ in 1980 totaled 7,784,334, or only 4.3 percent of the adult (over 14) population.

5. Some of the under-45 differences among families are due to variations in the average age of members of the families in this category. For example, the relatively low number of children born to younger Catholic women reflects in part their lower average age. Under-45 liberal Protestant women tend to be slightly older than the under-45 women in other religious groups.

6. The rates for other families are Jews, 90 percent; Catholics, 83 percent; black Protestants, 86 percent; conservative Protestants, 78 percent; moderate Protestants, 73 percent; no religious preference, 53 percent.

7. For a similar interpretation of trends in liberal Protestantism in Britain, see Bruce (1984).

8. Increased birth rates in the society at large, as occurred in the postwar period, and increased longevity, which continues for all social groups, might be expected to have an impact, but church leaders can do little to affect these changes.

3. The Extravasation of the Sacred and the Crisis in Liberal Protestantism

1. These data are from the 1973–80 General Social Surveys done by the National Opinion Research Center of the University of Chicago. I am grateful to Prof. Samuel Mueller of the University of Akron for making them available to me in this form.

4. Past Imperfect: History and the Prospect for Liberalism

1. I have made these calculations without including one denomination on the Carroll graph—the Lutheran Church in America—whose antecedents in earlier decades are too complex for reliable figuring. Inclusion of the LCA among the mainline bodies would decrease the gap between mainline and conservative growth rates for 1965–75.

2. The American Baptist figures, I realize, have risen partly because the data collection method they used in the sixties and seventies has been abandoned. (Baptist "losses" had been affected, earlier, by that method.) But there has been a gain of 20,000, or roughly 1.5 percent.

5. *Our Country:* One Century Later

1. See the Introduction by Jurgen Herbst to the modern reprint of the 1891 edition of *Our Country* (Cambridge, MA: Belknap Press, Harvard University Press, 1963).

2. Strong quoted de Tocqueville's warning in a footnote: "For if ever a permanent inequality of conditions and aristocracy again penetrate into the world, it may be predicted that this [capital-labor division] is the channel by which they will enter."

7. Campus Ministry and the Liberal Protestant Dilemma

1. I realize that the term "Liberal Protestantism" is imprecise. I use it here to refer to that historical group of churches commonly called "mainline" or "establishment" churches. There were churches which addressed issues of modernity in good faith rather than those which ignored them.

2. From unpublished interviews with campus ministers, October 1984.

3. From October 1984 interview with campus minister. It is interesting to note that "women of faith" are also being placed on campus. At a recent national meeting of campus ministers, approximately one third of those present were women.

4. From October 1984 interview with campus minister.

5. From October 1984 interviews with campus ministers.

8. Self-fulfillment and Culture Crisis: America's Search for Soul in the 1960s and 1970s

1. These remarks were made at a public lecture, "The Myth of the Great Search," given at the University of California, Santa Barbara, on November 14, 1983.

2. I am thinking of Erich Fromm's (1976) distinction between the having and being modes of existence. This distinction was also employed by Gabriel Marcel.

9. The Loss of Optimism as a Problem for Liberal Christian Faith

1. This observation is based on ten years of experience as director of congregationally oriented change projects involving more than 200 congregations and 17 theological schools.

2. Liberalism as a theological movement in America preceded Rauschenbusch. In some forms it was characterized by a growing individualism. That raised the problem of authority and truth. It also

developed into a highly personal privatistic psychology form of religion with all the attendant problems that that poses for biblical faith. Cf. Berger (1969), esp. ch. 7, pp. 155ff.

3. It should be noted that Rauschenbusch's emphasis on social reform as redemptive in history is much more akin to Kutter Ragaz than to Schleiermacher and Ritschl.

4. Rauschenbusch himself was deeply distressed by World War I. He saw it as evidence of a defect in all humanity and not simply as an episodic aberration. He died deeply disappointed and increasingly despondent about progress in history. See Robert Cross' Introduction, Rauschenbusch (1964), xix.

5. The usual term is "realism." I like "chastened optimism" better.

6. This is a Jewish perspective that has some similarities to the one I have mentioned.

7. McLoughlin (1968) argues that American Calvinistic evangelicalism quickly converted to an Arminian view. Human choice was always possible and the consequences of human choices were always significant for God's work in history as well as human destiny in the next world.

8. Although there are significant differences in their recommendations for social action, persons such as Stanley Hauerwas, Peter Berger, and Richard Neuhaus belong to this group. A growing number of socially concerned evangelicals, such as Ronald Sider, Hal Wallis, and Steven Mott, seem to be moving in the direction of an activist religious presence based on an individualistic evangelicalism. They may be the group of theological thinkers who at this point are closest to Walter Rauschenbusch's position. It will be interesting to see whether they develop an emphasis on the church as the corporate representative of God's salvific work in history. If they do, they would be the natural conversation partners for those persons most deeply influenced by Karl Barth.

10. Complementism: Liberal Protestant Potential Within a Fully Realized Pluralistic Cultural Environment

1. As part of a Lilly Foundation funded research team, I was involved in an in-depth analysis of mainline denominational periodicals in an attempt to discover what they had to say by way of diagnosis and prescription regarding their situation. The articles used in this essay are most representative of liberal Protestantism's own assessment of its predicament. Also, following the explanation given in the preface to this volume, throughout this essay I will use "liberal" rather than

"mainline" or "oldline" as a descriptive term for the type of Protestantism we are investigating.

2. Fritjof Capra considers the systems view of life as a new perceptual paradigm, which, in replacing the Cartesian-Newtonian paradigm of a "world-machine," will revolutionize thinking in all areas of human intellectual activity: biology, medicine, physics, ecology, and, of course, religion. As opposed to the mechanistic world view posited by Newton, which envisioned an atomistic material base bound up in a strict cause and effect scheme—like a giant clock—the systems view sees the world in terms of its "essential interrelatedness and interdependence of all phenomena—physical, biological, psychological, social and cultural" (Capra, *The Turning Point*, p. 265). Robert Bellah offers a clear description of old paradigmatic thinking in the social sciences: "mainstream social science is derived from Seventeenth Century English social thought and the French Enlightenment. . . . The underlying assumptions can be briefly listed: positivism, reductionism, relativism and determinism" (Robert Bellah on "Biblical Religion and Social Science" recorded by Rae Ann McLennan in October 1982 at Holy Spirit Chapel in Berkeley, California).

14. Can a Mainstream Change Its Course?
1. For the distinction between the church's right to *condemn* and its right to *legitimate*, see Berger (1981), 194–99.

Bibliography

Abbott, Andrew
    1983   "Religion, Psychiatry, and Problems of Everyday Life." Pp. 131–41 in Jeffrey K. Hadden and Theodore E. Long, eds., *Religion and Religiosity in America*. New York: Crossroad.

Ahlstrom, Sydney E.
    1960   "Theology and the Present-day Rival." *The Annals of the American Academy of Political and Social Science* 332 (November):20–36.
    1970   "The Radical Turn in Theology and Ethics: Why It Occurred in the 1960's." *The Annals of the American Academy of Political and Social Science* 387 (January):1–13.

Ajzenstat, Janet
    1984   "Collectivity and Individual Rights in 'Mainstream Liberalism.'" Journal of Canadian Studies 19 (Fall):99–111.

Anderson, Gerald
    1974   "A Moratorium on Missionaries?" *Christian Century* 91 (January 16):43–45.

Averill, Lloyd J.
    1967   *American Theology in a Liberal Tradition*. Philadelphia: Westminster Press.

Baily, J. Martin
    1982   "Recognizing the Signs of Hope." *A.D.* (November):5–8.

Becker, Ernest
    1973   *The Denial of Death*. New York: The Free Press.

Bellah, Robert
    1970   "Christianity and Symbolic Realism." *Journal for the Scientific Study of Religion* 9 (Summer):89–96.
    1974   "Civil Religion in America." In Russell E. Richey and

Donald Jones, eds., *American Civil Religion*. New York: Harper & Row.

1985a   *Habits of the Heart: Individualism and Commitment in American Life*. Berkeley: University of California Press.

1985b   "Is Individualism Out of Control in America?" In *Los Angeles Times*, pt. 2, February 15.

Berger, Peter

1967   *The Sacred Canopy*. Garden City, NY: Doubleday.

1969   *The Sacred Canopy*. Garden City, NY: Doubleday.

1977   "In Praise of Particularity: The Concept of Mediating Structures." In *Facing Up to Modernity: Excursions in Society, Politics and Religion*. New York: Basic Books.

1979   *The Heretical Imperative*. Garden City, NY: Anchor Press/ Doubleday.

1980   "From Secularity to World Religions." *Christian Century* (January 16):41–43.

1981   "The Class Struggle in American Religion." *Christian Century* (February 25):194–99.

1983   "From the Crisis of Religion to the Crisis of Secularity." Pp. 14–24 in Mary Douglas and Steven Tipton, eds., *Religion and America: Spirituality in a Secular Age*. Boston: Beacon Press.

Berger, Peter, and Richard Neuhaus

1977   *To Empower People: The Role of Mediating Structures in Public Policy*. Washington, DC: American Enterprise Institute for Public Policy Research.

Borowitz, Eugene B.

1982   "Harvard Divinity School Convocation Address." *Harvard Theological Review* 75 (July):267–72.

Bosch, David J.

1983   "An Emerging Paradigm of Mission." *Missiology: An International Review* 6 (4):485–506.

Braaten, Carl E.

1976   "The Christian Mission and American Imperialism." *Dialog* 15 (Winter):70–78.

Brinton, Crane

1965   "Utopia and Democracy." *Daedalus* (Spring):348–66.

Bronowski, Jacob

1958   *Science and Human Values*. New York: Julian Messner, Inc.

Bruce, Steven
    1984   "A Sociological Account of Liberal Protestantism." *Religious Studies* 20 (3):401–15.

Caplow, Theodore, Howard M. Bahr, Bruce A. Chadwick, Dwight W. Hoover, et al.
    1983   *All Faithful People: Change and Continuity in Middletown's Religion.* Minneapolis: University of Minnesota Press.

Capra, Fritjof
    1982   *The Turning Point.* New York: Simon & Schuster.

Carroll, Jackson W., et al
    1979   *Religion in America, 1950 to the Present.* San Francisco: Harper & Row.

Carroll, Jackson W., and Robert L. Wilson
    1980   *Too Many Pastors?* New York: The Pilgrim Press.

Cauthen, Kenneth
    1962   *The Impact of American Religious Liberalism.* New York: Harper & Row.

Christianity Today
    1985   "Members of Congress Hold Ties to 21 Religious Groups." (January 18):61–64.

Clecak, Peter
    1983   *America's Quest for the Ideal Self: Dissent and Fulfillment in the 60's and 70's.* New York: Oxford University Press.

Cobb, John, and Charles Birch
    1981   *The Liberation of Life.* Cambridge: Cambridge University Press.

Coggins, Wade T.
    1974   "What's Behind the Idea of a Missionary Moratorium?" *Christianity Today* 19 (November):7–8.

Commager, Henry Steele
    1950   *The American Mind.* New Haven, CT: Yale University Press.

Coote, Robert T.
    1982   "The Uneven Growth of Conservative Evangelical Missions." *International Bulletin of Missionary Research* (July):113–23.

Copeland, E. Luther
    1973   "The Crisis in Christian Mission." *Christian Century* 90 (April 11):416–18.

Cox, Harvey
    1984   *Religion in the Secular City. Toward a Postmodern Theology.* New York: Simon & Schuster.

Davis, James A.
    1984   *General Social Surveys, 1972–1984.* Chicago: National Opinion Research Center.

Douglas, Mary
    1983   "The Effects of Modernization on Religious Change." Pp. 25–43 in Mary Douglas and Steven Tipton, eds., *Religion and America: Spirituality in a Secular Age.* Boston: Beacon Press.

Douglas, Mary, and Steven Tipton, eds.
    1983   *Religion and America: Spirituality in a Secular Age.* Boston: Beacon Press.

Doyle, Don H.
    1977   "The Social Functions of Voluntary Associations in a Nineteenth-Century American Town." *Social Science History* 1 (Spring):333–55.

Duclaux, Mary
    1927   *Portrait of Pascal.* New York: Harper & Brothers.

Dupre, Louis
    1976   *Transcendent Selfhood: The Loss and Rediscovery of the Inner Life.* New York: Seabury Press.
    1983   "Spiritual Life in a Secular Age." Pp. 79–107 in Mary Douglas and Steven Tipton, eds., *Religion and America: Spirituality in a Secular Age.* Boston: Beacon Press.

Durkheim, Emile
    1975   "Individualism and the Intellectuals." In W.S.F. Pickering, ed., *Durkheim on Religion: A Selection of Readings with Bibliographies.* Boston: Routledge and Kegan Paul.

Ellul, Jacques
    1972   *Hope in Time of Abandonment.* New York: Seabury Press.

Fackenheim, Emil
    1970   *God's Presence in History.* New York: New York University Press.

Fewster, Lowell H.
    1981   "Evaluating Professional Preparation in a Theological Seminary." Unpublished M.S. thesis, Graduate School of Education and Human Development, University of Rochester.

Forman, Charles W.
    1982   "The Americans." *International Bulletin of Missionary Research* (April):54–56.

Fosdick, Harry Emerson
    1943   *On Being a Real Person.* New York: Harper and Brothers.

Foster, Charles I., and Gregory H. Singleton
    1975   "Protestant Voluntary Organizations and the Shaping of Victorian America." *American Quarterly* 27 (December):549–60.

Fromm, Erich
    1976   *To Have or to Be?* New York: Harper & Row.

Gallup, George Jr., and David Poling
    1980   *The Search for America's Faith.* Nashville: Abingdon Press.

Gaustad, Edwin Scott
    1983   "Did the Fundamentalists Win?" Pp. 169-78 in Mary Douglas and Steven Tipton, eds., *Religion and America: Spirituality in a Secular Age.* Boston: Beacon Press.

Gilkey, Langdon B.
    1969   "Religion and the Secular University." *Dialog* 8 (Spring):108–15.
    1981   *Society and the Sacred.* New York: Crossroads.

Gill, Robin
    1983   *Prophecy and Praxis.* London: Marshall, Morgan, and Scott.

Gouldner, Alvin
    1979   *Dark Side of the Dialectic,* vol. 2. New York: Seabury Press.
    1985   *Against Fragmentation: The Origins of Marxism and the Sociology of Intellectuals.* New York: Oxford University Press.

Gustafson, James
    1981   *Ethics from a Theocentric Perspective,* vol. 1. Chicago: University of Chicago Press.
    1984   *Ethics from a Theocentric Perspective,* vol. 2. Chicago: University of Chicago Press.

Hadden, Jeffrey K.
1969   *The Gathering Storm in the Churches.* Garden City, NY: Doubleday.

Hammond, Phillip E.
1966   *The Campus Clergyman.* New York: Basic Books.
1983   "In Search of a Protestant Twentieth Century: American Religion and Power Since 1900." *Review of Religious Research* 24 (4):281–94.
1984   "The Courts and Secular Humanism." *Society* (May/June):11–16.
1985   (ed.) *The Sacred in a Secular Age.* Berkeley and Los Angeles: University of California Press.

Hammond, Phillip E., and Robert Mitchell
1965   "Segmentation of Radicalism—The Case of the Protestant Campus Minister." *American Journal of Sociology* 71 (September):133–43.

Handy, Robert T.
1971   *A Christian America: Protestant Hopes and Historical Realities.* New York: Oxford University Press.
1984   *A Christian America: Protestant Hopes and Historical Realities.* New York: Oxford University Press. Second Edition. Revised and enlarged.

Hauerwas, Stanley
1977   *Truthfulness and Tragedy: Further Investigations in Christian Ethics.* Notre Dame: University of Notre Dame Press.
1983   *The Peaceable Kingdom: A Primer in Christian Ethics.* Notre Dame: University of Notre Dame Press.

Herberg, Will
1955   *Protestant-Catholic-Jew: An Essay in American Religious Sociology.* Garden City, NY: Doubleday.

Hillman, James
1967   *Insearch: Psychology and Religion.* Irving, TX: Spring Publications.

Hoge, Dean R., and David A. Roozen
1979   *Understanding Church Growth and Decline, 1950–1978.* New York: The Pilgrim Press.

Hogg, W. Richie
1977   "The Role of American Protestantism in World Mission." Pp. 354–402 in R. Pierce Beaver, ed., *American Missions in*

Bicentennial Perspective. South Pasadena, CA: William
Carey Library.

Holifield, E. Brooks
1983   A History of Pastoral Care in America: From Salvation to
Self-realization. Nashville: Abingdon Press.

Hughes, Philip
1975   "Radical Christianity." Living Church (November 9):10–11.

Hunter, James D.
1983   American Evangelism: Conservative Religion and the
Quandary of Modernity. New Brunswick, NJ: Rutgers University Press.

Hutcheson, Richard D. Jr.
1979   Wheel Within the Wheel: Confronting the Management Crisis of the Pluralistic Church. Atlanta: John Knox Press.
1981a   Mainline Churches and the Evangelicals: A Challenging
Crisis? Atlanta: John Knox Press.
1981b   "Will the Real Christian Program Please Stand Up?" Christian Century 98 (October 7):994–97.

Hutchison, William R.
1968   (ed.) American Protestant Thought: The Liberal Era. New
York: Harper & Row.
1976   The Modernist Impulse in American Protestantism. Oxford: Oxford University Press.
1981   "Crisis in Overseas Mission: Shall We Leave It to the Independents?" Christian Century (March):290–96.

Inbody, Tyron
1985   "What Liberals and Fundamentalists Have in Common." In
Marla Selvidge, ed., Fundamentalism Today: What Makes
It So Attractive? Elgin, IL: Brethren Press.

Jacquet, Constant H., ed.
1984   Yearbook of American and Canadian Churches. Nashville:
Abingdon Press.

Janowitz, Morris
1983   The Reconstruction of Patriotism: Education for Civic Consciousness. Chicago: University of Chicago Press.

Kelley, Dean M.
1972   Why Conservative Churches Are Growing. New York:
Harper & Row.

1977   *Why Conservative Churches Are Growing.* New York: Harper & Row.

1979   "Is Religion a Dependent Variable?" Pp. 334–43 in Dean R. Hoge and David A. Roozen, eds., *Understanding Church Growth and Decline.* New York: The Pilgrim Press.

Kelsey, Morton T.
1979   "Pastoral Counseling and the Spiritual Quest." *The Journal of Pastoral Care* 33 (2):124–34.

Krauthammer, Charles
1983   "The End of the World." *The New Republic* 188 (March 28).

Kristol, Irving
1983   *Reflections of a Neoconservative: Looking Back, Looking Ahead.* New York: Basic Books.

Kristol, Irving, and Daniel Bell, eds.
1981   *The Crisis in Economic Theory.* New York: Basic Books.

Lasch, Christopher
1984   *The Minimal Self: Psychic Survival in Troubled Times.* New York: W.W. Norton & Co.

Laszlo, Ervin
1972   *The Systems View of Life.* New York: George Braziller.

Leopold, Aldo
1966   *A Sand County Almanac and Other Essays.* New York: Oxford University Press.

Lindbeck, George A.
1984   *The Nature of Doctrine: Religion and Theology in a Postliberal Age.* Philadelphia: Westminster Press.

Luckman, Thomas
1967   *The Invisible Religion.* New York: Macmillan.

Luker, Kristin
1984   *Abortion and the Politics of Motherhood.* Berkeley: University of California Press.

Marsden, George
1982   *Fundamentalism and American Culture.* New York: Oxford University Press.

1983   "Preachers of Paradox: The Religious New Right in Historical Perspective." Pp. 150–65 in Mary Douglas and Steven Tipton, eds., *Religion and America: Spiritual Life in a Secular Age.* Boston: Beacon Press.

Marty, Martin E.
   1970   *Righteous Empire.* New York: Harper & Row.
   1979a   "Congregations Come Alive." *A.D.* 7 (April):28–33.
   1979b   "Shape of the Religion in the Me Decade." *A.D.* 8, 9 (December–January):19–23.
   1979c   "The Career of Pluralism in America." Pp. 51–77 in Jackson W. Carroll, et al., *Religion in America, 1950 to the Present.* San Francisco: Harper & Row.
   1981   "The Milieu of Campus Ministry: Higher Education." *CSCM Yearbook* IV:56.
   1984   *Pilgrims in Their Own Land: 500 Years of Religion in America.* Boston: Little, Brown.

Mather, Cotton
   1977   *Magnalia Christi Americana.* Cambridge, MA: Harvard University Press.

McElvaney, William K.
   1980   *Good News Is Bad News.* . . . Maryknoll, NY: Orbis.

McLemore, Clinton W.
   1982   The Scandal of Psychotherapy. Wheaton, IL: Tyndale.

McLoughlin, William G., ed.
   1968   *The American Evangelicals, 1800–1900.* New York: Harper & Row.

Menendez, Albert
   1983   "The Changing Religious Profile of Congress." *Church and State* (January):9–12.

Miguez Bonino, Jose
   1974   As quoted in Gerald Anderson, "A Moratorium on Missionaries?" *Christian Century* 91 (January 16):43–45.

Miller, Donald E.
   1981   *The Case for Liberal Christianity.* San Francisco: Harper & Row.

Miller, Perry
   1963   *Roger Williams: His Contribution to American Tradition.* Cleveland: Bobbs-Merrill.

Moratorium
   1973   "The Suggested Moratorium on Missionary Funds and Personnel." *Missiology: An International Review* (July):275–79.

Needleman, Jacob
  1982   *Lost Christianity*. New York: Bantam Books.

Nelson, William
  1974   "Serving in 1974: Between Despair and Hope." *A.D.* 2 (January):12–13.

Neuhaus, Richard
  1984   *The Naked Public Square*. Grand Rapids, MI: Eerdmans Publishing Co.

Niebuhr, H. Richard
  1929   *The Social Sources of Denominationalism*. New York: Henry Holt.
  1937   *The Kingdom of God in America*. New York: Harper and Brothers.

Niebuhr, Reinhold
  1929   *Leaves from the Notebook of a Tamed Cynic*. Chicago: Willett, Clark and Colby.
  1932   *Moral Man and Immoral Society*. New York: Charles Scribner's Sons.

Novak, Michael
  1975   "The Communal Catholic." *Commonweal* 101 (12):321.

O'Connor, Flannery
  1970   "The Teaching of Literature." In Sally and Robert Fitzgerald, eds., *Mystery and Manners*. New York: Farrar, Strauss and Giroux.

Olds, Glenn A.
  1964   "Religious Centers." In Erich A. Walter, ed., *Religion and the State University*. Ann Arbor: University of Michigan Press.

Osborn, Ronald E.
  1974   "A New Start in the Journey of Faith." *The Disciple* 1 (January 6):18–21.

Parsons, Talcott
  1963   "Christianity and Modern Industrial Society." Pp. 33–70 in E. A. Tiryakian, ed., *Sociological Theory, Values, and Sociocultural Change*. New York: The Free Press.

Pattison, E. Mansell
  1978a   "Psychiatry and Religion Circa 1978: Analysis of a Decade, Part I." *Pastoral Psychology* 27:8–25.

1978b   "Psychiatry and Religion Circa 1978: Analysis of a Decade, Part II." *Pastoral Psychology* 27:119–41.

Percy, Walker
1980   *The Second Coming.* New York: Farrar, Strauss and Giroux.

Pratt, James B.
1920   The Religious Consciousness: A Psychological Study. New York: Macmillan.

Princeton Religion Research Center and the Gallup Organization
1978   *The Unchurched American: Study Conducted for the Religious Coalition to Study Backgrounds, Values, and Interests of Unchurched Americans.* Princeton, NJ: Princeton Religion Research Center and the Gallup Organization.

Rauff, Edward A.
1979   *Why People Join the Church.* New York: The Pilgrim Press.

Rauschenbusch, Walter
1916   *Christianizing the Social Order.* New York: Macmillan.
1964   *Christianizing the Social Order.* New York: Harper Torchbooks.

Regas, George
1972   *The Church and the Moral Issue of War.* Ph.D. diss., School of Theology at Claremont.

Rieff, Philip
1966   *The Triumph of the Therapeutic.* New York: Harper & Row.

Robinson, Marilynne
1985   "Writers and the Nostalgic Fallacy." Pp. 3ff. in *New York Times Book Review* (October 13).

Rohde, Peter P., ed.
1960   *The Diary of Soren Kierkegaard.* New York: Philosophical Library.

Roof, Wade Clark
1978   *Commitment and Community.* New York: Elsevier.
1982   "America's Voluntary Establishment: Mainline Religion in Transition." *Daedalus* 111 (Winter):165–84.

Roof, Wade Clark, and Christopher Kirk Hadaway
1979   "Denominational Switching in the Seventies: Going Beyond Stark and Glock." *Journal for the Scientific Study of Religion* 18 (December):363–77.

Roof, Wade Clark, and William McKinney
  1986   *The New Shape of American Religion*. New Brunswick, NJ:
          Rutgers University Press.

Roozen, David, William McKinney, and Jackson W. Carroll
  1984   *Varieties of Religious Presence*. New York: The Pilgrim
          Press.

Rorabaugh, W.J.
  1979   *The Alcoholic Republic: An American Tradition*. New
          York: Oxford University Press.

Russell, Letty M.
  1979   "Clerical Ministry as a Female Profession." *Christian Cen-
          tury* 96 (February 7):125–26.

Scherer, James A.
  1982   "When Church and State Go Abroad." *Worldview* (Febru-
          ary):2–8.

Schrading, Paul
  1970   "A New Campus Ministry." *Theology Today* 26 (Janu-
          ary):471–75.

Sears, Jayne
  1963   *John Colet and Marsilio Ficino*. Aberdeen: Oxford Univer-
          sity Press.

Shedd, Clarence P.
  1938   *The Church Follows Its Students*. New Haven: CT: Yale
          University Press.

Sheppard, Gerald T.
  1977   "Biblical Hermeneutics: The Academic Language of Evan-
          gelical Identity." *Union Seminary Quarterly Review* 32
          (Winter):81–94.

Slotkin, Richard
  1973   *Regeneration Through Violence: The Mythology of the
          American Frontier, 1600–1860*. Middletown, CT: Wesleyan.

Smith, Gerald B.
  1928   *Current Christian Thinking*. Chicago: University of Chicago
          Press.

Smith, Timothy L.
  1957   Revivalism and Social Reform. Nashville: Abingdon Press.

Snyder, Howard
  1982   "Holding a Mirror to the Contemporary Church." *Christianity Today* 26 (September 17):20–23.

Stark, Rodney, and Charles Y. Glock
  1968   *American Piety.* Berkeley: University of California Press.

Strong, Josiah
  1963   *Our Country.* Cambridge, MA: Harvard University Press.

Sweet, Leonard I.
  1982   "Not All Cats Are Gray: Beyond Liberalism's Uncertain Faith." *Christian Century* 99 (June 23):721–25.
  1984a   "The Crises of Liberal Christianity and the Public Emergence of Evangelicalism." Pp. 29–45 in George Marsden, ed., *Evangelicalism and Modern America.* Grand Rapids, MI: Eerdmans.
  1984b   "Theology a la Mode." *The Reformed Journal* 43 (October).

Temple, William
  1943   *Christianity and Social Order.* New York: Penguin.

Thailand Statement
  1981   "The Thailand Statement 1980: Consultation on World Evangelization." *International Bulletin of Missionary Research* (January):29–31.

Time
  1963   "Churches: The Hidden Revival." (February 1):64–65.

Tobias, Michael, ed.
  1984   *Deep Ecology.* San Diego: Avant Books.

Tracy, David
  1983   "The Questions of Pluralism: The Context of the United States." *Mid-Stream* 22 (July/October):273–85.

Troeltsch, Ernst
  1931   *The Social Teachings of the Christian Churches,* vol. 2. Trans. by Olive Wyon. New York: Harper and Brothers.
  1960   *The Social Teachings of the Christian Churches,* vol. 1. Trans. by Olive Wyon. New York: Harper Torchbook.

Van Dusen, Henry P.
  1951   God in Education. New York: Charles Scribner's Sons.

Verghese, Paul.
  1970   "How My Mind Has Changed." *Christian Century* 87 (September 23):1118–19.

Wacker, Grant
   1984   "Searching for Norman Rockwell: Popular Evangelicalism in Contemporary America." In Leonard Sweet, ed., *The Evangelical Tradition in America*. Macon, GA: Mercer.

Walter, Erich A.
   1964   *Religion and the State University*. Ann Arbor: University of Michigan Press.

Walzer, Michael
   1968   *The Revolution of the Saints*. New York: Atheneum.

Ward, Ted
   1982   "Christian Missions—Survival in What Forms? *International Bulletin of Missionary Research* (January):2–3.

Weber, Timothy
   1979   *Living in the Shadow of the Second Coming*. New York: Oxford University Press.

Wilke, Harold
   1984   "A Painful Attempt at Autobiography—*My Marginal Life*." In Flavian Dougherty, ed., *The Deprived, the Disabled, and the Fullness of Life*. Wilmington, DE: Michael Glazier.

Willimon, William
   1982   "In but Not of the World." *Circuit Rider* 6 (November/December).

Wilson, Brian
   1976   *Contemporary Transformations of Religion*. New York: Oxford University Press.
   1977   "How Religious Are We?" *New Society* (October 27):176–78.

Wilson, Samuel
   1981   "Current Trends in North American Protestant Ministries." *International Bulletin of Missionary Research* (April):74–75.

Woodhouse, A.S.P., ed.
   1938   *Puritanism and Liberty*. London: J.M. Dent and Sons.

World Council of Churches
   1981   "Message from Melbourne: World Council of Churches' Conference on World Mission and Evangelism." *International Bulletin of Missionary Research* (January):29.

Wuthnow, Robert
    1976   "Recent Patterns of Secularization: A Problem of Genera-
            tions?" *American Sociological Review* 41 (October):850–
            67.

Yankelovich, Daniel
    1982   *New Rules: Searching for Self-fulfillment in a World
            Turned Upside Down.* New York: Bantam Books.